ORIGEN'S TREATISE ON PRAYER

ORIGEN'S TREATISE ON PRAYER

Translation and Notes with an account of the practice and doctrine of prayer from New Testament times to Origen

By
ERIC GEORGE JAY

WIPF & STOCK · Eugene, Oregon

Wipf and Stock Publishers
199 W 8th Ave, Suite 3
Eugene, OR 97401

Origen's Treatise on Prayer
Translation and Notes with an Account of the Practice and
Doctrine of Prayer from New Testament Times to Origen
By Jay, Eric George
Copyright©1954 SPCK
ISBN 13: 978-1-60899-735-0
Publication date 11/16/2010
Previously published by SPCK, 1954

This Edition reprinted by Wipf and Stock Publishers by
arrangement with SPCK, London.

To
GUY VERNON SMITH
Bishop of Leicester, 1940–53
to whose
friendship and encouragement I owe much.

CONTENTS

	page
PREFACE	ix

Part I. PRAYER IN THE EARLY CHURCH

Chapter
1. Prayer in the New Testament and Apostolic Fathers . 3
2. Prayer in the Apologists and Irenaeus . . . 13
3. Prayer in the Acts of the Martyrs, Hippolytus, and Tertullian 18
4. Prayer in Clement of Alexandria 26

Appendix
A. The Hours of Prayer 36
B. Posture at Prayer 41
C. Prayer and the Saints 43

Part II. ORIGEN

Chapter
1. Origen's Life and Works 47
2. Origen's Doctrine 52
3. Prayer in Origen 61

Appendix
D. The Date of Περὶ Εὐχῆς 72
E. Manuscripts and Editions 73

Part III. ORIGEN'S TREATISE ON PRAYER: TRANSLATION AND NOTES 79

Appendix
F. Ἐπιούσιος 220

INDEX OF SCRIPTURAL QUOTATIONS AND REFERENCES	225
INDEX OF PATRISTIC QUOTATIONS AND REFERENCES	230
GENERAL INDEX	233

ACKNOWLEDGEMENTS

Acknowledgements are due to the following for permission to quote from the works indicated:

The Clarendon Press, Oxford (E. C. E. Owen, *Some Authentic Acts of the Early Martyrs*); Messrs. T. & T. Clark (William Wilson, *Clement of Alexandria*, two volumes in the Ante-Nicene Christian Library); Macmillan & Co., Ltd. (J. B. Lightfoot and J. R. Harmer, *The Apostolic Fathers*); La Table Ronde, Paris (Jean Daniélou, *Origène*).

PREFACE

ORIGEN receives mention in text-books of church history and in the theological lecture-room for a variety of reasons. He was something of a youthful prodigy, becoming head of the famous Catechetical School at Alexandria at the age of seventeen. His scholarship and his many writings are duly recorded. He is usually reckoned the chief exponent of that method of interpreting Holy Scripture known as allegory. His fearless use of philosophy in the explication of Christian doctrine is discussed. But it is for his speculations about the origin and end of the soul that he is most famous, speculations which gave rise to controversies between his supporters and his opponents which lasted several centuries, making some of the dullest reading among the pages of church history, and which, by fastening on him the suspicion of heresy, deprived him of the canonization which otherwise would surely have been his. All these are the aspects of his life and work which have attracted the greatest attention, and comparatively little is said about him as a believing Christian and a man of devotion.

It seemed, therefore, worth while to attempt this translation of the *Treatise on Prayer* (Περὶ Εὐχῆς), in the hope that it might be more widely known that Origen was not only a great biblical and philosophical theologian, but also a practising Christian of rare devotion, a man of prayer, and one anxious to teach his brethren such secrets of prayer as he had himself discovered.

In order that this early work on prayer may be studied not in isolation but in its context within Christian thought on the subject, it is preceded by a short account of Christian teaching on the subject of prayer and of the practice of private prayer, so far as it can be gathered from Christian writings up to the time of Origen.

Koetschau's edition of the text of Origen has been used, as the best available. But since Migne's *Patrologia Graeca* is probably more accessible to the majority of students, Koetschau's divergences from Delarue's text in Migne have been fully noted.

In translating quotations from the Scriptures I have kept as close to the wording of the Authorized Version as the Greek seems to

PREFACE

warrant. Throughout I have followed this version's practice of using a small letter for the pronoun when it refers to the Divine Names, but in quoting authors or translators who use the capital letter I have let it stand. The section headings of the translation are my own.

I wish to express my thanks to the Rev. R. V. G. Tasker, Professor of New Testament Exegesis at King's College, London, for his help in translating several passages, to the Rev. H. Chadwick of Queens' College, Cambridge, for resolving a number of difficulties which I encountered, and to Dr W. Telfer, Master of Selwyn College, Cambridge, Dr G. W. Butterworth, and Dr G. L. Prestige, Canon of St Paul's, for generous help. It is due to them that errors are not more numerous. They are in no wise accountable for those that remain. I owe, too, a debt of gratitude to Mr W. D. Bowen for his meticulous work in preparing the typescript for publication. Typographical and grammatical errors, and obscurities of language which survive are to be attributed to the obstinacy of the author. I am also grateful to the librarians of the Bibliothèque Nationale in Paris and of Trinity College, Cambridge, for their courteous and helpful replies to my questions.

For this work the writer was awarded the degree of Doctor of Philosophy in the Faculty of Theology of the University of London in 1951.

E. G. J.

Part I

PRAYER IN THE EARLY CHURCH

Chapter One

PRAYER IN THE NEW TESTAMENT AND APOSTOLIC FATHERS

No full treatise on the subject of Christian prayer was written, so far as we know, until the third century. Then within fifty years three works on prayer, each of them including a commentary on the Lord's Prayer, were written, and, curiously enough, their authors were all men born on the southern shores of the Mediterranean, Tertullian and Cyprian in the Roman province of Africa, and Origen in Alexandria. Tertullian's *De Oratione* was written at the very beginning of the century, Origen's Περὶ Εὐχῆς between A.D. 231 and 250, and Cyprian's *De Oratione* about A.D. 250.

But Christian literature of the first two centuries by no means ignores the subject of prayer. It would be difficult to cite any work by a Christian author in this period which has not some reference to prayer. It could not have been otherwise, for the Apostles and their successors were men who would have subscribed wholeheartedly to Heiler's assertion: "Prayer is the central phenomenon of religion, the very hearthstone of all piety." [1]

The New Testament

That prayer is integral to religion was taught both by the precept and by the example of Jesus. From every strand of the gospel tradition, Synoptic and Johannine, can be adduced examples of Jesus' own regular practice of prayer, his teaching about the spirit and attitude of mind in which prayer must be made, about the need for regularity and fervour, and his insistence upon its objective efficacy. The "Ask, and it shall be given you" of the Synoptics (Matt. 7. 7; Luke 11. 9) is paralleled by the "Ask, and ye shall receive, that your joy may be full" of John 16. 24.

The Master's lessons were not unheeded. The New Testament is the literature of a community for whom prayer was an essential part

[1] Friedrich Heiler, *Prayer*, English translation (O.U.P., 1932), p. 1.

of life. The pages of the Acts of the Apostles abound in instances of Christians at prayer: common prayer in the synagogue and in their own assemblies, private prayer, special prayer when important decisions were to be made and in times of crisis both for the community and for individuals. From the simple and unemphatic way in which this prayer is mentioned we may gather that it was regarded as a natural and normal part of the Christian life.

The Epistles strengthen the evidence that prayer was seen to be of the essence of the Christian life. Not one of the Epistles is without some assurance to its readers of the writer's prayers, some request for their prayers, or some reference to prayer. Many of them include prayers, blessings, and thanksgivings, some of them, like 1 Peter 1. 3–4, so carefully and beautifully phrased that they raise the question whether in them we have fragments of the earliest Christian liturgical uses, whilst some of them, like the "Peace be to thee" of 3 John 14, are so simple that they may be examples of the regular greetings between Christians. Christian earnestness and sincerity infused a deep spirituality into the ancient convention by which a letter began or ended with a prayer. We are made to realize that these were letters passing between men who knew themselves to be united by the spiritual bond of prayer. The prayers for grace and peace and the thanksgivings with which the Epistles begin and end are quite naturally introduced and indicate how naturally Christians of the first generation regarded prayer.

The Doctrine of Prayer in the Epistles

(*a*) *The Co-operation of the Holy Spirit.* Prayer is essentially a simple thing, the communing of a man with God. The Epistles show that Christians regarded prayer as a normal part of their lives. They were conscious of a greater freedom in their prayers, and of being closer to God in them than they had been before. They probably thought of this as but one of the effects of Christ's atoning work, and there was little attempt, at least in their writings, to provide any rationale of Christian prayer. There are, however, one or two passages in which we may see the beginnings of a theology of Christian prayer. It is a development of the Pauline doctrine of Christ's deliverance of his people from slavery, that they become sons of God. Becoming sons, they have a greater freedom of approach to God. The difference between the pre-Christian and the Christian approach to God in prayer is comparable with the difference between a slave's address to his master, and a son's to his father. Paul's explanation of this in Galatians 4. 4–7 is that the Spirit of him who is the eternal Son of God has been given to the hearts of Christians, enabling them to approach God as Father: "God hath sent forth the Spirit of his Son into your hearts, crying, Abba, Father." The παρρησία, confident freedom of speech, which is the mark of prayer in the New Testament, is due to the atoning work of Christ, and to the work of his Spirit in the Christian soul.

In Romans 8. 26, 27, Paul boldly develops this idea. Here he interprets the phenomenon of glossolalia, the ecstatic utterances of Christians in the assembly of prayer, as due to the fact that the Holy Spirit is at work in the heart of him who prays. "For we know not what we should pray for as we ought: but the Spirit itself maketh intercession for us with groanings which cannot be uttered." These wordless sounds, therefore, whilst meaningless to men, are not meaningless to God, for they are the outward expression of the Spirit's prompting of men to pray worthily of God.[1]

The doctrine of Christian prayer as the co-operation of the Holy Spirit with the human spirit is again glanced at in Ephesians 2. 18: "through him (Christ) we both (Jew and Gentile) have access by one Spirit unto the Father"; and in so diverse a work as Jude, whose readers are exhorted to keep themselves in the love of God "praying in the Holy Ghost" (Jude 20).

(*b*) *The Assistance of Christ.* Whilst Christian prayer, with its boldness and intimacy, was regarded as being the work of the Spirit of Christ in the Christian heart, it was felt also to receive strength from the prayers of the risen Christ himself, "who is even at the right hand of God, who also maketh intercession for us" (Rom. 8. 34). The prayer of confession, too, is taken up by the risen Christ on man's behalf: "if any man sin, we have an advocate with the Father, Jesus Christ the righteous" (1 John 2. 1). Christ's heavenly intercession is also one of the main themes of the Epistle to the Hebrews. The great High Priest, eternally offering in the heavenly Holy of Holies his one sacrifice for man, also presents his intercessions before the Father. "He

[1] There is here no real incompatibility with St Paul's seeming disparagement of glossolalia in 1 Cor. 14, where he has in mind the edification of man, for which glossolalia is of little use. He reminds the Corinthians that "he that speaketh in an unknown tongue speaketh not unto men, but unto God: for no man understandeth him; howbeit in the spirit he speaketh mysteries" (1 Cor. 14. 2); "if I pray in an unknown tongue, my spirit prayeth, but my understanding is unfruitful" (14. 14). It is from the point of view of the listener that this kind of prayer is less valuable (14. 15, 16).

is able also to save them to the uttermost that come unto God by him, seeing he ever liveth to make intercession for them" (Heb. 7. 25; cf. also 9. 24).

The secret, then, of the joyous and confident prayer of Christians of the first century is their faith that the Holy Spirit, the Spirit of Christ's own Sonship, was in their hearts, prompting their words, and their knowledge that Jesus Christ, risen, ascended, glorified, was praying with them. Prayer sweetens the whole atmosphere of the world in which Christians of the first century lived. There is little cause for wonder that the seer of the Apocalypse symbolizes the prayers of the saints by golden vials full of odours (Rev. 5. 8) and thinks of them as ascending before God together with incense from a golden censer held in an angel's hand (Rev. 8. 3, 4).

The Apostolic Fathers

In the Apostolic Fathers,[1] a body of writings which covers roughly the first half of the second century, we breathe very much the same devotional atmosphere as in the New Testament. Christians of the subapostolic age were as vividly conscious as those of the Apostles' time that there had been opened up for them a new way of approach to God, and this constantly finds expression in their writings. Clement of Rome repeatedly exhorts the Corinthians to prayer, thanksgiving, confession of their sins, and intercession for the sins of others.[2] Ignatius of Antioch gives us a picture of the Churches of Syria, Asia Minor, and Rome linked together by the invisible bonds of prayer. He asks for prayers for the Church in Syria from which he has been led a prisoner;[3] he thanks the Churches of Philadelphia and Smyrna, and Bishop Polycarp, for their prayers on behalf of the Syrian Church, through which that Church was already at the time of his writing beginning to enjoy peace once more;[4] and he asks for prayers for himself that he may face his ordeal in Rome bravely, and make a good martyrdom.[5] All the literature associated with the name of Polycarp shows this venerable bishop as a man of prayer, one who had taken to heart Ignatius' early admonition, "Give thyself to unceasing prayers"

---

[1] The quotations in this section are from J. B. Lightfoot and J. R. Harmer, *The Apostolic Fathers* (London, 1891).

[2] *I Clem.* XXIX, XXXVIII, XLI, XLVIII, LIII, LV, LVI. Clement's epistle thus has references to all four parts of prayer listed by Origen, *De Orat.* XXXIII.

[3] *Eph.* XXI; *Mag.* XIV; *Trall.* XIII; *Rom.* IX.

[4] *Phil.* X; *Smyrn.* XI; *Polycarp* VII.

[5] *Trall.* XII; *Rom.* III.

(Ignatius, *Polycarp* 1). In his letter to the Philippians Polycarp enjoins upon them the duty of wide intercession (XII). His own practice is amply illustrated in the letter of the Smyrnaeans which records the prayer, two hours long, in which, before his arrest, he remembered "all who at any time had come in his way, small and great, high and low, and all the universal Church throughout the world".

The little manual of Christian practice known as the *Didache* gives great prominence to the duty of prayer. The value of its evidence in matters such as the development of the Christian ministry and the early history of the sacraments of Baptism and the Eucharist is difficult to assess because of the lack of certainty concerning its place of origin and date. Its provenance is generally assumed to be Syria, but there is debate whether it comes from the main stream of church life in Syria, or is representative, as Harnack thought, of an insignificant backwater of Christianity. Lightfoot says that the work is "obviously of very early date"; Streeter puts it between A.D. 90 and 100; Vokes in *The Riddle of the Didache* [1] puts it between A.D. 167 and 233; W. Telfer [2] considers the writer was a leader of the Church in Antioch who, being concerned to recall the Church to primitive standards of holiness, reconstructed what he conceived to be the order and discipline of the Church laid down by St Peter for the congregations of Syria and Cilicia. He dates the *Didache* between A.D. 135 and 180. But whatever its date and place of origin, the *Didache* had a very wide influence, being used, in part at least, by the compilers of many of the Church Orders of later centuries. The question of its place of origin hardly affects the value of what the *Didache* has to say about prayer; for if the work comes from some prominent Syrian or Palestinian Church we have evidence that as much prominence was given to the practice of prayer in that Church as in other Churches; whilst if it comes from some insignificant Church, we have evidence that however different that Church may have been from others in its ministry or its administration of the sacraments, it valued the practice of prayer as highly as any other Church in Christendom. In the beginning, where the writer sets in front of his readers the Two Ways, of life and of death, prayer is twice mentioned as the practice of those who are treading the Way of Life: "Thou shalt not hate any man, but some thou shalt reprove, and for others thou shalt pray, and others

[1] London, 1938.
[2] *J.T.S.*, Vol. XL, Nos. 158–159 (April and July 1939).

thou shalt love more than thy life" (II); "In church (ἐκκλησία) thou shalt confess thy transgressions, and shalt not betake thyself to prayer with an evil conscience" (IV). In the *Didache* we have the first definite evidence (unless the work is to be assigned to the very latest possible date) of a rule of prayer laid upon members of the Church: "Neither pray ye as the hypocrites, but as the Lord commanded in His Gospel, thus pray ye: Our Father, which art in heaven, hallowed be Thy name; Thy kingdom come; Thy will be done, as in heaven, so also on earth; give us this day our daily bread; and forgive us our debt, as we also forgive our debtors; and lead us not into temptation, but deliver us from the evil one; [1] for Thine is the power and the glory for ever and ever. Three times in the day pray ye so" (VIII). This ordinance of the *Didache* is sometimes quoted as very early evidence of the establishment of daily offices of prayer in the Church. But it is to be noted that nothing is said here of public prayer, and in the absence of specific directions about meeting in assembly the natural way to take the passage is to refer it to private prayer.[2] Doubtless the custom of daily prayer privately at set times, a practice which, as we shall see, was soon by no means confined to the area to which the *Didache* may be presumed to have been addressed, was one of the factors which led to the establishment of a scheme of daily common prayer. To admit this, however, is not to hold that daily offices, recited in the assembly, were already in being. A recent writer who argues for the early establishment of the offices, as taking the place of the Jewish synagogue services, admits that there is little evidence for the regular hours of Christian prayer in assembly until the fourth century.[3] It is daily private prayer that the *Didache* enjoins, and the prayer which Christ taught his disciples must be at the heart of such prayer: "Your prayers and your almsgivings and all your deeds so do ye as ye find it in the Gospel of our Lord" (xv). This is the heart of the matter.

The Epistle of Barnabas, a work which repels the modern Christian reader by reason of its anti-Jewish tone and its misapprehension of the place of the Jews in the divine purposes, has nevertheless several

[1] The *Didache* here quotes the Lord's Prayer of Matt. 6. 9 ff. with only slight verbal alterations.
[2] See "The Choir Offices" by E. C. Ratcliff in *Liturgy and Worship*, S.P.C.K., 1932.
[3] C. W. Dugmore, *The Influence of the Synagogue upon the Divine Office* (O.U.P., 1944), Chapter III. 4, "Daily Services". There may well have been daily assemblies for prayer in many local churches, but it is private prayer that concerns most of the early writers on the subject.

passages which show that not even this somewhat uncharitable Christian failed to realize something of the true Christian spirit, and that the secret of the Christian life lay in the new free and open access to God made possible by the atoning work of Christ. The most important passage in this connection follows an attack upon the idolatrous veneration of the Temple by the Jews, as a consequence of which, the writer contends, it was destroyed. "But let us enquire whether there be any temple of God. There is; in the place where He Himself undertakes to make and finish it. For it is written; 'And it shall come to pass, when the week is being accomplished, the temple of God shall be built gloriously in the name of the Lord.' I find then that there is a temple. How then shall it be built in the name of the Lord? Understand ye. Before we believed on God, the abode of our heart was corrupt and weak, a temple truly built by hands; for it was full of idolatry and was a house of demons, because we did whatsoever was contrary to God. 'But it shall be built in the name of the Lord.' Give heed then that the temple of the Lord may be built gloriously. How? Understand ye. By receiving the remission of our sins and hoping on the Name we became new, created afresh from the beginning. Wherefore God dwelleth truly in our habitation within us ... opening for us who had been in bondage unto death the door of the temple, which is the mouth, and giving us repentance leadeth us to the incorruptible temple. ... This is the spiritual temple built up to the Lord" (xvi). "Barnabas" thus shares with other Christian writers of the second century the conviction that the Christian possesses in his heart a temple wherein a closer devotion to God and more effective prayer may be raised than was ever possible for the Jew.

"*The Shepherd*" *of Hermas*. A prominent place is given to prayer in the widely read and popular work known as *The Shepherd*.[1] It consists of a series of visions experienced by the writer, Hermas, a slave, culminating in the appearance of "a man glorious in his visage, in the garb of a shepherd", who imparts to Hermas teaching by means of precepts or mandates (ἐντολαί) and allegories or parables (παραβολαί). Recent scholarship [2] has detected a great deal of artificiality

[1] It is quoted by Irenaeus, Tertullian, Clement of Alexandria, and Origen, and is mentioned in the Muratorian fragment. The high regard in which *The Shepherd* was held is shown by the fact that the four Fathers mentioned quote it as Scripture.
[2] Daniel Völter, *Die Visionen des Hermas*, Berlin, 1900; Martin Dibelius in the Ergänzungsband to Lietzmann's *Handbuch zum Neuen Testament*.

in this work, but the claim that Hermas makes is that these visions were experienced whilst he was at prayer. The meaning of them sometimes only became known to him after further periods of prayer.[1]

The Shepherd is probably to be dated in the fifth decade of the second century. For our present purpose it is particularly interesting for its evidence that Christians of those days were not unconscious of intellectual difficulties connected with prayer. In Mandate ix two problems are discussed. The first is that of those who were doubtful whether, in view of their sins, they were worthy to bring their petitions to God. "He (the Shepherd) saith to me; 'Remove from thyself a doubtful mind and doubt not at all whether to ask of God, saying within thyself, How can I ask a thing of the Lord and receive it, seeing that I have committed so many sins against Him?'" And the Shepherd goes on to recommend great boldness in prayer.

The second problem is that of so-called unanswered prayer. "If, after asking anything of the Lord, thou receive thy petition somewhat tardily, be not of doubtful mind because thou didst not receive the petition of thy soul at once." Hermas's solution of this difficulty is naïve: "For assuredly it is by reason of some temptation or some transgression, of which thou art ignorant, that thou receivest thy petition so tardily."

The great secret of effective prayer, according to Hermas, is confident faith: "Faith is from above from the Lord, and hath great power; but doubtful-mindedness is an earthly spirit from the devil, and hath no power" (Mandate ix). But there are other necessary conditions. Cheerfulness is one. "'Clothe thyself in cheerfulness, which hath favour with God always, and is acceptable to Him, and rejoice in it ... the sad man is always committing sin. In the first place he committeth sin, because he grieveth the Holy Spirit, which was given to the man being a cheerful spirit; and in the second place, by grieving the Holy Spirit he doeth lawlessness, in that he doth not intercede with neither confess unto God. For the intercession of a sad man hath never at any time power to ascend to the altar of God.' 'Wherefore,' say I, 'doth not the intercession of him that is saddened ascend to the altar?' 'Because,' saith he, 'sadness is seated at his heart. Thus sadness mingled with the intercession doth not suffer the intercession to ascend pure to the altar. For as vinegar when mingled with wine in the same vessel hath not the same pleasant taste, so

---

[1] E.g. Vision I. 1 ; II. 1.

THE N.T. AND APOSTOLIC FATHERS   11

likewise sadness mingled with the Holy Spirit hath not the same intercession. Therefore cleanse thyself from this wicked sadness, and thou shalt live unto God; yea, and all they shall live unto God, who shall cast away sadness from themselves and clothe themselves in all cheerfulness'" (Mandate x). This would seem, on the face of it, a little unfair to a genuine mourner. But there seems little doubt that Hermas means by $\lambda v\pi\eta$ what the later theologian called "accidie".

Another necessary condition is that a man must be detached from mundane affairs. He must live as one that serves God, and not be distracted about business. "'For they that busy themselves overmuch, sin much also, being distracted about their business, and in no wise serving their own Lord. How then,' saith he (the Shepherd), 'can such a man ask anything of the Lord and receive it, seeing that he serveth not the Lord? They that serve Him, these shall receive their petitions, but they that serve not the Lord, these shall receive nothing'" (Parable iv). "Whosoever is a servant of God, and hath his own Lord in his heart, asketh understanding of Him, and receiveth it, and interpreteth every parable . . ." (Parable v. 4). One of the outward signs of serving the Lord is fasting. After giving various injunctions about fasting, the Shepherd assures Hermas that "all those, who shall bear and observe them, shall be blessed, and whatsoever things they shall ask of the Lord, they shall receive" (Parable v. 3).

Hermas's solutions of these current problems of prayer are over-simplifications. Christian experience does not substantiate his assertion that the servant of God who prays with confidence will "receive all things and lack nothing of his petitions". It needs to be pointed out that the Christian must pray "through Jesus Christ our Lord"; and that if he asks for such things as Christ would not ask, God in his wisdom will overrule those petitions, however fervently they may be made. Had Hermas been more explicit on this point he would have given even greater practical help to the "average Christian" for whom he writes. But the merit of his work is that he does recognize the problems of prayer, and according to his ability attempts to solve them. His recurrent condemnation of accidie in prayer is a warning needed by the lip-servants of prayer in all generations. "As many as are sluggish and idle in intercession, these hesitate to ask of the Lord. But the Lord is abundant in compassion, and giveth to them that ask of Him without ceasing" (Parable v. 4).

In one passage Hermas gives us a vivid picture of early Christian society in which all, rich and poor, acknowledge each his dependence on the other, and are bound together in a fellowship of prayer. This is the second Parable, that of the elm and the vine. The vine bears its best fruit when it has some sturdy support such as that of the elm. So "the rich man hath much wealth, but in the things of the Lord he is poor, being distracted about his riches, and his confession and intercession with the Lord is very scanty . . . When then the rich man goeth up to the poor, and assisteth him in his needs, believing that for what he doth to the poor man he shall be able to obtain a reward with God—because the poor man is rich in intercession and confession, and his intercession hath great power with God—the rich man then supplieth all things to the poor man without wavering. But the poor man being supplied by the rich maketh intercession for him, thanking God for him that gave to him. And the other is still more zealous to assist the poor man, that he may be continuous in his life: for he knoweth that the intercession of the poor man is acceptable and rich before God." [1]

There is, of course, a danger here that the rich man may think he can buy his way into heaven, and consider himself exempt from prayer and the other Christian duties. But provided that the rich man is persevering in his devotions, there is an attractiveness in this picture of mutual service, in which "the poor, by interceding with the Lord for the rich, establish their riches, and again the rich, supplying their needs to the poor, establish their souls", and "both are made partners in the righteous work".

[1] Cf. *I Clem.* xxxviii: "Let the rich minister aid to the poor; and let the poor give thanks to God, because He hath given him one through whom his wants may be supplied."

Chapter Two

PRAYER IN THE APOLOGISTS AND IRENAEUS

The Apologists

When we turn to the writings of the Apologists,[1] we find ourselves in a different atmosphere. There are no longer the frequent ascriptions of praise, prayers for grace, exhortations to prayer, and requests for prayer, which abound both in the Apostolic Fathers and in the New Testament letters. The reason for this change of atmosphere is to be found in the different purpose for which the Apologists wrote. They were concerned to defend the Christian religion from the varied attacks of Jews and heathen. They believed that attack was the best form of defence, and they devoted a great deal of space to exposing the absurdities and errors of current paganism. As against the Jews, they largely employed the argument from prophecy, and we find pages of wordy exegesis of the Old Testament. In all this the devotional note is necessarily not prominent.

Yet there are indications that the Apologists were well aware of the importance and of the power of prayer. Indeed, the prayer life of Christian people, beautiful in its calmness and simplicity, and particularly the spectacle of Christians praying for their persecutors, provided them with one of their more effective arguments.[2]

---

[1] Apologies were addressed to Hadrian (Emperor A.D. 117–138) by Quadratus and Aristides (Eusebius, *Historia Ecclesiastica* IV. 3). Apologies were frequent throughout the remainder of the second century, a period in which Christianity was facing both intellectual attack from pagan teachers like Celsus, and also outbursts of mob violence. One of the ways in which Christians attempted to combat such attacks was by explaining Christian teaching in these "Apologies".
The term "Apologist" is usually applied to these second-century writers, including Tertullian, who, however, had much wider interests than apologetics. We shall treat Tertullian separately. Apologies appear in later centuries, e.g. the *Contra Celsum* of Origen in the third century.

[2] E.g. Justin Martyr, *Apology* I. 13 (Migne, *Patrologia Graeca* VI. 345), *Dialogue with Trypho* XCVI. 2–3, CVIII, CXXXIII. 6; Athenagoras, *Legatio pro Christianis* XI (Migne, *P.G.* VI. 912). Quotations from Justin Martyr's *Dial. with Trypho* in this chapter are taken from the English translation by A. Lukyn Williams (S.P.C.K., 1930).

On the other hand the argument from Christian prayer is strangely absent in some passages where its use would seem to be specially appropriate. However, it must be remembered that the mind of the twentieth-century apologist works differently from that of his second-century predecessor. A case in point is the first book of the *Apologia ad Autolycum* of Theophilus of Antioch (died *c.* A.D. 185), in which he sets out to satisfy the request of Autolycus, "Show me your God". A modern apologist, in addressing himself to this request, could hardly avoid using the argument from religious experience. But the first book *ad Autolycum* will be searched in vain for a single reference to prayer.[1] However, in the second book we find Matthew 5. 44 quoted to illustrate the Christian's love of his enemies. Theophilus goes on to press his argument that Christians are law-abiding citizens and an asset to the State: "The Divine Word bids us even to be subject to principalities and powers, and to pray for them that we may live a calm and peaceful life" (v).[2]

Apart from the apologetic interest in prayer as one indication of the superiority of Christianity over other religions, there are occasional references to prayer from which we can glean a certain amount of information about second-century Christian belief in the efficacy of prayer. Justin Martyr speaks of contrite prayer as being particularly efficacious: "For who of you does not know that prayer uttered with lamentations and tears, and the prayer of one who sinks down with body bent and on his knees, especially propitiates God?"[3]

An instance of the kind of story related by Christians to illustrate the power of prayer is provided by the story of the Thundering Legion, which gained much currency towards the close of the second century. It relates to the campaign of Marcus Aurelius against the Quadi. The Roman army had been cut off from its water supply, and was in danger of defeat. But the soldiers of the twelfth legion who were Christians prayed for rain, and immediately there occurred a violent thunder-storm which had the double effect of providing water for the thirsty Romans, and disorganizing the Quadi to such an extent

---

[1] Migne, *P.G.* VI. 1023 ff.   [2] Ibid. 1139–40.
[3] *Dialogue with Trypho* XC. 5. This appears in a passage in which the prayer of Moses in a different posture, his arms supported by Aaron and Hur, whilst Joshua fought the Amalekites, is explained as being typical of the Cross: "If he remained in this position, so long was Amalek overcome, and as he prevailed he prevailed by the cross" (Lukyn Williams, pp. 192–3). Cf. *Epistle of Barnabas* XII.

THE APOLOGISTS AND IRENAEUS

that they were easily defeated. Such was the Christian account of the event. It is related by Tertullian in his *Apology*, Chapter v, and by Eusebius (*H.E.* v. 5), who cites in support of its truth the evidence of a contemporary, Claudius Apollinaris. The letter of Marcus Aurelius which describes the event, and which is appended to Justin Martyr's first Apology,[1] is clearly spurious. There are also pagan accounts of the incident which claim the miraculous storm as the result of the prayers either of an Egyptian magician or of the Emperor himself. There are certainly discrepancies in each account of the event, but there seems to be a core of truth in the story. However that may be, it was certainly related confidently by Christians as evidence for the efficacy of their prayers.[2]

Among the Apologists, Justin Martyr has the deepest conception of prayer. In his writings can be found references to praise (*Dial. with Trypho* LXXIV. 3; *Apol.* I. 13), thanksgiving (*Apol.* I. 13), and confession (ibid. I. 61) as well as intercession and petition. He realizes the importance of the principle which Origen was later to make the theme of his treatise on prayer: "Ask for the great things; ask for the heavenly things." Expounding Psalm 22 as a prophecy of Christ he writes: "And his asking that his soul might be saved from sword, and from lion's mouth, and from dog's paw, was a prayer that no one should lord it over his soul, that, when we come to the end of this life, we may ask the same of God, who can turn back every shameless and evil angel from seizing our soul.... God also teaches us by His Son, that we should do our utmost by all means to become righteous, and at our death to ask that our souls do not fall under any such power. For when He gave up His spirit on the cross He said: 'Father, into Thy hands I entrust My spirit'." [3]

He glances at an important principle of prayer, that of the interrelation of prayer and work, when he says "He therefore that loves his neighbour will both pray and work for that to happen to his neighbour as for himself".[4]

---

[1] Migne, *P.G.* VI.
[2] The second-century historian Hegesippus, writing on the martyrdom of James of Jerusalem, illustrates the converting power of a Christian's prayer for his enemies. "'I beseech thee, Lord, God and Father, forgive them; for they know not what they do.'... One of the priests... thereupon cried 'Cease; what are you doing? Justus is praying for you'" (fragment in Eusebius, *H.E.* II. 23: Migne, *P.G.* V. 1312–3).
[3] *Dialogue with Trypho* cv. 3–5 (Lukyn Williams, pp. 219–20).
[4] Ibid. XCIII. 3 (Lukyn Williams, p. 198).

Irenaeus

In the Apologists there is nothing which can be described as a doctrine of prayer, but Irenaeus,[1] in the fourth book of the *Contra Haereses*, widens the conception of prayer to include the whole life of the Christian as being conscious of God's presence and of the possibility of communion with him. Prayer is thought of not so much as an activity which a man may or may not decide to pursue; it is rather a necessity of man's life, without which he ceases to be truly human: "As God is in need of nothing, so man is in need of communion with God. For this is the glory of man, to persevere and abide in the service of God" (*Contra Haereses* IV. 14).[2] God was teaching mankind this through the example of the lives of the prophets. "But God prepared the prophets beforehand upon the earth, thus accustoming mankind to bear his Spirit and to have communion with God, he himself, indeed, being in need of nothing; but to those who need him he offers communion with himself" (*C.H.* IV. 14).[3] This communion with God is not confined to the time a man spends in prayer in the narrow sense of the word; it extends to the whole of life. After citing a number of the Old Testament passages which attack the institution of sacrifice, Irenaeus concludes: "From all of which it is clear that God was seeking from them not sacrifices and whole burnt-offerings, but faith and obedience and justice, for the sake of their salvation" (*C.H.* IV. 17).[4]

Yet there must be particular moments in this life of communion with God when the mind is consciously directed towards him, for otherwise there would be a danger, at least for less devout souls, that the Godward direction of human life should be forgotten altogether. There is, then, a Christian sacrifice, the pure offering which Malachi had foretold: "For from the rising of the sun even unto the going down of the same my name shall be great among the Gentiles; and in every place incense shall be offered unto my name, and a pure offering" (Mal. I. 11). This prophecy, argues Irenaeus, is fulfilled in that the name of God is now glorified throughout the world in the Church; for Christ's name is God's name.[5] And as for the prophecy "'In every

---

[1] C. A.D. 133–203. His great work, *Contra Haereses*, is an exposure of the Gnostic sects.
[2] Migne, *P.G.* VII. 1010.   [3] Ibid. 1011.   [4] Ibid. 1023.
[5] Justin Martyr, *Dial. with Trypho* CXVII, uses a similar argument against the Jewish contention that Malachi's prophecy was fulfilled in the prayers of the Diaspora. He says: "Your race is not even now 'from the rising of the

place incense is offered to my name, and a pure offering', now John in the Apocalypse says that incense is the prayers of the saints" (*C.H.* IV. 17).[1] This leads to a discussion (IV. 18) of the Eucharist, in which, Irenaeus contends, Malachi's prophecy of the pure offering is fulfilled. Yet the offering of the Eucharist is not to be dissociated from the whole life of prayer and service of the Christian. For Irenaeus reminds us again that God does not need things from us, but wishes us to perform acts of mercy (cf. Matt. 25. 34 ff., which he cites) "lest we should be unfruitful". So also God's people are to offer oblations "although he does not need them, in order that they may learn to serve God. So also for that reason he wishes us to offer a gift at the altar frequently and without intermission. There is, then, an altar in heaven (for thither our prayers and oblations are directed), and a temple, as John says in the Apocalypse, 'And the temple of God is open' (Rev. 11. 19), and a tabernacle, 'For behold,' he says, 'the tabernacle of God in which he will dwell with men' (Rev. 21. 3)."[2] It seems clear that Irenaeus's discussion of the Eucharist has broadened out again into a discussion of the Christian prayer-life in general. The offering which is to be made at the altar "frequently and without intermission" cannot be the Eucharist regarded in isolation. There is no evidence for a daily Eucharist in the second century, and even if there were, "without intermission" would hardly be applicable. On the other hand, in this context in which the Eucharist has been so fully discussed, a reference to it here cannot be entirely excluded. Irenaeus's meaning appears to be that the offerings made by Christians at the altar in the Eucharist must be thought of as particular and explicit expressions of what is implicit in the whole Christian life, namely service of God, without intermission directed to Almighty God in heaven. The life of the true Christian is a life in which prayer and service are woven together, and in which specific acts of public worship, as in the Eucharist, complete the pattern.

---

sun unto its setting', for there are nations among which none of your race has ever yet dwelt. But there is not one race of men at all—barbarians or Greeks or persons addressed by any name whatever, or Waggon-livers, or so-called Homeless men, or Cattle-rearers dwelling in tents—among whom prayers and thanksgivings are not made to the Father and Maker of the universe through the name of Jesus who was crucified" (Lukyn Williams, pp. 242–3).

[1] Migne, *P.G.* VII. 1023–4.
[2] Ibid. 1029.

Chapter Three

PRAYER IN THE ACTS OF THE MARTYRS, HIPPOLYTUS, AND TERTULLIAN

Prayer in the Acts of the Early Martyrs

There is another class of literature which affords some interesting evidence about the practice of prayer, namely the Acts of the Martyrs. These are accounts of martyrdoms purporting to be compiled by the Churches to which the martyrs belonged. Their number is legion, and few of them have a just claim to authenticity. But in those which are probably genuine [1] we observe that prayer was a potent source of strength to these Christians facing the fiercest of all trials. Much of the time of waiting before their execution they spent in prayer, and most of the Acts record that they died with words of praise and thanks to God upon their lips. These brave Christians were very conscious of the all-embracing providence of God, and their prayers are the expression of their faith.

Of special interest is *The Passion of SS. Perpetua and Felicitas* (A.D. 203), of which the following is an account. The quotations are from E. C. E. Owen, *Some Authentic Acts of the Early Martyrs*.

During the persecution Perpetua's father endeavoured to dissuade her from Christianity. "Then I thanked the Lord for being parted a few days from my father, and was refreshed by his absence. During those few days we were baptized, and the Holy Spirit bade me make no other petition after the holy water save for bodily endurance" (III).

Shortly afterwards Perpetua was imprisoned, together with her baby and certain other Christians. Perpetua was evidently known as

[1] Reference may be made to E. C. E. Owen, *Some Authentic Acts of the Early Martyrs*, Oxford, 1927. See especially *The Acts of SS. Carpus, Papylus and Agathonica* (A.D. 161–9); *The Acts of SS. Justin and his Companions* (A.D. 163–5); *The Letter of the Churches of Vienne and Lyons concerning the Martyrdom of SS. Pothinus and Others* (A.D. 177); *The Acts of the Scillitan Saints* (A.D. 180). See also *The Acts of S. Apollonius* (A.D. 180–5) in Kidd, *Documents*, Vol. I, pp. 130 ff.

one whose prayers sometimes received visions in answer. "My brother said to me: 'Lady sister, you are now in great honour, so great indeed that you may well pray for a vision and may well be shown whether suffering or release be in store for you.' And I who knew myself to have speech of the Lord, for whose sake I had gone through so much, gave confident promise in return, saying: 'Tomorrow I will bring you word.' And I made request, and this was shown me...." There follows an account of a vision of a ladder which Saturus and Perpetua mount. It is taken to indicate their approaching martyrdom (IV).

After condemnation, and whilst waiting for execution, the Christians prayed. "After a few days, while we were all praying, suddenly in the middle of the prayer I spoke, and uttered the name Dinocrates; and I was astonished that he had never come into mind till then; and I grieved thinking of what had befallen him. And I saw at once that I was entitled, and ought, to make request for him. And I began to pray much for him, and make lamentation to the Lord." Dinocrates was Perpetua's brother who had died unbaptized at the age of seven. On the same night Perpetua dreamed that in the place where Dinocrates was, a font of water stood, from which her brother was unable to drink. "And I woke and recognized that my brother was in trouble, and I prayed for him every day until we were transferred to the garrison prison. . . . And I prayed for him day and night with lamentations and tears that he might be given me" (VII). Shortly afterwards Perpetua experienced another dream in which she saw Dinocrates "clean in body, well-clothed and refreshed". The font was now within his reach and he drank from it. "And when he had drunk enough of the water, he came forward being glad to play as children will. And I awoke. Then I knew that he had been released from punishment" (VIII). This extract is of great interest as a very early instance of prayer for the departed.

Another martyr of this group was St Felicitas, who, being pregnant, feared lest her martyrdom should be delayed, since it was against the law for pregnant women to be executed. "Her fellow-martyrs too were deeply grieved at the thought of leaving so good a comrade and fellow-traveller behind alone on the way to the same hope. So in one flood of common lamentation they poured forth a prayer to the Lord two days before the games [i.e. the date of execution]. Immediately after the prayer her pains came upon her" (xv).

The last chapters, which possibly were written by Tertullian, describe how the martyrs met death in the way each desired: "He who had said: 'Ask and ye shall receive' had granted to those who asked Him that death which each had craved" (xix).

Such stories are a reminder that these were days when prayer was much more than a religious exercise accepted as a duty. For the second-century Christian it was the breath of the Christian life and it gave him strength and courage in death.

Hippolytus

Since the publication in 1916 of R. H. Connolly's *The So-called Egyptian Church Order and Derived Documents* (Cambridge Texts and Studies VIII. 4), it has been widely recognized that the Ἀποστολικὴ Παράδοσις (*Apostolic Tradition*) which appears in the list of the titles of the works of Hippolytus inscribed on the statue of him discovered in the sixteenth century is the original work at the base of the Egyptian Church Order in its various versions,[1] and of the other documents derived from it.[2]

The exact status of Hippolytus in Rome at the beginning of the third century is in dispute. Döllinger (*Hippolytus und Kallistus*) considered that he was an anti-pope, consecrated in opposition to Callistus, whose laxity of discipline he attacks in his *Refutation of All Heresies*. Lightfoot held that he was Bishop of Portus, with the oversight of the Greek-speaking Christians of Rome, Callistus being the bishop of the Latin-speaking Roman Christians.

Gregory Dix in *The Treatise on the Apostolic Tradition of St Hippolytus of Rome* (S.P.C.K., 1937) dates this first reasonably complete Church Order "a year or two either way of A.D. 215". In it Hippolytus was concerned to recall the Church from laxity to a stricter discipline and practice. Dix argues that we may accept the *Apostolic Tradition* as reliable evidence of old Roman Christian customs, since Hippolytus's case against the laxity of his opponents could not have stood if he had merely given an account of his own preferences. Hippolytus's argument rests on the appeal to former practice.

The evidence of the *Apostolic Tradition* about the times of daily prayer will be considered in Appendix A, page 36. Hippolytus also provides some evidence that instruction in prayer was given to catechumens. There is a hint of this in Justin Martyr (*Apol.* I. 61): "As many as are persuaded and believe that those things which are

[1] Latin (fragmentary), Ethiopic, Arabic, Sahidic, and Bohairic.
[2] *Apostolic Constitutions*, Book VIII; *The Epitome of Ap. Cons.* VIII; *The Testament of our Lord*; *The Canons of Hippolytus*.

taught and declared by us are true, and give promise that they are able to live thus, are taught to pray." Hippolytus speaks of catechumens praying after their instructions: "Each time the teacher finishes his instruction let the catechumens pray by themselves apart from the faithful." [1] He does not here definitely say that they were given instruction in prayer, but in view of the fact that these catechumens were required to occupy themselves in prayer at the close of each instruction, it is probable that such was the case, and *A.T.* XXXVI. 15 bears this out. There, after giving an account of the proper times of prayer, Hippolytus writes: "These things, therefore, all ye faithful, if ye perform them and remember them and instruct one another and encourage the catechumens to do them ye will not be able to be tempted or to perish, having Christ always before your minds." [2]

Tertullian

Tertullian of North Africa (c. A.D. 160–240),[3] the first great Latin Father, was the first to write a treatise solely devoted to the subject of prayer. This work, which "can never be read without profit", and which contains some of the gems of his writing,[4] shows a very different side of Tertullian's character from that which is usually taken to be characteristic of him, namely his fierce and sarcastic ridicule and denunciation of all that he held to be false in heathenism and heresy, or slack in the Church itself. *De Oratione* was written before the intolerance and impatience, of which Tertullian himself was well aware (*De Patientia* I), gripped him completely, and led him into the schism of Montanism. It is a systematic, if brief, commentary on the clauses of the Lord's Prayer, followed by a discussion of various contemporary practices in connection with prayer.

The polemic nature of the bulk of Tertullian's writing provides comparatively few contexts in which the subject of prayer is conveniently mentioned. But there is enough evidence to allow us to say that mysticism is absent and that his doctrine of prayer is eminently practical. The treatise *De Oratione* bears this out. His teaching may best be summarized under the headings of the four main topics of

---

[1] *A.T.* XVIII. 1 : Dix, p. 29.   [2] Dix, p. 68.
[3] In order to leave Clement of Alexandria's doctrine of prayer for consideration immediately before that of his great successor Origen, we take Tertullian here, although he was born and died later than Clement.
[4] J. M. Fuller, art. "Tertullianus" in Smith and Wace, *Dict. of Christian Biography*.

prayer later laid down by Origen: praise, thanksgiving, confession, and intercession.

Praise. His comments on the first two clauses of the Lord's Prayer (*De Orat.* II, III) show that he holds that to "honour God" is the Christian's first duty in prayer. God's name, which is always holy in itself, is continually hallowed by the angelic "Holy, holy, holy", and must be likewise hallowed in the Christian's life and prayers.

Thanksgiving. It is "most fitting that God should be blessed everywhere and always for the remembrance of His benefits" (*De Orat.* III).[1]

Confession. The topic of confession is given a larger place in what Tertullian has to say about prayer (see *De Orat.* VII on "Forgive us our debts"). Confession, he points out, is especially appropriate in candidates for Baptism, who should prepare for their initiation "with frequent prayers, fastings, genuflexions and vigils, and with confession of all their past sins" (*De Baptismo* XX).

In cases of grievous sin after Baptism (discussed in *De Poenitentia* VII–XII) Tertullian allows a second repentance, but it must be by way of public confession, and after days and nights spent in weeping, fasting, and prayer. The penitent ought to fall to the earth and implore the help of the presbyters, to spend hours on his knees before God's altars, and to implore the brethren to pray for him.

Petition and Intercession. Tertullian interprets the clause "Thy will be done in heaven and in earth" as in reality a petition for the things which will make our salvation sure. "We ask, therefore, that He supply us with the nature and power of His will, that we may be safe both in heaven and on earth ... we are praying for our own benefit" (*De Orat.* IV). Like all responsible teachers on prayer he thus holds that petition should be for spiritual before material gifts.[2]

In accordance with this he considers that the petition for bread in the Lord's Prayer should be taken in a spiritual sense as a prayer "to live perpetually in Christ and undivided from His body". But he does not entirely exclude the literal sense of the petition, and remarks on the modesty of the request: "For He commands that bread be sought, which is all the faithful need" (*De Orat.* VI). With this may be

---

[1] Translation of passages from Tertullian's *De Oratione* and *De Baptismo* is from A. Souter, *Tertullian's Treatises Concerning Prayer and Concerning Baptism* (S.P.C.K., 1919).

[2] Cf. also *De Baptismo* XX, where the newly baptized are enjoined to "spread out your hands for the first time" and ask that "the gifts of grace, the partitions of spiritual endowments be added" to the grace of Baptism.

THE ACTS OF THE MARTYRS

compared a passage in *De Jejunio* xv, where, as a Montanist, Tertullian argues against the justification by churchmen, whom he scornfully calls "Psychics", of their meagre fasts on the score that our Lord was one who ate and drank, reminding them that the Lord in his prayer taught us to ask for bread, and not for the riches of Attalus.

In *De Oratione* x Tertullian says that "since there are things to be asked in view of the circumstances of each individual, they that approach have the right, after dispatching first the regular and standard prayer by way of a foundation, to build on it outside petitions embodying their desires, always remembering, however, the prescribed requests". Some of these "outside petitions" are enumerated in the last chapter of *De Oratione* (xxix): "Righteous prayer turns away all the wrath of God, keeps watch in face of the enemy, 'begs for the persecutors'. Is there any wonder that it can wring water from the sky, seeing that it could obtain even fire? Prayer is the only thing that can prevail with God, but Christ willed that it should work no evil. All the power He conferred upon it sprang from good. So it has no power except to recall the souls of the dead from the very way of death,[1] to restore the maimed, to cure the sick, to purge the victims of evil spirits, to open the bars of the prison, to loosen the bonds of the upright. It also washes away sins, drives back temptations, quenches persecutions, consoles the downhearted, cheers the courageous, attends upon the traveller in distant lands, subdues waves, confounds robbers, nourishes the poor, guides the rich, raises the fallen, supports the falling, and upholds them that do stand."

Prayers for the Emperor and the State are twice mentioned in the *Apology*. In xxxii Tertullian says that one reason for this practice is that at the end of the Roman Empire Antichrist will appear, and the world come to an end: "We have also another and a greater need to pray for the Emperors, and, moreover for the whole estate of the Empire, and the fortunes of Rome, knowing as we do, that the mighty shock which hangeth over the whole world, and the end of time itself, threatening terrible and grievous things, is delayed because of the time allowed to the Roman Empire. We would not, therefore, experience these things, and while we pray that they may be put off, we favour the long continuance of Rome."[2] This is nothing if not a frank admission that there was an ulterior motive in Christian prayer for

---
[1] One of the earliest clear references to the practice of prayer for the departed.
[2] Quoted in Kidd, *Documents*, Vol. I, No. 90.

the Emperor. Again in XXXIX there is mention of prayers for the Emperor, but here the reference is clearly to common prayer: "We are a body formed by our joint cognizance of Religion, by the unity of discipline, by the bond of hope. We come together in a meeting and a congregation as before God, as though we would in one body sue Him by our prayers. This violence is pleasing to God. We pray also for Emperors, for their ministers and the powers, for the condition of the world, for the quiet of all things, for the delaying of the end." [1]

The value that Tertullian attaches to intercession for others is shown by his request at the end of *De Baptismo*, "I only pray that, when ye ask, ye may also remember Tertullian, a sinner", as well as by his advice to those seeking reconciliation after post-baptismal sin to implore the prayers of the presbyters and of the brethren (*De Poenitentia* IX).

One passage in the last chapter of *De Oratione* is important as showing that Tertullian regarded the psychological effect of prayer as one of its valuable results: "Even the prayer of the olden times freed men from fire and wild beasts and starvation, and yet it had not received its pattern from Christ. But how much more does Christian prayer work! It does not plant the angel of moisture 'in the midst of the fire' or 'stop the mouths of lions' or bring country fare to the starving; it turns away no feeling of suffering by the gift of grace,[2] but furnishes sufferers and the victims of intense feeling and pain, with the power to endure; it extends grace to include courage, that faith may know what it is to get from the Lord, realizing what it is suffering for God's name." The objective result prayed for may be denied by the wisdom of God, but the subjective result of inward strengthening is assured to Christian prayer.

It is very often said that the great difference between the Christianity of the West and that of the East is that the latter is more speculative in doctrinal matters and more mystical in its devotion, whilst Latin Christianity is more concerned to systematize doctrine, and inculcates

---

[1] Quoted in Kidd, *Documents*, Vol. I, No. 92. The reference to prayer for the delaying of the end here and in *Apol.* XXXII is inconsistent with the thought of *De Orat.* v, where Tertullian says that Christians eagerly wait and pray for the end of the world, for it means "to the Christians answered prayer, to the heathen disgrace, to the angels rapture".

[2] Other passages, e.g. later in the same chapter, make clear that Tertullian did not, in fact, regard such objective results of prayer as impossible.

a more practical outlook in devotion. Tertullian's doctrine of prayer certainly bears this out. It is severely practical, and we find none of the mysticism which we are to meet in certain forms in the Christian Platonists of Alexandria, Clement and his successor, Origen, who was a younger contemporary of Tertullian.

Chapter Four

PRAYER IN CLEMENT OF ALEXANDRIA

"THE specifically Christian doctrine of prayer first assumes something like systematic consistency in the writings of Clement of Alexandria." So writes A. L. Lilley in his *Prayer in Christian Theology*.[1] Certainly Clement [2] has a great deal more to say on the subject of prayer than any previous Christian writer, and in the seventh book of the *Stromateis* or *Miscellanies* he endeavours to set out a coherent doctrine of prayer. It is certain that this has had a great influence on later Christian mysticism, but equally certain that it has had little influence on prayer as practised by the majority of faithful Christians.

Clement, as is evident from the diverse learning displayed in his writings, was a typical scholar. He was deeply influenced by the philosophy of Plato with its emphasis on the intellect as the significant faculty of man, able to bring him into touch with reality. The highest aim of man is to acquire knowledge, knowledge of the Form of the Good, the source of all goodness. Consequently virtue is thought of as consisting in true knowledge, and vice as consisting precisely in ignorance. "The highest thing, is then," says Clement, "the knowledge of God; wherefore also by it virtue is so preserved as to be incapable of being lost."[3] This intellectualism predominates in Clement's system, and it greatly affects his doctrine of prayer.

Hence, for Clement, the true Christian is what he calls the Gnostic, the man who has attained to the greatest possible degree of knowledge of God. Faith, "an internal good (which) without searching for God confesses His existence, and glorifies Him as existent",[4] is the be-

---

[1] S.C.M., 1925: a small book which has not received the attention it deserves.

[2] Clement of Alexandria, c. A.D. 150–214, was a teacher in, and almost certainly for a period head of, the Catechetical School in Alexandria.

[3] *Stromateis* VII. 7. Clement's works are translated in the Ante-Nicene Christian Library in two volumes (Edinburgh, 1867–9). Quotations given here are from this translation, which is by William Wilson.

[4] Ibid. VII. 10.

ginning of the process. "Starting from this faith, and being developed by it, through the grace of God, the knowledge respecting Him is to be acquired as far as possible." [1] There is need of "very great preparation and previous training",[2] and this includes acquaintance with the philosophers, but above all with the Lord's teaching. Knowledge elevates the soul "to what is akin to the soul, divine and holy, and by its own light conveys man through the mystic stages of advancement; till it restores the pure in heart to the crowning place of rest; teaching to gaze on God, face to face, with knowledge and comprehension. For in this consists the perfection of the gnostic soul, in its being with the Lord, where it is in immediate subjection to Him." [3] There is, however, another stage in the process of the Christian life, and that is the growth into the life of love. "The first saving change is that from heathenism to faith . . . and the second, that from faith to knowledge. And the latter terminating in love, thereafter gives the loving to the loved, that which knows to that which is known." [4] Clement then goes on to describe the Gnostic's way of life in terms which make it clear that he by no means thought of the ideal Christian life as a barren intellectualism.[5]

In such a scheme it will be evident that prayer, defined by Clement as "converse with God",[6] plays a prominent part.

Prayer as Constant Companionship with God

Again and again Clement repeats that prayer is a continual state in which a man realizes the end of his existence, namely fellowship with God. "Man has been . . . constituted by nature, so as to have fellowship with God. . . . We invite him—born, as he is, for the contemplation of heaven, and being, as he is, a truly heavenly plant—to the knowledge of God, counselling him to furnish himself with what is his sufficient provision for eternity, namely piety. Practise husbandry, we say, if you are a husbandman; but while you till your fields, know God. Sail the sea, you who are devoted to navigation, yet call the whilst on the heavenly Pilot. Has knowledge taken hold of you while engaged in military service? Listen to the commander, who orders what is right" (*Exhortation to the Heathen* x. 28).

His final exhortation in the same work includes the appeal: "Let us become God-loving men, and obtain the greatest of all things

[1] *Strom.* vii. 10. [2] Ibid. [3] Ibid.
[4] Ibid. [5] Ibid. vii. 11–14. [6] Ibid. vii. 7.

which are incapable of being harmed—God and life. . . . Having learned that we are the most excellent of His possessions, let us commit ourselves to God, loving the Lord God, and regarding this as our business all our life long" (ibid. xii. 34).

Clement reiterates this conception of prayer in *Strom.* vi. 14: "Lauding, hymning, blessing, praising, such a soul is never at any time separated from God"; again in vii. 7: "Holding festival, then, in our whole life, persuaded that God is altogether on every side present, we cultivate our fields, praising; we sail the sea, hymning"; and in vii. 12: "Not only on rising in the morning and at noon, but also when walking about, when asleep, when dressing and undressing . . . he is ever giving thanks to God."

True prayer, then, according to Clement, is a constant intercourse with God. But God is a God who knows and perceives all things, and thoughts as well as words. "The divine power, with the speed of light, sees through the whole soul" (*Strom.* vii. 7). Thus prayer is expressed in the Gnostic's thoughts rather than by words: "The subjects of requests are the objects of desires." Clement works this conception out fully in *Strom.* vii. 7, using the typical language of mysticism: "God hears continually all the inward converse. So also we raise the head and lift the hands to heaven, and set the feet in motion at the closing utterance of the prayer, following the eagerness of the spirit directed towards the intellectual essence; and endeavouring to abstract the body from the earth, along with the discourse, raising the soul aloft, winged with longing for better things, we compel it to advance to the region of holiness, magnanimously despising the chain of the flesh."

Again, "God does not wait for loquacious tongues, as interpreters among men, but knows absolutely the thoughts of all; and what the voice intimates to us, that our thought, which even before the creation He knew would come into our mind, speaks to God. Prayer, then, may be uttered without the voice, by concentrating the whole spiritual nature within on expression by the mind, in undistracted turning towards God."

And once more, "He does not use wordy prayer by his mouth . . . If he but form the thought in the secret chamber of his soul, and call on the Father 'with unspoken groanings' (Rom. 8. 26), He is near, and is at his side, while yet speaking."

A quotation which Clement gives as from "Scripture", but the source of which is uncertain, is made by him the text of this doctrine of "prayer by thought". It is first cited in *Strom.* vi. 9: "The Lord will not wait for the voice of this man (the Gnostic) in prayer. 'Ask,' He says, 'and I will do it; think, and I will give.'" Again in *Strom.* vi. 12 we have the same quotation, illustrated by a scriptural example: "To those, then, who have repented and not firmly believed, God grants their requests through their supplications. But to those who live sinlessly and gnostically, He gives, when they have but merely entertained the thought. For example, to Anna, on her merely conceiving the thought, conception was vouchsafed of the child Samuel. 'Ask,' says the Scripture, 'and I will do. Think, and I will give.'" [1]

Clement's Doctrine of Prayer in relation to the normal Christian Prayer Scheme

It is not easy to see how a doctrine of prayer as continual intercourse with God expressed on the man's part by his thoughts can be accommodated to the normal Christian practice of prayer. And it is here that we perceive a certain indecision on Clement's part. For this reason a number of his passages on prayer are impossible to reconcile.

On the one hand he compares the Gnostic's prayer with that of other Christians, who pray at special times of the day, in terms that show something of arrogance. "Now, if some assign definite hours for prayer—as, for example, the third, and sixth, and ninth—yet the Gnostic prays throughout his whole life, endeavouring by prayer to have fellowship with God. And, briefly, having reached to this, he leaves behind him all that is of no service, as having now received the perfection of the man that acts by love" (*Strom.* vii. 7). Yet on the other hand the Gnostic must condescend to pray with other Christians: "But also it becomes him to make all his prayers gently along with the good. For it is a dangerous thing to take part in others' sins. Accordingly the Gnostic will pray along with those who have more recently believed, for those things in respect of which it is their duty to act together" (ibid.). Yet, since this sharing in the devotions of other Christians is a matter of condescension, the principle is kept, that true prayer is something other than the normal devotions of Christians.

We next ask whether the prayer of the true Gnostic has any points of contact with the usual topics of normal Christian prayer.

[1] This is quoted again in *Strom.* vii. 12.

Praise and Thanksgiving are to be prominent notes in the true Gnostic's prayer. The "Let God be magnified" of Psalm 70. 4 [1] and the resounding praise of Psalm 150 [2] are taken as models for the Gnostic's prayer. "If thou shalt love the Lord thy God ... let its first manifestation be towards God in thanksgiving and psalmody" (*Paed.* II. 4). Clement singles out particular moments at which it is appropriate to give thanks: at the partaking of food and drink, and on retiring for the night (*Paed.* II. 4, 9). It is evident that Clement does not entirely regard as unimportant definite moments of fully conscious prayer. Nor does he despise a man's natural gratitude for material gifts: "Thanksgiving has place not for the soul and spiritual blessings alone, but also for the body, and for the good things of the body." [3] Yet it is "knowledge" which enables the Gnostic to utter the perfect thanksgiving. His knowledge of God gives him an insight into the purpose of all that befalls, and he is able to see that it is, contrary often to appearance, by God's arrangement for the good of souls. "The form of his prayer is thanksgiving for the past, for the present, and for the future as already through faith present. This is preceded by the reception of knowledge." [4]

Confession. There are few references in Clement to confession of sins in prayer. [5] In the other writers whom we have considered above, references to confession are also fewer than to the other topics of prayer, but none of these deals with the subject of prayer to anything like the same extent as does Clement. The absence of this note in Clement, apart from a brief reference or two, is surely significant. The fact is that Clement's Gnostic is presumed to be as near to perfection as is possible for one who is still in the flesh. He knows God, and this knowledge is virtue. The Gnostic souls are "likened to the consecrated virgins who wait for the Lord ... saying 'Lord, for long have we desired to receive Thee; we have lived according to what Thou hast enjoined, transgressing none of Thy commandments'". [6] "He who holds converse with God must have his soul immaculate and stainlessly pure, it being essential to have made himself perfectly good." [7] There is little wonder, then, that confession of sin will have but an insignificant place in the Gnostic's prayer.

---

[1] *Exhortation to the Heathen* x. 29.   [2] *Paed.* II. 4.
[3] *Strom.* v. 10.   [4] Ibid. VII. 12.
[5] Ibid. v. 3, VII. 12, and VII. 13, where brief references occur, are the only examples I have found.
[6] Ibid. VII. 12.   [7] Ibid. VII. 7.

Clement seems to forget that, on his own showing, a considerable amount of training is necessary before the Christian attains Gnostic status. During this period, before the knowledge in which virtue consists is given, the Christian must be in ignorance on many matters, and consequently he must be a sinner. Clement seems to ignore the prayers of such people. When he speaks of prayer, it is almost always the prayer of the Gnostic that he has in mind. He has nothing to say of the prayer of the ordinary persevering Christian, and to what extent confession must form a part of it.

The prayers of unworthy men constitute a special problem for Clement, which we will discuss later. But he gives no hint that confession may render them more worthy. In spite of all the qualifications and allowances which can justly be made, Clement's teaching on prayer gives little help to any who are incapable of the long sustained intellectual effort he demands.

Intercession and Petition. It might be doubted whether Clement's conception of prayer as essentially an intellectual intercourse with God could include petition. Most religious philosophers have felt an incongruity between their conception of God's unchangeable nature, and any idea of prayer as able to influence God.[1] But Clement appears to feel no such difficulty, and a great deal of what he has to say about prayer is concerned with intercession and petition. To him, it would seem, "specific requests are the most fully conscious moments of prayer, the moments of most energetic aspiration towards God of the total character formed by habitual converse with Him".[2]

Like every Christian teacher of prayer, Clement has much to say about praying for spiritual rather than material gifts:[3] "The Gnostic, who has reached the summit, will pray that contemplation may grow and abide, as the common man will for continual good health." In *Strom.* I. 24 he quotes with approval the verse from an unknown source which Origen was to make the text of his treatise on prayer: "Seek what is great, and the little things shall be added." The Gnostic is to pray for others: "He will pray that as many as possible may become like him, to the glory of God, which is perfected through knowledge. For he who is made like the Saviour is also devoted to saving."[4] He may also pray for the material wants of others: "In the

---

[1] See Heiler, *Prayer*, Chapter IV, "Critique and Ideal of Prayer in Philosophical Thought".
[2] Lilley, *Prayer in Christian Theology*, p. 24.
[3] *Strom.* VII. 7 *passim.*   [4] Ibid. VI. 9.

case of his brethren in want, the Gnostic will not ask himself for abundance of wealth to bestow, but will pray that the supply of what they need may be furnished to them. For so the Gnostic gives his prayer to those who are in need, and by his prayer they are supplied, without his knowledge, and without vanity." [1]

Such teaching on petition and intercession brings Clement's doctrine close to traditional practice in prayer. But it diverges again in his insistence that the petitions of the Gnostic are always granted. The Gnostic knows "what things are really good, and what are to be asked, and when and how in each individual case. It is the extremest stupidity ... to ask those things which are not beneficial." [2] "The only really holy and pious man is he who is truly a Gnostic according to the rule of the church, to whom alone the petition made in accordance with the will of God is granted, on asking and on thinking. For as God can do all that He wishes, so the Gnostic receives all that he asks." [3]

The success which invariably attends the prayer of the true Gnostic depends on the refined nature of his prayer. "The Gnostic will ask the permanence of the things he possesses, adaptation for what is to take place, and the eternity of those things which he shall receive. And the things which are really good, the things which concern the soul, he prays that they may belong to him, and remain with him. And so he desires not anything that is absent, being content with what is present. For he is not deficient in the good things which are proper to him; being already sufficient for himself, through divine grace and knowledge. But having become sufficient in himself, he stands in no want of other things. But knowing the sovereign will, and possessing as soon as he prays, being brought into close contact with the almighty power, and earnestly desiring to be spiritual, through boundless love, he is united to the Spirit" (*Strom.* VII. 7).

The Gnostic's petition is again declared in *Strom.* VII. 12 to be invariably attended with success. "His whole life is prayer and converse with God. And if he be pure from sins, he will by all means obtain what he wishes. For God says to the righteous man, 'Ask, and I will give thee; think, and I will do'. If beneficial, he will receive it at once; and if injurious, he will never ask it, and therefore he will not receive it. So it shall be as he wishes."

Such passages prompt the comment that there is a distinct *naïveté*

---

[1] *Strom.* VII. 13.   [2] Ibid. VII. 7.   [3] Ibid.

in Clement's doctrine of prayer. If his premiss is granted, that the Gnostic completely knows the will of God, it must follow that the Gnostic will ask nothing amiss in his petitions. But Clement gives little guidance to the ordinary Christian. He tells us that perfect prayer is prayer in accordance with the will of God and will be answered, but gives little help to one who may want to know what the will of God is. To be told that this is part of the knowledge of the Gnostic is of little help to the majority of Christians who are not Gnostics.

The Petitions of the Unworthy. Discussion of the success attending the Gnostic's petitions prompts Clement to discuss also the petitions of the unworthy. Almost every passage in which the former is treated contains a reference to the contrasting ineffectiveness of the prayers of the unworthy.

As we have seen, the good success of the Gnostic's prayer arises from the fact that he knows the right things to ask. Consequently, failure attends the petitions of those who are ignorant of the will of God and of the good life. "It is clear, then, that those who do not perform good actions, do not know what is for their own advantage. And if so, neither are they capable of praying aright, so as to receive from God good things; nor, should they receive them, will they be sensible of the boon; nor, should they enjoy them, will they enjoy worthily what they know not; both from their want of knowledge how to use the good things given them, and from their excessive stupidity, being ignorant of the way to avail themselves of the divine gifts" (*Strom.* VI. 14). Clement here admits that the unworthy sometimes receive what they pray for; and this fact constitutes a problem for him, to which he offers two solutions. The first is that no real advantage comes to the wicked when they receive their petitions: "In the case of wicked men, therefore, prayer is most injurious, not to others alone, but to themselves also. If, then, they should ask and receive what they call pieces of good fortune, these injure them after they receive them, being ignorant how to use them. For they pray to possess what they have not, and they ask things which seem, but are not, good things" (*Strom.* VII. 7). The second suggested solution is more ingenious: "But if one say to us, that some sinners even obtain according to their requests, (we should say) that this rarely takes place, by reason of the righteous goodness of God. And it is granted to those who are capable of doing others good. Whence the gift is not made for the sake of him that asked it; but the divine dispensation, foreseeing that one would be saved by his means, renders the boon again righteous" (*Strom.* VII. 12).

But according to Clement, it only "rarely takes place" that the unworthy receives his petition. The general principle is that "God knows those who are and those who are not worthy of good things; whence He gives to each what is suitable. Wherefore to those that are unworthy, though they ask often, He will not give; but He will give to those who are worthy" (*Strom.* VII. 7).

Enough has been said to show that in spite of the tendency towards an intellectual mysticism in Clement's doctrine of prayer, he still regards it, for a great part of the time, as does the "average" Christian, as the converse of the soul with God, expressing its wonder at God's greatness in praise, its gratitude for God's goodness in thanksgiving, its sense of unworthiness in confession, and its needs in petition. Clement the pedant, attempting to make prayer an intellectual exercise of the *élite*, does not in the end quite deceive Clement the Christian, who cannot after all help thinking of prayer as the generations of Christians before him had thought of it, as the forthright speech of man with his Maker.

Prayer and Good Works. In justice to Clement's doctrine of prayer it must be said that he does not entirely overlook the importance of good works as substantiating the sincerity of a man's prayer. In most passages his emphasis on the function of the intellect in prayer leaves no room for consideration of the function of the will and its fruit in good works. But a passage or two shows that Clement does not entirely forget that prayer is hypocrisy if a man's life does not exemplify his aspirations in prayer. "'Good works are an acceptable prayer to the Lord', says the Scripture.[1] And the manner of prayer is described. 'If thou seest', it is said, 'the naked, cover him; and thou shalt not overlook those who belong to thy seed. Then shall thy light spring forth early, and thy healing shall spring up quickly; and thy righteousness shall go before thee, and the glory of God shall encompass thee.' What, then, is the fruit of such prayer? 'Then shalt thou call, and God will hear thee; whilst thou art yet speaking, He will say, I am here'" (*Paed.* III. 12).

With this may be compared the continuation of the passage quoted above (p. 31) from *Strom.* VI. 9: "(The Gnostic) will pray that as many as possible may become like him, to the glory of God, which is perfected through knowledge. For he who is made like the Saviour is

[1] The source of this quotation is not known.

also devoted to saving; performing unerringly the commandments as far as the human nature may admit of the image. And this is to worship God by deeds and knowledge of the true righteousness. The Lord will not wait for the voice of this man in prayer. 'Ask,' He says, 'and I will do it; think, and I will give.'"

An important principle of prayer is glanced at in the following: "The Gnostic . . . makes his prayer and request for the truly good things which appertain to the soul, and prays, he himself also contributing his efforts to attain to the habit of goodness" (*Strom.* VII. 7). Unwillingness to devote one's own endeavours, so far as possible, towards the attainment of what is asked in prayer betrays insincerity.

These last passages help to keep Clement's doctrine of prayer within the orbit of traditional Christian teaching and practice.

Appendix A

THE HOURS OF PRAYER

The Didache. "Thus pray ye: Our Father . . . Three times in the day pray ye so" (VIII). In the absence of any specific directions about meeting in assembly this passage must be taken to refer to private prayer. No hint is given of the exact times of day intended.

Hippolytus. The *Apostolic Tradition* of Hippolytus mentions seven hours of prayer.

(1) *Morning Prayers.* "As soon as they (the faithful) wake and are risen" (XXX. 1; cf. also XXXV. 1: Dix, *The Apostolic Tradition of Hippolytus*, pp. 57, 61).

(2) *Terce.* "Pray at the third hour and praise God . . . For in this hour Christ was seen nailed upon the tree" (XXXVI. 2, 3: Dix, pp. 62, 63).

(3) *Sext.* "Pray also likewise at the sixth hour, for at that hour when Christ had been hanged upon the wood of the Cross the daylight was divided and it became darkness" (XXXVI. 4: Dix, p. 63).

(4) *None.* "And at the ninth hour also let prayer be protracted and praise be sung . . . For in that hour Christ was pierced in His side" (XXXVI. 5, 6: Dix, p. 64).

(5) *Night Prayers.* "Pray also before thy body rests upon thy bed" (XXXVI. 7).

(6) *Mattins.* "And at midnight rise and wash thy hands with water and pray" (XXXVI. 8). ". . . because in this hour every creature hushes for a brief moment to praise the Lord . . . And testifying to this the Lord says thus, Behold a cry was made at midnight of them that said, Behold the Bridegroom has come" (XXXVI. 12, 13).

(7) *Cockcrow.* "And at the hour when the cock crows, likewise rise and pray, because at the hour of cockcrow the children of Israel denied Christ" (XXXVI. 14).

The strong implication is that this scheme of seven hours of daily prayer had been the normal custom of Christians at Rome for many years. Hippolytus, writing against what he considered to be the laxity of the times, is setting down the apostolic tradition. His case would have been destroyed if his readers had been able to point to any novelty in the practices which he was advocating.

Hippolytus's scheme of seven hours of prayer is so like that of the later offices of the Church, systematized by the monks, that it is tempting to assume that in the *Apostolic Tradition* we have our earliest evidence for the daily offices said in assembly by the Church. Yet it is to be noticed that, apart from provision for daily morning instruction in the assembly which the faithful are to attend if possible, in preference to private prayer at home, nothing whatever is said to indicate that Hippolytus envisages a gathering together of Christians for common prayer at the stated hours. In the case of prayer at the third hour, prayer before retiring, at midnight, and at cockcrow, it is clear that he has in mind private prayer, and the same is to be presumed in the case of the other hours.

This question is admirably summarized by E. C. Ratcliff: [1] "There is as yet no trace of Offices. Prayer, 'which is the duty of all', is still private. Yet, although this is so, Hippolytus's outlook is noticeably different from that of earlier writers. Regimen has replaced recommendation; and the importance of the *Apostolic Tradition* lies in the fact of its wide acceptance and the consequent diffusion of the changed outlook. In its systematization of daily private prayer and in the imposition of its system as obligatory, the *Apostolic Tradition* gave a new direction to the movement of Christian life and ideal of practice, and originated a process of which the logical conclusion was a liturgical system of daily public prayer. Common prayer at stated times in church is the next step to obligatory private prayer at the same time at home, and the step is easier when the custom is already established of resorting daily to church for instructions. There is, also, but a short distance between direction to say prayers, and direction as to what prayers to say."

Clement of Alexandria. Six hours of prayer are mentioned by Clement. *Strom.* VII. 7 speaks of three: "Now, if some assign definite hours for prayer—as, for example, the third, and sixth, and ninth—yet the Gnostic prays throughout his whole life."

There are also references to prayer before sleep (*Paed.* II. 4;

[1] Chapter "The Choir Offices" in *Liturgy and Worship* (S.P.C.K., 1932) p. 259.

Strom. II. 23), during the night (*Paed.* II. 9; *Strom.* VII. 7), and at dawn or upon rising (*Strom.* II. 23, VII. 12).

Thus there is evidence that at Alexandria six definite hours of prayer were kept by Christians. There is nothing, however, to show that the majority of Christians kept these hours, or that there were any who kept them all.

Tertullian. Tertullian knows of six hours of prayer: at the beginning of the day, the third, sixth, and ninth hours, at the beginning of the night, and during the night. The relevant passages are:

De Oratione XXV. "Concerning time, however, the keeping also of certain hours will not be useless from an external point of view —I mean of these common hours that mark the intervals of the day, the third, sixth and ninth, which in Scripture are to be found the most usual ... of course, quite apart from the regular prayers which without any reminder are due at the beginning of day and night."

De Jejunio X has reference to prayer at the third, sixth, and ninth hours.

Ad Uxorem II. Tertullian asks, with Christian women married to heathen husbands in mind, "Will not thy rising in the night to pray be interpreted to be some act of magic?"

Origen. De Oratione XII. 2: "What is usually called 'prayer' ... ought not to be performed less than three times each day." These three times are midnight, noon, and in the evening. See note on pp. 115–6 below.

The Origin of the Christian Hours of Prayer

It is almost certain, although Hippolytus and other early Christian writers were unaware of it, and would have repudiated the suggestion, that the origin of the hours of prayer is, at least in part, to be found in the daily Jewish synagogue services.[1] The majority of the Christians of the first generation were Jews who would have continued to take part in the worship of the synagogue. When the break with the synagogue came, possibly hastened by the inclusion about A.D. 90, in the daily blessings, of a declaration against heretics which was especially aimed at Christians,[2] the institution of daily prayer at set

---

[1] For a full discussion of this see C. W. Dugmore, *The Influence of the Synagogue upon the Divine Office* (O.U.P., 1944).
[2] Cf. Justin Martyr, *Dial. with Trypho* XCVI.

THE HOURS OF PRAYER

times was regarded as so valuable a part of the Christian life that the practice survived the disruption.

Morning and Evening Prayers. The times of the synagogue services were probably determined by the times of the sacrifices daily in the Temple, which were in the morning between dawn and sunrise, and in the evening between sunset and dark. Local Jewish communities were represented in turn at the Temple sacrifices by a deputation (*Ma'amad*). At the same times there was an assembly of the faithful for prayer in the local community thus represented in Jerusalem, and in this Dugmore sees the origin of the synagogue services.

The priests of the Herodian Temple altered the time of the evening sacrifice from sunset to 3.0 p.m. The synagogue conservatively continued to observe the older times of dawn and sunset, when the *Shema'* was recited.[1] But Pharisaic influence soon enforced the recital of Benedictions at the exact time of the Temple sacrifices, and synagogue prayers at sunset became voluntary, until Gamaliel II made them compulsory some time between A.D. 90 and 110.

The three times of the synagogue services, therefore, were:

(1) Dawn to sunrise, when the *Shema'* and the *Tefillah*[2] were recited.

(2) 3.0 p.m., the *Tefillah*.

(3) Sunset to dark, *Shema'* and *Tefillah*.

There is no evidence that there was at any time midday prayer in the synagogue, or a midday sacrifice in the Temple.

It follows from this that the Christian custom of prayer at the third, sixth, and ninth hours (9.0 a.m., midday, and 3.0 p.m.) is not derived from the Jewish synagogue, although the contrary has been commonly assumed. On the other hand it is most probable that Christian prayer at dawn and nightfall is to be traced back to a Jewish origin. Tertullian (*De Oratione* xxv)[3] uses language which attributes a higher status to morning and evening prayer than to prayer at the other hours. His phrasing suggests that morning and evening prayer was an old and well-established practice, which may well have been the unbroken

---

[1] *Shema'*, "Hear", the first word of the Jewish statement of faith, Deut. 6. 4 ff.

[2] *Tefillah*, "the Prayer", known also as the Benedictions or *Shemoneh 'Esreh*, the Eighteen.

[3] See p. 38 above.

tradition of Christians from the time that daily synagogue worship was the norm.

The origin of prayer at the third, sixth, and ninth hours must, therefore, be sought elsewhere. Such evidence as we have points to a purely Christian origin for these hours. Tertullian in *De Orat.* xxv has several suggestions to make about the reasons why Christians pray at these hours. As a reason for prayer at the third hour he suggests that the gift of the Spirit was then given (Acts 2. 15). Peter prayed at the sixth hour (Acts 10. 9), and at the ninth hour Peter and John went to the Temple (Acts 3. 1).[1] Again, Tertullian instances Daniel's prayer three times a day (Dan. 6. 10); but two of the times referred to here are almost certainly dawn and sunset, the times of the Temple sacrifices, and therefore, while they might be referred to as prototypes of Christian morning and evening prayer, they have no connection with the day-hours. The other time at which Daniel prayed was probably noon, but no particular significance can be attached to this. Tertullian puts forward yet another reason in the suggestion that prayer not less than thrice a day is appropriate for those who are "debtors to the three, Father, Son, and Holy Spirit". Dugmore (op. cit.) considers, however, that Tertullian hints at the real origin of the three day-hours when he calls them "these common hours that mark the intervals of the day". They marked the main divisions of the day in the Roman world, and were announced publicly in populous places. It was natural, Dugmore urges, for Christians to fasten upon these hours, hallowed as they were by the events of the Crucifixion.

Hippolytus, as we have seen, assigns the reason for these hours of prayer to the Crucifixion. In the third hour "Christ was seen nailed upon the tree"; in the sixth hour "when Christ had been hanged upon the wood of the Cross the daylight was divided and it became darkness"; in the ninth hour "Christ was pierced in His side with a lance and shed forth blood and water".

It seems clear, then, that prayer at the third, sixth, and ninth hours was of Christian origin. In all the above attempts to assign a reason for these hours the only hint of an origin other than Christian is Tertullian's reference to Daniel's prayer, which we have seen to be irrelevant. We may rightly presume Jewish influence to this extent, that the already existing practice of devout Jews of praying in the synagogue

---

[1] This would surely have been for the evening sacrifice, and cannot legitimately be used as a precedent for private prayer or common office.

THE HOURS OF PRAYER

or at home at set times during the day provided a precedent. Morning and evening prayer may well be direct descendants of the Jewish synagogue prayers at the times of the morning and evening sacrifices in the Temple. But the choice of the third, sixth, and ninth hours was due to the Christian conviction of the appropriateness of prayer at those hours which marked the events of their Lord's Crucifixion.

Midnight and Cockcrow. For the other two hours of prayer taught by Hippolytus, midnight and cockcrow, we have no earlier evidence, except the reference to midnight prayer by Paul and Silas in prison at Philippi (Acts 16. 25). Psalm 119. 62 suggests that midnight prayer was the practice of the devout Jew who walked in the law of the Lord: "At midnight I will rise to give thanks unto thee because of thy righteous judgments." It is noteworthy that Hippolytus is the first Christian writer to give a scheme of prayer which conforms to the same psalmist's practice: "Seven times a day do I praise thee because of thy righteous judgments."[1] But apart from a possible desire on Hippolytus's part to conform to this scriptural ideal, he was also probably concerned most of all to inculcate a stricter rule of devotion than was kept by the majority of Christians in Rome. We have already mentioned his opposition to the laxity of the times. Yet prayer at midnight cannot have been unknown to the Church, since Hippolytus insists that it was part of the ancient tradition: "Truly those men of holy memory who handed on the Tradition to us taught us thus."[2] Hippolytus adduces no such support for prayer at cockcrow; but again it must be remembered that the practice of prayer at this hour cannot have been a mere innovation of Hippolytus, for his whole thesis is that the plan he outlines is the ancient tradition of the Church.

Appendix B

POSTURE AT PRAYER

Tertullian. From *De Oratione* XVII we learn that the attitude of prayer was to stand with hands "not raised on high, but raised moderately and fitly, without the presumptuous raising of the face either". In XIV Tertullian is more explicit. Christians do not merely

[1] Ps. 119. 164.   [2] *A.T.* XXXVI. 12: Dix, pp. 66, 67.

raise the hands "but also spread them out, and we make our confession to Christ, while we represent the Lord's passion and likewise pray". Compare *De Idolatria* VII, where, speaking of Christians employed as makers of idols, he points out the incongruity of raising to God the Father hands which were the "mothers of idols"; in *De Spectaculis* he asks "How can hands raised in prayer to God occupy themselves in clapping the actor?"

Kneeling is appropriate when confessing sins (*De Orat.* XXIII).

That it was customary in North Africa to turn to the east at prayer is suggested in a passage in the *Apology* in which Tertullian rebuts the charge that Christians worship the sun, an idea which may have originated in the Christian practice of turning to the east.

The sign of the Cross was evidently frequently made by Christians, but Tertullian does not explicitly say that this was done at prayer: "In all our travels and movements, in all our coming in and going out, in putting on our shoes, at the bath, at the table, in lighting our candles, in lying down, in sitting down, whatever employment occupieth us, we mark our forehead with the sign of the cross" (*De Corona Militis* III).[1]

Clement of Alexandria. Clement is not much interested in this subject. To him prayer is a thing of the intellect. However, in one passage he defers to the tradition in the matter of facing east: "And since the dawn is an image of the day of birth, and from that point the light which has shone forth at first from the darkness increases, there has also dawned on those involved in darkness a day of the knowledge of truth. In correspondence with the manner of the sun's rising, prayers are made looking towards the sunrise in the east" (*Strom.* VII. 7).

Origen. Origen is conservative on the subject of posture at prayer: "That which involves the stretching out of the hands and the uplifting of the eyes is to be preferred before all." [2] This involves standing, but sitting or lying down is permitted to those in sickness and to those in cramped circumstances, for example on a voyage. Kneeling is, however, appropriate during confession. (*De Orat.* XXXI. 2-3.)

Any place may be suitable for prayer, though Origen takes it for granted that a man's own home will be the usual place (*De Orat.* XXXI. 4). But a discussion follows (XXXI. 5-7) which leads him to the

[1] Quoted in Kidd, *Documents*, Vol. I, No. 97.
[2] Cf. also *Comm. on John* XXVIII. 4., where Origen comments on John 11. 41, "And Jesus lifted up his eyes".

POSTURE AT PRAYER

conclusion that a common meeting-place for prayer is preferable, since it is also the meeting-place of the power of the Lord, angels, and departed saints.

He is firm on the question of the direction in which a man should face when he prays. It is to the east. He deals very sharply with the objection or excuse of the man whose house does not open towards the east and who claims that it is better to pray towards the light than towards a blank wall. (*De Orat.* xxxii.)

Appendix C

PRAYER AND THE SAINTS

The Apostolic Fathers. Two passages bear on the question of the place of departed saints in the prayers of the Church. One passage is a strong denial of any tendency towards saint-worship in the Christian Church (*Martyrdom of Polycarp* xvii). After the death of Polycarp, the "Evil One... managed that not even his poor body should be taken away by us, although many desired to do this and to touch his holy flesh. So he put forward Nicetes... to plead with the magistrate not to give up his body, 'lest', so it was said, 'they should abandon the crucified one and begin to worship this man'—this being done at the instigation and urgent entreaty of the Jews, who also watched when we were about to take it from the fire, not knowing that it will be impossible for us either to forsake at any time the Christ who suffered for the salvation of the whole world of those that are saved—suffered though faultless for sinners—nor to worship any other. For Him, being the Son of God, we adore, but the martyrs as disciples and imitators of the Lord we cherish as they deserve for their matchless affection towards their own King and Teacher."

But there is one passage in *I Clement* which appears to commend the practice of intercession to the saints: "Therefore let us also make intercession for them that are in any transgression... For so shall the compassionate remembrance of them with God and the saints be fruitful unto them, and perfect." [1] But it would be rash to argue that

[1] οὕτως γὰρ ἔσται αὐτοῖς ἔγκαρπος καὶ τελεία ἡ πρὸς τὸν θεὸν καὶ ἁγίους μετ' οἰκτιρμῶν μνεία (LVI).

this isolated and not very clear sentence implies any considered doctrine of prayers to the saints, nor from it can it be assumed that the practice was widespread.

Clement of Alexandria. There are two brief passages which speak of the Christian consciousness of the assistance of the saints as well as the angels in prayer: "By these (i.e. prayers, praises, psalms, and hymns, at set times) he unites himself to the divine choir" (*Strom.* VII. 7); "(The Gnostic) prays in the society of angels, as being already of angelic rank, and he is never out of their holy keeping; and though he pray alone, he has the choir of the saints[1] standing with him" (*Strom.* VII. 12).

Origen. De Oratione XXXI. 5 alludes to the presence and assistance of angels and departed saints when the Christian is at prayer. The place of prayer is "the place of the coming together of the faithful, and, as one may reasonably believe, of angelic powers who are present at the gatherings of the faithful, and of the power of our Lord and Saviour himself, and moreover of holy spirits[2] also (I believe both those who have fallen asleep, and also, as is clear, those who remain alive), even if it is not easy to say how". Later in the same section Origen argues that if St Paul, "when still clothed in the body", and then being at Ephesus, considered himself to be united in spirit with Christians at Corinth (1 Cor. 5. 4), "we must not give up hope that thus also the blessed who have departed are present in spirit at the gatherings of the Church, perhaps more so than one who is in the body".[3]

That allusion is made to this aspect of the doctrine of the Communion of Saints by Clement and Origen alone among early writers suggests that the subject was of special interest in Alexandria.

[1] ἁγίων. But an inferior reading has ἀγγέλων.
[2] Or possibly "of the spirits of the saints".
[3] Cf. also *Hom. in Levit.* XIV. 3, where again Origen asserts that Christ, the angels, and the holy dead are all present at the public worship of the Church. See also *Hom. in Luc.* XXIII.

Part II
ORIGEN

Chapter One

ORIGEN'S LIFE AND WORKS

The Life of Origen

The main authority for the life of Origen is Eusebius.[1] Origen was born in Alexandria about A.D. 185. His name is derived probably from that of the Egyptian god Hor, and means "child of Hor", the god of light. In spite of his heathen name, it appears that his parents were Christians at the time of his birth, and from his early childhood he was educated as a Christian. Eusebius says "he had been conversant with the Holy Scriptures even when a child". At the age of seventeen, we read, Origen encouraged his father Leonidas, a victim of the persecution of Severus, not to waver, and, fired as he was with the spirit of martyrdom, was only prevented himself from becoming a martyr by his mother's endeavours. She, with admirable forethought (and insight into her son's characteristic modesty), hid his clothes. At this early age, then, Origen already possessed a faith which needed more than persecution to shake.

Origen owed much to the education given him by his parents. They insisted that he should learn whole passages of Scripture before he was introduced to the study of the liberal sciences and Greek literature. This early training is reflected in all Origen's writings. Deeply concerned as he was with philosophy, he could never get very far from some scriptural text.

The city in which Origen spent his youth and early manhood is worth a brief description, for it was there that he imbibed most of his ideas. Alexandria was the seat of a great pagan "university"; there were three great libraries, and a large staff of professors. "Though the hope of imperial favour drew the more ambitious teachers of philosophy and rhetoric irresistibly towards Rome, letters were still cultivated, and the exact sciences flourished as nowhere else by the banks of the Nile."[2] There was every opportunity, therefore, for the young Origen

---

[1] *H.E.* vi. 1–39.
[2] Charles Bigg, *Christian Platonists of Alexandria*, Lecture I.

to gain knowledge of Greek literature and philosophy, encouraged by the whole atmosphere of the city. But, side by side with all this, the Christian Church in Alexandria had been growing. Special buildings had been constructed for worship, land was most probably held by the Church, and a school for catechumens was in existence. The Church in Alexandria in Origen's day was in a flourishing and comparatively stable condition. This, however, was being threatened by the fact that many young Christian men who, as was natural, attended lectures at the University were lapsing into Hellenism and Gnosticism. The Catechetical School, to the mastership of which Origen, when not yet eighteen years of age, was appointed by Bishop Demetrius, was organized to meet this threat, and to provide instruction for students, who would thus be less likely to come into contact with heathen professors trained to criticize the apparent crudeness of the Scriptures and Christian doctrine. The general course of study in this school began with geometry, physiology, and astronomy. Then came philosophy, the teacher being careful to point out "how the partial light vouchsafed to Plato or Aristotle was but an earnest of the day-spring from on high".[1] After philosophy, ethics was taught. The dialectical method was used, students being given such words as "good", "evil", "justice", to define, and their definitions being then discussed by the class. The teacher was careful to emphasize virtue as something to be practised and not merely to be discussed. Theology crowned the list of the subjects. Origen, therefore, as master of such a school had no small responsibility, and must have had a reputation, even at his early age, for wide knowledge in many branches of study.

For some thirteen years Origen devoted himself continually to the work of teaching, whilst he lived a life of extreme austerity. He was living at this time, Dr Bigg remarks, in bondage to the letter, determined to take the precepts of the Gospel in their literal sense. He strictly limited his food, clothing, and sleep. Going even farther in his literalism, he acted upon the words of Matthew 19. 12b; and this self-mutilation robbed him of the respect of many people. Yet his simplicity of life attracted many students to the school, and his lectures were frequented by non-Christians as well as Christians and catechumens. He was also constantly sought out privately for advice. During this period, broken only by a short visit to Rome, and one to Arabia, Origen was also busy upon the first stages of his Hexapla, an edition of the Old Testament comparing the Septuagint and other Greek

[1] Charles Bigg, *Christian Platonists of Alexandria*, Lecture II.

ORIGEN'S LIFE AND WORKS 49

versions with the Hebrew. In order to produce this work he learned Hebrew. During the same period he did not neglect the tendencies of non-Christian thought, and, though criticized for it in some quarters, attended the lectures of Ammonius Saccas. To lighten his burden he now brought one of his old pupils in to help with the work of the school, Heraclas, afterwards Bishop of Alexandria.

About A.D. 215, after an outburst of persecution in Alexandria, Origen visited Caesarea in Palestine. Here his reputation was high, and his friends, Alexander, Bishop of Jerusalem, and Theoctistus, Bishop of Caesarea, invited him to expound the Holy Scriptures in church. Demetrius, Bishop of Alexandria, being informed of this, objected on the ground that Origen was a layman, and recalled him to Alexandria, whither he returned about A.D. 219.

Origen now began to devote the greater part of his time to writing, especially works expounding the Bible, while Heraclas took over more of the teaching work in the Catechetical School. A wealthy friend, Ambrosius, whom Origen had restored to orthodoxy from heresy, encouraged him, and supplied shorthand writers and scribes. Among his earlier works were the first five books of the *Commentary on John*, and *De Principiis*. From the time of the publication and instant success of these works, strained relations grew up between Origen and his bishop, whether because of jealousy on Demetrius's part, or because he considered it his duty to restrain the speculative questings of Origen's mind. But Origen remained in Alexandria until, probably between A.D. 226 and 230, he accepted an invitation to visit Greece to combat heresy there. On the way he stayed at Caesarea, and was ordained presbyter there by his old friends, the Bishops of Jerusalem and Caesarea. This incurred the strong disapproval of Demetrius, who called together a synod which decided that Origen should not henceforth be allowed to teach in Alexandria. A little later he was excommunicated by Demetrius. At the conclusion of his mission to Greece, Origen went to Caesarea (A.D. 230 or 231), where his excommunication was disregarded and he was warmly received. Alexandria made no overtures to recall Origen, even when his two old pupils Heraclas and Dionysius successively became bishops there, although the latter certainly,[1] and Heraclas probably also, corresponded with him in friendly fashion.

In Caesarea, Origen's literary and preaching work went on. Ambrosius was with him to encourage and to finance the publication

[1] Eusebius, *H.E.* VI. 46.

of books. A new Catechetical School was instituted, to which came a number of distinguished students, among them Gregory Thaumaturgus, afterwards Bishop of Neocaesarea, who in his *Panegyric* has left us an intimate picture of Origen as a friend and teacher, and an invaluable sketch of his teaching method. A great deal of time was also devoted by Origen to expounding the Scriptures publicly, and there were few days when he was not in church at least once for this purpose. He refused to allow these homilies to be taken down and published until near the end of his life. But meanwhile commentaries on almost every book of the Bible were being written.

The persecution of Maximin (A.D. 235–237) in which Ambrosius suffered, although he was not martyred, caused Origen to retire to Cappadocia, where he was the guest of a Christian lady named Juliana. Firmilian, Bishop of Caesarea in Cappadocia, was an old supporter of Origen. But by A.D. 238 Origen was back in Palestinian Caesarea, which remained his headquarters to the end of his life. He paid visits to different parts of Palestine and to Athens, and twice to Arabia, both times by invitation of the Church, a fact which shows that his excommunication, although according to Jerome it received acknowledgement at Rome, was widely disregarded by the Church in the East. Origen's first visit to Arabia was in order to convince Beryllus, Bishop of Bostra, that his views on the Incarnation were erroneous, and the second to combat some errors on the resurrection. On both occasions Origen was completely successful.

In A.D. 250 the fierce persecution of the Emperor Decius broke out, a swing of the pendulum after the peace of the preceding reign of Philip, with whom, and with whose wife, Severa, Origen is said to have had some correspondence. In this persecution Origen's friend, Alexander of Jerusalem, died in prison, and Origen himself suffered cruel torture, which, according to Eusebius, he endured with great courage. On the death of Decius in 251, Origen was released, but his health had evidently been weakened by his sufferings, and he died at Tyre in 253, "having completed seventy years save one" (Eusebius, *H.E.* VII. 1). He was buried there and his tomb was preserved and honoured until the city was destroyed by the Saracens in the thirteenth century.

Origen's Works

A mere list of Origen's works will serve to show the versatility of the scholar.

(a) *Critical.* The Hexapla, an edition of the Old Testament, comparing, by means of six columns, the Septuagint and other Greek versions with the Hebrew. Fragments only remain.

(b) *Exegetical.* Commentaries on nearly every book of the Bible, of which are extant, either wholly or in great part, those on John, Matthew, the Epistle to the Romans, and the Song of Songs.

(c) *Homiletic.* Homilies on nearly every book of the Bible, for the most part taken down by his disciples and afterwards published. There remain substantially those on Genesis, Exodus, Leviticus, Numbers, Joshua, Judges, Psalms 36–38, Isaiah, Jeremiah, Ezekiel, and Luke, but for the most part in the Latin translation of Rufinus.

(d) *Dogmatic Works.* On the Resurrection, of which fragments only remain. *De Principiis (On First Principles)*, a systematization of the Christian faith. This is Origen's best-known work.

(e) *Apologetic Works. Contra Celsum*, an answer to an attack on Christianity made by an educated Greek some fifty years before. This work is almost as well known as *De Principiis.*

(f) *Practical Works. De Oratione (On Prayer)* and the *Exhortation to Martyrdom*, addressed to Ambrosius and a companion in the persecution of Maximin at Caesarea, to bid them stand fast.

(g) *Letters.* Of Origen's many letters, only two remain entire. One is to Gregory Thaumaturgus, bidding him use his gifts in the service of God and the Christian religion. The other is to Julius Africanus on the authenticity of the History of Susanna.

(h) Difficult to classify are the *Stromateis (Miscellanies)*, ten books written on a variety of subjects. The three extant fragments deal with such widely differing topics as truthfulness, the stories of Susanna and Bel in the Book of Daniel, and an interpretation of Galatians 5. 13.

The extant writings of Origen occupy several volumes of all the modern editions of the Fathers. "Voluminous", though a hackneyed word, is the only suitable adjective with which to describe his total output.

Chapter Two

ORIGEN'S DOCTRINE

THOSE who are but beginning their acquaintance with Origen may find it convenient to have here a summary of Origen's teaching. But a word of warning is first needed. So widely ranging is his thought, and sometimes so intricate and speculative, and so many are the books he wrote, that there can hardly be a single statement in any summary of his work which will not need amplification, comment, and even modification. The reader must seek a fuller account of Origen's system of thought elsewhere, and he may be advised to consult B. F. Westcott's article "Origenes" in Volume IV of Smith and Wace, *A Dictionary of Christian Biography* (1887—printed also in the one-volume edition of 1911), a piece of scholarship of lasting value, even though some details need to be modified in the light of more recent work on Origen. Of Charles Bigg's *The Christian Platonists of Alexandria* (1886) the same may be said. More recent work on Origen from which a comprehensive view of his doctrine may be gained includes E. de Faye, *Origen and his Work* (English translation from the French, by F. Rothwell, 1926); the Introduction to G. W. Butterworth's *Origen on First Principles*, 1936; the lecture on Origen in G. L. Prestige's Bampton Lectures, *Fathers and Heretics*, 1940; and, for those who read French, R. Cadiou, *Introduction au Système d'Origène*, 1932, and J. Daniélou, *Origène*, 1948.

Origen as Systematic Theologian. Origen has several claims to greatness, but chief among them stands his work in the fields of systematic theology and biblical exegesis. Although Pantaenus and Clement of Alexandria had previously attempted something of the sort, Origen's *De Principiis* is the first attempt to provide a complete system of Christian doctrine. The doctrine of the Trinity, of creation, of man, of the Incarnation, and of the resurrection, judgement, and final destiny, is presented as an integrated whole. The best philosophical thought of the day is called in to demonstrate the rationality of the truths of Scripture. The Christian faith is shown to provide a cosmic view capable of satisfying the demands of contemporary intellectuals far more completely than the other systems presented for their acceptance.

Origen as Biblical Interpreter. Origen's importance in the history of biblical scholarship lies in the fact that he was the first Christian writer to provide clear rules for interpreting the Scriptures. A mind as acute as Origen's was not unaware of the obscurities of the Bible, and the factual and moral contradictions which it contained. But having been brought up on the Bible from his early boyhood, he was convinced that it was God's revelation and that every part of it contained a meaning important for the soul. The difficulty in many passages was to discover what that meaning was. Origen here makes great use of the allegorical method which Greek philosophy had long applied to the ancient stories of the gods. Precedent for the Christian use of the method was supplied by St Paul, for example in Galatians 4. 22 ff.; and Philo, the Alexandrian Jew, over a century before, by his wide use of it in interpreting the Old Testament, had given the method currency in the intellectual circles of Alexandria. Origen lays down that Scripture has three senses, the bodily or literal, the psychical or moral, and the spiritual or allegorical, corresponding to body, soul ($\psi v \chi \acute{\eta}$), and spirit ($\pi v \epsilon \hat{v} \mu a$) in man.[1] Any passage lacking literal sense, or having a literal sense repugnant to reason, must have a moral or spiritual meaning which it is the duty of the Christian to discover. By the use of the allegorical method of interpretation Origen believed that the profoundest truths of God were to be unveiled.

To those who know something of the principles of biblical criticism to-day, such a method of interpretation may seem fantastic. But its value in the third century is not to be minimized. The allegorical method "enabled the Old Testament to be claimed as Christian literature as against Jewish controversialists, and both Testaments to be defended against the destructive criticism of educated Hellenists. And by saving the Bible, it gave security to the historical foundation of the Christian faith and permanence to the evangelical standard of Christian values" (Prestige, op. cit., p. 122).

Origen's Purpose: to vindicate Christian Doctrine. Origen's mighty endeavours in the two spheres of philosophic theology and biblical exegesis, which appear at first to be so disparate, were occasioned by a single purpose. This was to commend the Christian religion to the

---

[1] Cf. note on *De Orat.* II. 3 (p. 85, n. 1, below), where a fuller treatment of Origen's principles of scriptural interpretation is given.

minds of men. The *Contra Celsum* is Origen's one example of what is technically called an "apology". But in a wider sense all his work was apologetic. Out of a burning love for truth and a pastoral desire that all men should know the truth of God revealed in the Holy Scriptures and the tradition of the Church, and no less from a practical desire to fortify his young Christian students set in the midst of a contemptuous pagan world, Origen took in hand the work of proving the intellectual respectability of Christianity. Two major obstacles confronted him. In the first place paganism seemed to have monopolized the resources of Greek philosophy. Until Clement of Alexandria Christian teachers had been too content to leave the exercise of rational thought and the application of the great and fruitful truths of Greek philosophy to the teachers of the Academy and the Stoa. Christian teachers had seemed to connive at and even to lend substance to the sneers which lecturers in the pagan schools were wont to cast at Christianity as being intellectually beneath contempt. Clement of Alexandria first staked out the Christian claim in the territory of Greek rational thought, and Origen proceeded to make good the claim by his bold use of rationalism in the explication of the Christian tradition.

The second obstacle was the contemptuous opinion of the Scriptures held by Origen's contemporaries among the intellectuals. Compared with the dialogues and the letters of a Plato and the lectures of an Aristotle they seemed poor stuff. Those who took the trouble to glance at them found there a great number of contradictions, and not a few stories whose ethical value obviously compared badly with the teaching of, for example, the Stoics. It was in the face of this obstacle that Origen constructed his theory of the interpretation of Scripture.

"The Church owes it to Origen, first and foremost," writes G. L. Prestige (op. cit., p. 133), "that, whenever Christianity is true to itself, it is a rational faith. The whole educated world is in his debt for the preservation of the old Hellenic intellectual culture, which he transformed by his genius into the beginnings of a *philosophia perennis* for Christendom."

Origen's System of Thought. The resulting system, which is Origen's lasting legacy to Christian thought, is breath-taking in its width of range. The following summary of it is given largely in Origen's own words in *De Principiis* (in the English translation of G. W. Butterworth).[1]

---

[1] Butterworth translates Koetschau's reconstruction of the text of *De Principiis*. Words which are not Origen's are in italics.

THE HOLY TRINITY. God is spirit. *He* must not be thought to be any kind of body, but to be a simple intellectual existence, the mind and fount from which originates all intellectual existence or mind. *He is invisible, for* to see and to be seen is a property of bodies; to know and to be known is an attribute of intellectual existence.

Christ is the only-begotten Son of the Father. *In him* there is one nature, his deity. *But there is also* another human nature, which in very recent times he took upon him to fulfil the divine purpose. *He is* the Wisdom of God, *and it is not to be supposed* that God the Father ever existed, even for a single moment, without begetting this wisdom. In this very subsistence of wisdom there was implicit every capacity and form of the creation that was to be. *Human analogies fail to represent the relation between the Father and the Son, for it consists in* an eternal and everlasting begetting as brightness is begotten from light.

The Holy Spirit *is revealed in the Scriptures as having* personal existence. *He* proceeds from the Father *and* is of so great authority and dignity that saving baptism is not complete except when performed by the naming of Father, Son and Holy Spirit. He had always been Holy Spirit. These terms, such as "always" or "has been", must be interpreted with reservations and not pressed; for they relate to time, but the matters of which we are speaking transcend all idea of time.

RELATION OF THE TRINITY TO CREATED BEINGS. The universe was created by God. There is no substance which has not received its existence from him. The God and Father who holds the universe together is superior to every being that exists, for he imparts to each one from his own existence that which each one is; the Son, being less than the Father, is superior to rational creatures alone; the Holy Spirit is still less and dwells within the Saints alone. So that in this way (*i.e. in extent of function, not as regards essence*) the power of the Father is greater than that of the Son, and that of the Son is more than that of the Holy Spirit. God the Father bestows the gift of existence; Christ confers the natural gift of reason. *The Holy Spirit's work is* that those beings who are not holy in essence may be made holy. *Yet* there is no separation in the Trinity. *The three Persons work together* at every stage of man's progress *so that* we may perchance just succeed at last in beholding the holy and blessed life, *and may* hold fast the Father, the Son and the Holy Spirit, *which is man's true end.*

THE DECLENSION OF RATIONAL BEINGS. *The possibility of such progress involves the possibility of falling away.* All rational creatures if they become negligent gradually sink to a lower level and take to themselves bodies suitable to the regions into which they descend. The position of every created being (*angel, man, daemon*) is the result of his own work and his own motives. *The angel* has obtained his degree of dignity in proportion to his own merits, *while* ranks in wickedness have been assigned to impure spirits in proportion to their bad conduct. *The same is true of* those spirits who are judged fit by God to replenish the human race.

PRE-EXISTENCE OF THE HUMAN SOUL. *The souls of human beings exist before bodies.* Whole nations of souls are stored away somewhere in a realm of their own. As long as the soul continues to abide in the good it has no experience of union with a body. But by some inclination towards evil these souls lose their wings and come into bodies.[1]

THE SOULS OF HEAVENLY BODIES. *The sun, moon, and stars which move with such majestic order and plan are living and rational beings whose souls will finally share in the deliverance from the bondage of the body at the consummation.*

THE CONSUMMATION. The end of the world and the consummation is known to God alone. The goodness of God through Christ will restore his entire creation to one end, even his enemies being conquered and subdued. The end is always like the beginning. God shall be all in all.

THE VISIBLE WORLD. The whole world is arranged in diverse parts and functions. Since the world is so very varied and comprises so great a diversity of rational beings, what else can we assign as the cause of its existence except the diversity in the fall of those who decline from unity in dissimilar ways? God willed matter to exist, and to be at the call and service of the Creator in all things. Material substance possesses such a nature that it can undergo every kind of transformation. *In the* lower beings *it is* formed into the grosser and more solid condition of body. But when it ministers to more perfect and blessed beings it shines in the splendour of "celestial bodies" and adorns either the "angels of God" or the "sons of the resurrection" with the garments of a "spiritual body". The tragic tale of human miseries, from which some are free while others are involved in them, *and* the differences that exist among men on earth *arise* from the decision of the creature's own freedom, *and are* such as the principle of equity

[1] There are different opinions as to whether Origen held the doctrine of transmigration of souls in the strict sense (i.e. that souls could enter the bodies of animals and plants). Rufinus acquits Origen of holding this doctrine.

and righteousness demands. *They do not imply injustice in God, or a dual system of control of the world. Such is the setting of the soul's struggle.* Whoever purges himself when placed in this life will be prepared for every good work in the future, whereas he who does not purge himself will be a "vessel unto dishonour".

THE INCARNATION. But the aid of the Author and Creator himself was demanded in order to restore the capacity to obey. *The Son of God united to himself a pre-existent soul which had* clung to God from the beginning of the creation and ever after in a union inseparable and indissoluble, *and which,* receiving him wholly, was made with him in a pre-eminent degree one spirit. This soul acting as a medium between God and the flesh, there is born the God-man. *An illustration is used:* a lump of iron placed in a fire becomes completely changed into fire provided the fire is never removed from it. *Yet the iron is still iron.* So, that soul which was for ever placed in the Word, in God, is God in all its acts and feelings and thoughts. *Yet* the nature of his soul was the same as that of all souls.

FUTURE AGES. *If the soul's purification is not achieved in this world by the grace of God and the aid of Christ and the Holy Spirit* there will yet be further "ages to come". Rational creatures are never deprived of free will. *Even when subjected to God* they might forget that they had been placed in that final state of blessedness by the grace of God and not by their own goodness. These movements would again be followed by a variety and diversity of bodies, out of which a world is always composed.[1] The end of this world is the beginning of the world to come. We learn this plainly from Paul himself when he says "that in the ages to come he might show the exceeding riches of his grace in kindness towards us".

THE ASCENT OF THE SOUL. *But the normal progress of the soul is from stage to stage,* passing through the series of those abiding places which the Greeks have termed spheres, but which the divine scripture calls heavens. *Each is* a place of instruction, a school for souls: they will perceive the causes of things and the perfection of God's creation; *and then* they will come to "the things which are not seen". And so the rational being, growing at each successive stage, advances to perfect knowledge, *being nourished by its proper* food, which must be understood to be the contemplation and understanding of God, *supplied in* measures suitable to a nature which has been made and created.

[1] But Origen did not hold the Stoic doctrine of the cyclic recurrence of identical worlds.

THE LAST THINGS OF HOLY SCRIPTURE. *This progress of the soul,* according to the threatenings of the holy scriptures and the contents of the Church's teaching, *involves* the resurrection of the body, the day of judgement, punishment, *and finally the possession of* the promises. Implanted in our bodies is the life-principle which contains the essence of the body; and although the bodies die, that same life-principle raises them up from the earth and restores and refashions them, just as the power which exists in a grain of wheat refashions and restores the grain, after its corruption and death, into a body with stalk and ear. *It is* a spiritual body, which can dwell in the heavens.[1]

In the judgement the mind or conscience will see exposed before its eyes a kind of history of its evil deeds. Then the conscience is harassed and pricked by its own stings, and becomes an accuser and witness against itself. *Punishment follows because* God our physician, in his desire to wash away the ills of our souls, makes use of penal remedies *by which* the soul is undoubtedly wrought into a condition of stronger inward connexion and renewal. Punishment is not everlasting. For when the body is punished, the soul is gradually purified. For all wicked men, and for daemons too, punishment has an end, and both wicked men and daemons shall be restored to their former rank.[2]

FREE WILL. *Underlying the whole of Origen's system is the doctrine that* the rational animal can choose good and avoid evil, that deeds worthy of praise or of blame lie within our own power. *But the soul's free will is not unlimited.* It is neither in our power to make progress apart from the knowledge of God, nor does the knowledge of God compel us to do so unless we ourselves contribute something towards the good result. Our perfection does not come to pass without our doing anything, and yet it is not completed as a result of our efforts, but God performs the greater part of it.

THE SOUL'S STRUGGLE WITH DAEMONS. Opposing powers and the Devil himself are engaged in a struggle with the human race, provoking and inciting men to sin.

BUT SIN IS WITHIN. The simpler sort of believers suppose that all the sins that men have committed come from the persistent influence of the contrary powers. *This cannot be so, for it would mean that* if there were no devil, no man would ever sin at all. We derive the beginnings and what we may call the seeds of sin from those desires which are

---

[1] Origen's doctrine of the resurrection of the body is thoroughly Pauline.
[2] There is little doubt that Origen held that the Devil would finally be saved.

given to us naturally for our use. The hostile power incites and urges us, striving to extend the sin over a larger field. It is possible to resist, and it is possible when a divine power has urged us on to better things not to follow its guidance. Our faculty of free will is preserved to us in either case.[1]

SUCCESSIVE AGES. The soul always possesses free will, both when in the body and when out of the body; and the will's freedom always moves in the direction either of good or of evil, nor can the rational sense, that is the mind or soul, ever exist without some movement either good or evil. *This fact provides another reason why* after the dissolution of this world there will be another one. *But* the entire creation cherishes a hope of liberty, a hope of being "delivered from the bondage of corruption", when the "children of God", who had both fallen and become scattered, have been gathered into one. The perfect restoration of the entire creation will be accomplished through certain means and courses of discipline and periods of time: not by the pressure of some necessity, nor by the use of force, but by word, by reason, by teaching, by the exhortation to better things, by the best methods of education.

THE CONSUMMATION. So then the end is renewed after the pattern of the origin, and that condition restored which rational nature once enjoyed when it had no need to eat of the tree of the knowledge of good and evil, so that all consciousness of evil has departed and given place to what is sincere and pure, and he alone who is the one good God becomes all things to the soul. Then truly God will be all in all.

Origen's Humility. There is much in Origen's system of thought which seems fanciful to the modern reader. He laboured, of course, under the handicap of having no conception of development, of physical and biological evolution, of historical progress, of progressive revelation. These are modern categories of thought, and Origen must not be belittled because he did not possess them. Yet it must be said that his intellectual honesty is apparent to all who will read the *De Principiis* in full. An illustration or two may be given. After discussing the pre-existent soul of Jesus he writes: "If there be anyone who can

[1] Westcott comments: "Such a doctrine, so far from tending to Pelagianism, is the very refutation of it. It lays down that the essence of freedom is absolute self surrender; that the power of right action is nothing but the power of God. Every act of man is the act of a free being, but not an exercise of freedom." (*D. C. B.*, art. 'Origenes.')

discover something better and prove what he says by clearer statements out of the holy scriptures, let his opinion be accepted in preference to mine" (II. vi. 7). After a discussion of the consummation he writes: "We have outlined, then, to the best of our knowledge, these three opinions about the end of all things and the supreme blessedness. Each of our readers must judge for himself, with all care and diligence, whether one of them may be approved and adopted" (II. iii. 7). There are many such passages. Origen never dogmatizes, except upon the facts of the Christian tradition as he sets them forth at the beginning of *De Principiis* (Preface to Book I). Every suggestive theory wrought in his brilliant mind is presented at the bar of Holy Scripture for examination, and humbly commended to the reader. Origen is, no doubt, often in error as to the extent to which his ideas are ratified in the Bible. But he never fails in humility. Perhaps, after all, that is his best claim to greatness.

Chapter Three

PRAYER IN ORIGEN

Two very different points of view about prayer can be detected in the writings of Origen. On the one hand he appears to be a true successor of Clement of Alexandria in what may be called his intellectual mysticism. Origen's Platonism led him to consider the intellect as the most important faculty in man. The end, for man, is to become an incorporeal intelligence, enjoying a full and unhindered knowledge of the mysteries of God. This is clear throughout *De Principiis*. It is by his intellect that man can enter into union with God, and the highest activity of man upon earth is to advance "from a knowledge of small to a knowledge of greater things and from things visible to things invisible", and "from things of sense, which are bodily, to things beyond sense perception, which are incorporeal and intellectual".[1] Spiritual men will attain some degree of success in this in the present life, and *De Principiis* is written to provide the proper intellectual food for those "who are beginning to 'see God', that is, to understand him through 'purity of heart'".[2] But the perfection of the intellect lies beyond this life in the world to come. Origen thinks of eternal bliss as the perfect functioning of the intellect, at last finding complete fulfilment in the contemplation of God.

But on the other hand, Origen does not, as Clement seems to do, forget the needs of Christians who are less advanced. In his one book which is concerned wholly with the subject of prayer, the treatise Περὶ Εὐχῆς, there is a great deal of advice which any beginner in the devotional life would find practical and helpful. The mystical note is subdued throughout.

Modern Interest in Origen's Mysticism. Great interest has recently been shown in the mystical element in Origen's writings, and this has been largely due to the publication at Tübingen in 1931 of Walter

---

[1] *De Principiis* iv. iv. 10: Butterworth, p. 327.
[2] *De Princ.* ii. xi. 7: Butterworth, p. 154.

Völker's book *Das Vollkommenheitsideal des Origenes*, an investigation of the ascetic and mystical language used by Origen. Völker "sees in Origen a great mystic",[1] and "devotes a number of pages in his book to establishing the existence of mystical ecstasy in his writings".[2] Jean Daniélou in his *Origène*, p. 287, gives a list of the continental writers who have written on the subject, some in support of Völker's thesis, others to oppose it.

The presence of a mystical element in Origen's work is not a twentieth-century discovery. Charles Bigg in *The Christian Platonists of Alexandria* recognized it. After discussing the mysticism of Clement of Alexandria, which he holds not to be a true mysticism, since it is not of the emotions, but of the intellect, he writes: "The time for a purely Christian mysticism . . . had not yet arrived. Yet Clement laid the fuel ready for kindling. The spark that was needed was the allegorical interpretation of the Song of Songs. This was supplied, strange to say, by Origen, the least mystical of all the divines."[3] The surprise expressed by this profound scholar at the presence of the mystical note at all in Origen, and the estimate of him as "the least mystical of all the divines", should inspire caution in those who are inclined to go the whole way with Völker and hail Origen as the Father of Christian Mysticism.

Meaning of Mysticism. The word "mysticism" is frequently used very loosely. Sometimes it means little more than a tendency to use allegory. Thus John Keble in No. 89 of *Tracts for the Times, On the Mysticism attributed to the Early Fathers of the Church*,[4] refers to those who in using the word "mysticism" appear to denote "a disposition first to regard things as supernatural which are not really such, and secondly to press and strain what may perhaps be really supernatural in an undue and extravagant way". He distinguishes four elements in this popular conception of mysticism: fanciful interpretation of Scripture; a tendency to read one's own theories into familiar objects and ideas; a predilection to discern providential interference in the daily round of life; and "finally, they (the Fathers) are blamed for Mysticism, properly so-called, in their moral and devotional rules; i.e. for dwelling too much on counsels of perfection, tending (as is

---

[1] J. Daniélou, *Origène* (Paris, 1948), p. 287.
[2] Daniélou, *Platonisme et Théologie Mystique* (Paris, 1944), p. 278.
[3] Lecture III, p. 132 (1913 ed.).
[4] James Parker, 1868, pp. 4 ff.

affirmed) to contemplation rather than action, to monastic rather than social and practical virtue". Only in this last point does this use of "mysticism" approach, and then not very closely, the strict meaning of the word. It was, in fact, and still to some extent is, a term of abuse or ridicule. Thus the adjective "mystical" was applied by W. S. Gilbert, in the Mikado's song, to German divines for whose theorizings the practical Englishman of the nineteenth century had little use. He speaks of "mystical Germans who preach from ten till four".

The *Shorter Oxford English Dictionary*, relegating this use of "mysticism" as a term of reproach to the second place, defines it as: "The opinions, mental tendencies, or habits of thought and feeling, characteristic of mystics; belief in the possibility of union with the Divine nature by means of ecstatic contemplation; reliance on spiritual intuition as the means of acquiring knowledge of mysteries inaccessible to the understanding." And a mystic is defined there as: "One who seeks by contemplation and self-surrender to obtain union with or absorption into the Deity, or who believes in the spiritual apprehension of truths inaccessible to the understanding."

Albert Farges [1] defines mystical science as "the experimental and rational study, in accordance with revelation, of all states in which the soul is *passive* in relation to God". He quotes also [2] another definition, given by the Abbé Ribet: [3] "It is the science which treats of the supernatural phenomena, either inward or outward, which prepare, accompany or follow the *passive* attraction of souls towards God and by God, that is to say, divine contemplation." Farges himself points out that "the great mystics of past ages have not taken these definitions as the starting-point of their works", and probably few who have studied the mystics would agree that either of these two definitions is altogether adequate. Yet they do broadly indicate what is meant by "mysticism" in theological parlance, and we shall here try to estimate the extent to which mysticism in this sense is to be found in the writings of Origen.

Use of the Language of Mysticism in Origen. There can be no doubt that Origen uses some of the principal thought-forms of typical mysticism, nor that his writings were successfully quarried for mystical material by the Father who is "the true founder of mystical theo-

[1] *Mystical Phenomena* (Burns Oates, 1926), p. 9.
[2] Ibid.   [3] *La Mystique Divine*, 1878.

logy",[1] Gregory of Nyssa. Daniélou in his *Origène*, in the fourth book which is entitled "La Mystique d'Origène", gives a concise account of the mystical ideas to be found in Origen.

The common idea of the journey of the soul from worldliness to heavenly bliss is described in three stages.[2] The first stage is conversion, when the soul first realizes its true dignity, and that its destiny is to be with God; it begins to long for the recovery of the image of God in which it was created, but which it has lost by sin (*Hom. in Gen.* 1. 13, 15).

The second stage roughly corresponds to what is called in classical mysticism "the purgative way". Origen finds in the biblical account of the exodus, the crossing of the Red Sea, the journey of the Israelites in the wilderness, their trials and temptations, and their approach to the Promised Land, an allegorical account of the soul's conquest of temptation and the trials of life, its casting off of the life of the flesh and its progressive awakening to the life of the spirit. As the Israelites dwelt, not in permanent abodes, but in tents which were erected afresh at each stage of the journey, so the soul is never permanently at rest, but is always advancing in the knowledge of God. This advance of the soul is described in the greatest detail in the twenty-seventh *Homily on Numbers*.

The third stage is the union of the soul with the Word of God. Origen sees in the Song of Songs [3] the type of the soul "whose every desire is to be joined in fellowship with the Word of God, and to enter into the mysteries of his wisdom and knowledge, as into the chamber of a heavenly bridegroom".[4] The soul, having in its journey acquired those kinds of knowledge which the Greeks classified as ethical ($\dot{\eta}\theta\iota\kappa\dot{\eta}$) and physical ($\phi\upsilon\sigma\iota\kappa\dot{\eta}$), has now become capable of the contemplation of the eternal truths ($\theta\epsilon\omega\rho\eta\tau\iota\kappa\dot{\eta}$); [5] "purified in morals,

---

[1] *Platonisme et Théologie Mystique*, p. 185.

[2] It is to be noted that this conception of the life of the soul as a journey is by no means confined to mystical theologians. It is the common stock of Christian preachers and teachers.

[3] The *Commentary on the Song of Songs* (four books and a preface) comes down to us in a Latin translation by Rufinus. Useful extracts are accessible to the English reader in R. B. Tollinton, *Selections from the Commentaries and Homilies of Origen*, S.P.C.K, 1929.

[4] *Comm. on Song* 91: Tollinton, op. cit., p. 82.

[5] The three kinds of knowledge are made by Origen to correspond to the three books of Solomon: Proverbs with its ethical rules, Ecclesiastes with its musings on the causes and nature of things, and the Song of Songs.

and trained in the discernment of natural things, it is able to ... lift itself up to the contemplation of divinity by a pure and spiritual love",[1] and "having seen the beauty of the Word of God it loves his splendour and receives of him an arrow and wound of love".[2]

The doctrine of the spiritual senses, developed by St Gregory of Nyssa, St Bernard, St Bonaventure, and St Theresa, and very prominent in the mystical experiences of St Catherine of Genoa,[3] is also to be found in Origen in the *Commentary on the Song of Songs* and elsewhere.[4] As knowledge of natural things is mediated through the five senses, so the knowledge of God is regarded analogously as being given through five spiritual senses: spiritual sight to behold intellectual objects, hearing to distinguish sounds beyond the range of an earthly ear, taste to savour the Living Bread, smell to perceive the sweet odour of Christ, and spiritual touch to handle, like John, the Word of Life.

Fruitful as this doctrine was in subsequent mysticism, it is not in itself mystical. Its origin is in Holy Scripture, in such passages as "Taste and see that the Lord is good" of Psalm 34. 8, and "Now mine eye seeth thee" of Job 42. 5. To work such biblical texts into a system of "spiritual senses" is not necessarily more than the device of a skilful teacher desirous of giving his readers useful topics for meditation.

Völker attempted to prove that Origen wrote of mystical ecstasy as the soul's closest union with the Word.[5] But the texts adduced in which the noun ἔκστασις and the verb ἐξίστημι are used (e.g. *Hom. in Num.* XXVII. 12 and *Comm. on John* I. 30) have been shown by H.-Ch. Puech to refer not to ecstasy properly so called, but to an astonishment of the mind in the presence of unprecedented wonders. In Origen ecstasy is not a departure out of (ἔκστασις, literally "standing out from") oneself, a possession by the Spirit and the suspension of one's own faculties. It is an ἔκστασις or departure from earthly things as the soul is captivated by the wonder of things heavenly. There is no depersonalization.[6]

Absence of the Marks of a Thorough Mysticism in Origen. Just as there is no recognition in Origen of mystical ecstasy as a desirable state

---

[1] *Comm. on Song* 78.
[2] Ibid. 67.
[3] See also St Augustine, *Confessions* x. 27.
[4] See *De Princ.* I. i. 7–9.
[5] *Vollkommenheitsideal des Orig.*, pp. 134 ff.
[6] See Daniélou, *Origène*, pp. 295–6, and *Platonisme et Théologie Mystique*, pp. 278–9.

of the soul, so also certain other features and tendencies of mysticism are entirely absent from his writings. The argument from silence should never be pressed too far, but it must be allowed its due weight, especially when positive arguments on the other side are lacking.

For instance, Origen makes no use of the conception of spiritual darkness. Although he describes the journey of the soul in terms of the wandering of the Israelites, he yet attaches little significance to the Mount Sinai episodes, unlike Philo and Clement of Alexandria before him, and Gregory of Nyssa afterwards. Daniélou writes: "Origen's mysticism does not embrace darkness. It is a mysticism of light. And that perhaps is its limitation. It is more a speculative mysticism of the illumination of the spirit by gnosis than an experimental mysticism of the hidden presence of God laid hold on in obscurity by the soul's touch."[1]

Daniélou emphasizes this point elsewhere. Comparing Origen's treatment of the third stage of the soul's ascension, θεολογία, or contemplation, with that of Gregory of Nyssa, he says: "For Origen, the third way is still a noetic activity. For Gregory it is hyper-noetic and properly mystical."[2] He points out that the summit of the spiritual life for Origen was a full and unbounded gnosis, but for Gregory there was a stage beyond, that of ecstasy.[3] In agreeing with H.-Ch. Puech's criticisms of Völker's attempt to attribute ecstasy to Origen, Daniélou writes: "It is certain that Origen's mysticism is orientated towards intellectual contemplation rather than towards that transformation of the soul by love and that experience of the presence of God which Gregory of Nyssa describes. His mysticism remains a mysticism of instruction which culminates in the contemplation of the mysteries. It will be reserved for Gregory of Nyssa to lay the foundation of mystical theology properly so called, in describing the entry of the soul into the darkness where beyond all thought-forms, by love, it gains an obscure experience of the presence of God."[4] Origen stays in the domain of gnosis.

One danger of a thoroughgoing mysticism is that it tends so to emphasize the doctrine of the immanence of God in the soul that it not infrequently incurs the accusation of Pantheism. It would be tedious to examine all the passages in Origen which speak of the relation of the soul to God. But no competent student of Origen has ever accused him of Pantheism. His doctrine of the origin of souls is a doctrine of creation, not of emanation. "Rational beings, called either

[1] *Origène*, p. 291.   [2] *Platonisme et Théologie Mystique*, p. 128.
[3] Ibid., p. 157.   [4] *Origène*, p. 296.

minds or souls . . . are definitely outside the Godhead, as the Son and Spirit are definitely within." [1] Origen speaks of the end of the soul as a perfect unity in God, but he nowhere blurs the distinction between the Creator and the creature. The unity is one in which the soul's rational faculties are not submerged; indeed they are brought to the peak of fulfilment. There is no absorption of the soul into God to the loss of its own identity, even in that consummation when God shall be all in all.[2]

Again, Origen's writings, including those passages where he uses the language of mysticism, are strikingly lacking in that feeling after passivity which is another tendency of a thoroughgoing mysticism. Von Hügel,[3] in discussing the passivity practised and taught by Catherine of Genoa, describes the process as involving four experiences: "Utter unification of the soul's functions, indeed utter unity of its substance: i.e. the soul does one single thing, and seems to do it by one single act; itself is simply one, and expresses itself by one sole act. Passivity of the soul: i.e. the soul does not apparently act at all, it simply *is* and receives—it is now nothing but one pure immense recipiency. Immediacy of contact between the soul and God: i.e. there seems to be nothing separating, or indeed in any way between, the soul and God. And, finally, an apparent coalescence of the soul and God: i.e. the soul *is* God, and God *is* the soul." The fourth point, incidentally, well illustrates the pantheistic tendency of mysticism.

No such desire for quietude is discoverable in Origen. For him the soul is always in possession of free will, whether in or out of the body, and always moves in the direction of good or evil. So strongly does Origen hold this that it is one of the reasons which led him to believe in a succession of worlds: the soul must always be in motion. And thus the ideal life which Origen places before his readers is not after all that of the contemplative, but, as Daniélou remarks: "The spiritual man, for Origen, does not have contemplation for his end. God fills him with his light and power so that he can undertake the great battles of God, which are those of the apostolate." [4] The true sons of God, even those who, by being conformed to the Word of God, have recovered the lost image of God, continue in good works precisely because they

---

[1] Butterworth, *Origen on First Principles*, p. xxxiii.
[2] The relations between mysticism, Pantheism, and the immanence of God are discussed at length by Von Hügel in *The Mystical Element of Religion* (Dent, 1909), Vol. ii, Ch. XIV.
[3] Op. cit., Vol. ii, pp. 129 ff.   [4] *Origène*, p. 295.

are in the image of him who created, who makes the sun to rise on the evil and on the good, and sends rain on the just and on the unjust.[1]

Non-mystical Character of "De Oratione". Nor can it be without significance that when Origen comes to write a treatise wholly devoted to the subject of prayer, he draws little upon his stock of mystical language. The fact that the Περὶ Εὐχῆς is a work of his maturity must also be weighed. This treatise is a thoroughly practical guide to the practice of prayer, setting forth instruction on the proper disposition of the mind in preparation, the division of prayer into praise, thanksgiving, confession, and intercession, the proper posture, place, and times for prayer, as well as a detailed commentary on the Lord's Prayer. He agrees with Clement (see pp. 27 ff.) that true prayer demands more than setting aside a certain time of the day for its practice. It is rather a constant activity of the whole man: "The man who links together his prayer with deeds of duty and fits seemly actions with his prayer is the man who prays without ceasing, for his virtuous deeds or the commandments he has fulfilled are taken up as a part of his prayer. For only in this way can we take the saying 'Pray without ceasing' as being possible, if we can say that the whole life of the saint is one mighty integrated prayer" (XII. 2). It is not easy to detect a mystical note here.

There are a few passages, however, in which language approaching the mystical is used. IX. 2 describes the soul properly prepared for prayer as a "soul which is lifted up, which follows after the Spirit, and is separated from the body, and which not only follows after the Spirit, but is actually in the Spirit . . . assuredly such a soul which lays aside its being becomes spiritual." But such a passage must not be treated apart from its context. As the very next paragraph (IX. 3) makes clear, the soul must not "lay aside its being" to the extent of forgetting that there are other prerequisites of prayer, and that one of them is to forgive others.

In discussing the phrase "Hallowed be thy name", Origen compares with it Psalm 34. 3, "Let us exalt his name together", and comments that we are here bidden to "attain to the true and lofty knowledge of God's essence. For this is to 'exalt the name of God together', when a man partakes of an effluence of divinity by being lifted up by God, and by having overcome his enemies, who are thus unable to rejoice at his fall, and exalts the very power of God of which

[1] *De Orat.* XXII. 4.

he has obtained a share" (*De Orat.* XXIV. 4). Here too, superficially, there is the language of mysticism. But Chapter XXIV argues that God's name stands for his essence, and his essence is holiness. Thus the "knowledge of God's essence", and the "share" in "the very power of God", of which this passage speaks is a knowledge of God's holiness. And this is not regarded by Origen as simply an intellectual experience, for it involves a "journey towards perfection", and that men "strive forward unceasingly" (XXV. 2); it is not the present possession of the soul in ecstasy or rapture. It can only "be true for us if we make ourselves worthy of obtaining God who hears our prayer for all these things" (XXVI. 2). A man may be "in earth", and yet have his citizenship in heaven and thus be "of heaven and the heavenly world, which is better than this"; but this is only true of a man "by reason of his will" (XXVI. 5). Origen's doctrine of the soul's unceasing possession of free will makes impossible for him the conception of any state of man in which the will is suspended.

The end of man's journey is to be the restoration of the image of God in him. This comes about by man's being conformed to the Word of God who is the image of the invisible God, and this involves "being transformed by the renewing of the mind" (XXII. 4). He "who studies to become spiritual" does so "by his contemplation of truth" (XXX. 3). The Περὶ Εὐχῆς certainly contains such assertions of the importance of the intellect in man's achievement of unity with God. But it is equally emphatic about the need for penitence and for continunace in good works.

Origen not a Mystic. It is, therefore, doubtful whether "mysticism" is a term which can be properly applied to Origen's thought. We have used the expression "intellectual mysticism" (e.g. on p. 61). Daniélou speaks of his "speculative mysticism of illumination of the spirit by gnosis".[1] But since upon examination the typical ideas and tendencies of the thoroughgoing mystic are seen to be absent in Origen, it must be doubted whether such terms are strictly appropriate. That he uses thought-forms which were to become the normal vehicles of expression of the later mystics is not denied. But this does not make Origen a mystic. The reason for his use of these ideas is not hard to find. It was in those terms that the Gnostics taught. In much the same way that a preacher in the nineteenth century might have employed the theory of evolution, or in the twentieth century might draw his illustrations from the realm of nuclear physics, so Origen was using

[1] *Origène*, p. 291.

the current intellectual coin of the third century. But he put it to a Christian use; and he was the more able to do this, since, shorn of extravagance, there was much that was scriptural in many of the Gnostic ideas. The escape from slavery to the flesh, the conquest of spiritual powers of evil, man's advance to a state of incorruption, are all biblical ideas. That Origen incorporates them into a system which has points of contact with Gnostic systems is significant only of his pastoral anxiety to win men from a false to a true and Christian gnosticism. Origen is no more to be regarded as a mystic than is, for example, the writer of the twenty-third Psalm who, in brief compass, puts before us the same conception of the journey of the soul.

In the books of Origen, says Jules Lebreton, "we do not look for the description, or even the mention, of any privileged mystical experience, vision, ecstasy, or rapture; but what we see most clearly is a life of contemplation and prayer wholly reaching out towards God and Christ, and which endeavours to draw with it all those whom it can touch. This is the secret of that influence, which was so profound, of the teacher of Alexandria and Caesarea upon his pupils. If he lifts them up, it is by the warmth of his love, and not by the attraction of a brilliant speculation." [1] These words well sum up the question.

De Oratione. In the epistle to his pupil, Gregory Thaumaturgus, Origen writes: "Give careful attention to the reading of the divine Scriptures . . . knock and the porter will open to you . . . and be not content with knocking and seeking; for what is most necessary also for understanding divine truth is prayer. To this end the Saviour, when he exhorted us, not only said, Knock and it shall be opened unto you, and, Seek and ye shall find, but also, Ask and it shall be given to you." [2] In *De Oratione* Origen is insistent on the efficacy of this prayer of asking, which is the prayer of the simple Christian. At the outset of the treatise he faces one of the perennial objections urged against prayer, and one which often puzzles the simple believer: "God knows all things before they come into being . . . What need then is there to send up prayer to him who knows what we need even before we pray? . . . Just as, if anyone were to pray for the sun to rise, he would be deemed foolish for thinking that what would happen without his prayer comes to pass through his prayer, in the same way a man would be out of his wits who thought that those things which

[1] *La Source et le Caractère de la Mystique d'Origène,* Analecta Bollandiana, Tome LXVII: Mélanges Paul Peeters, Tome I, Brussels, 1949.
[2] *Ep. ad Greg.* IV: *Origenis Philocalia,* ed. J. A. Robinson, 1893, pp. 66–7.

assuredly would happen even if he did not pray, come to pass because of his prayer" (v. 2–3).

Origen's answer is to remind his readers, first, that man has a large measure of free will. The fact that we blame servants and censure children shows that it is our experience that a great deal of human activity is within our power. If, then, man has free will, and God has foreknowledge, the movements of man's free will, which include his readiness or his refusal to pray, are known beforehand by God, who arranges what is appropriate accordingly. It is as though God says: "Such and such things will I do to this man who shall pray, for it is fitting that I should do so since his prayer will be blameless, nor will he behave himself carelessly in the matter of prayer; and to this man who will pray at some length I will give such and such things exceeding abundantly above what he asks or thinks" (vi. 4). In other words, God's foreknowledge takes into consideration man's prayers, or his failure to pray. Thus, for Origen, prayer is no mere subjective conditioning of a man's own mind. He holds prayer to be objectively efficacious. No man thinking as Origen does can dare to neglect his prayers with the excuse that they can make no difference to God's ordering of things. The prayer thus left unsaid may be a vital part of the conditions God desires to bring his will to pass.[1]

Yet Origen insists throughout *De Oratione* that the proper objects of petition are "the great things" and "the heavenly things", spiritual benefits which enable men to inherit the kingdom of heaven. The material benefits which in various passages of Scripture are recorded as having been given in answer to prayer are interpreted by the allegorical method as typical in each case of some spiritual grace (xiii). We may believe that God will supply our material wants (the "small and earthly things") according to our needs. It is in line with this that Origen interprets the petition for bread in the Lord's Prayer as a petition not for material bread, but for the True Bread which is Christ. The verse of unknown origin, "Ask for the great things, and the small things shall be added unto you; ask for heavenly things and earthly things shall be added unto you", may be said to express the main theme of *De Oratione*. It is a high ideal of prayer which Origen puts before his readers, but it is a kind of prayer which the *simpliciores* (whom Origen ever bears in mind) can understand, and which needs no unusual gifts, but only faithfulness, for its accomplishment.

[1] Heiler (*Prayer*, p. 101) considers that Origen in this passage was the first to attempt a really profound defence of prayer.

Appendix D

THE DATE OF ΠΕΡΙ ΕΥΧΗΣ

In XXIII. 4 Origen writes: "We have discussed these points (i.e. points connected with Genesis 3. 8–9) at greater length in our examination of the contents of the Book of Genesis." There were twelve (according to Eusebius) or thirteen (according to Jerome) books of the *Commentary on Genesis*, which according to Origen himself (*Contra Celsum* VI. 670) only proceeded as far as Genesis 5. 1. This is verified by Jerome, who mentions that the thirteenth book contained a discussion of Gen. 4. 15.

We know from Eusebius that the first eight books only of the *Commentary on Genesis* were written before Origen left Alexandria. It is sufficiently probable that Gen. 3. 8–9 was discussed in a later book than the eighth to justify us in dating the Περὶ Εὐχῆς after A.D. 231, when Origen had made Caesarea his headquarters.

Since the four books of *De Principiis* appear to have been written after the first book on Genesis and before the fourth,[1] we are safe in assuming that Περὶ Εὐχῆς was later than both the *Commentary on Genesis* and *De Principiis*.

The work is addressed to Ambrosius, Origen's patron, who died before Origen, probably about A.D. 250, and that date must be the *terminus ad quem*. Most scholars incline towards the earlier part of the period of nineteen years in which the book may have been written. Bigg, for instance, dates it "about 236". The hope expressed by Origen in the last paragraph that he may have opportunity to treat the subject of prayer again at a later date certainly suggests that the work was composed by a man who did not consider his life's work to be nearing the end.

[1] In *De Princ.* II. iii. 6 Origen refers to his commentary on Genesis 1. 1 as already written. But in *De Princ.* I. ii. 6 he promises to expound Genesis 1. 26 when he reaches it in the Commentary. This he does in the fourth book.

Appendix E

MANUSCRIPTS AND EDITIONS

Codex Holmiensis. There is only one manuscript extant which contains the whole of Origen's treatise Περὶ Εὐχῆς. This is the Codex Holmiensis in the Library of Trinity College, Cambridge. The manuscript contains also fragments of the Greek text of Origen's *Commentary on Matthew.* It is numbered in Trinity College Library B.8.10. Delarue complains in the preface of his edition that it has many lacunae, and is spoiled by frequent abbreviations, so that "it seems to require a prophet rather than a reader". Koetschau describes the manuscript in the introduction to his edition of Origen (*Origenes Werke,* Vol. I, Leipzig, 1891, pp. lxxxiii ff.).

M. R. James, in his catalogue of the Trinity College manuscripts, dates this copy of the Περὶ Εὐχῆς as fifteenth-century. It has had an adventurous history. We first hear of it as in the Library at Worms, and when that city was sacked it came into the hands of a soldier, who sold it to a man called Rumf, physician to Elizabeth of Bohemia. He sold it to Isaac Voss at the Hague. Voss gave it to Herbert Thorndike, a Fellow of Trinity, and afterwards Canon of Westminster. Thorndike, one of the foremost Cambridge scholars of the seventeenth century, being dispossessed under the Protectorate, had decided to use his enforced leisure by collecting material for an edition of Origen. The restoration of the monarchy found him happily back at Trinity, but with no leisure to complete his project. From Thorndike the manuscript passed to Thomas Gale, another Fellow of Trinity with whom he sat at Trinity high table between 1661 and 1668. It was perhaps Thorndike's hope that Gale or somebody else at Trinity would continue the work on Origen. Thorndike died in London in 1672. When Gale, who had become Dean of York, died in 1702, the manuscript together with other books was given by his son, Roger Gale, to Trinity College, where it has remained since. It is referred to in the notes accompanying the translation following as "codex MS.".

Codex Colbertinus. Delarue discovered part of the Περὶ Εὐχῆς (xxxi to end) in a manuscript which he calls Codex Colbertinus 3607. This is known to-day as Codex Parisinus 1788, and is in the Bibliothèque Nationale in Paris. Koetschau regards it as a copy of Codex Holmiensis.

Oxford Edition. In 1686 there was published at Oxford an edition of the Περὶ Εὐχῆς, together with a Latin translation. This edition is based on Codex Holmiensis, but it is not very carefully done.

Wetstein. An edition by Wetstein was published at Amsterdam in 1694. This also is based on Codex Holmiensis.

Reading. In 1728 William Reading, librarian of Sion College, London, published an edition. He "added also the notes of a certain learned but anonymous Englishman (*Anglus*), notes partly critical, partly explanatory of difficult passages" (Delarue). Anglus's notes were added also as an appendix to Delarue's edition of Περὶ Εὐχῆς in his *Origenis Opera Omnia* (see below). They are to be found in Migne, *P.G.* xi. 1631–88. The identity of Anglus is unknown. But if we consider those who might have written these notes we are immediately confronted with the name of Thorndike. He is known to have possessed the only extant manuscript of Περὶ Εὐχῆς. It is extremely likely that a scholar like Thorndike, who spent the last years of his life in Westminster, visited Sion College, and not unlikely that any scholarly papers he left would have found their way there, where Reading would have had access to them. It is a tempting guess, therefore, that Thorndike was "Anglus".[1]

Delarue. The Benedictine, Charles Delarue, began a complete edition of Origen's works in three volumes, *Origenis Opera Omnia*, and published the first volume in 1733. He died in 1739 and his nephew, Vincent Delarue, completed the work, and published the third volume in 1759. Περὶ Εὐχῆς was in Vol. I. Delarue set beside the Greek a Latin translation by Claude Fleury, the church historian who had died in 1725. Anglus' notes, having been published by Reading, were accessible, and Delarue added them in an appendix. Two others greatly helped Delarue in his edition of Περὶ Εὐχῆς. One was Richard Bentley, Master of Trinity College, Cambridge, the founder of critical literary scholarship in England, who, Delarue claims, "restored to health almost all the passages which needed a healing hand". Bentley's emendations certainly carry conviction for the most part. The other was the Rev. John Walker, Fellow of

[1] Dr W. Telfer, Master of Selwyn College, Cambridge, brought this possibility to my notice.

Trinity, who compared the Trinity manuscript with the Oxford edition. It is clear, therefore, that in our knowledge of the Περὶ Εὐχῆς we owe a great deal to English scholars of the seventeenth and eighteenth centuries, and especially to those of Trinity College, Cambridge.

Lommatzsch. The edition of Origen's works, *Origenis Opera Omnia*, by Lommatzsch (Berlin 1831–48) is largely based on Delarue.

Koetschau. By far the most valuable edition of Origen's works, including the Περὶ Εὐχῆς, is that of Paul Koetschau in the series *Die griechischen christlichen Schriftsteller der ersten drei Jahrhunderte, herausgegeben von der Kirchenväter-Commission der Königl. preussischen Akademie der Wissenschaften* (Leipzig). He provides very complete critical notes.

Part III

TRANSLATION AND NOTES

ORIGEN'S
TREATISE ON PRAYER

Only God's grace can enable man to grasp what is beyond his natural capability

I.—1. Things which cannot be grasped by rational and mortal kind because they are vast and superhuman, and far surpass our perishable nature, nevertheless by the will of God become capable of being so grasped by reason of the abundant and immeasurable grace of God poured out from him towards men through Jesus Christ, the minister of boundless grace towards us, and through the Spirit, his fellow-worker. To acquire the wisdom by which all things have been fashioned is impossible for human nature (for God, according to David, made all things in wisdom (Psalm 104. 24)); but what is impossible becomes possible through our Lord Jesus Christ who was made unto us wisdom from God, righteousness and sanctification and redemption (1 Cor. 1. 30). For what man shall know the counsel of God? or who shall think what the will of the Lord is? For the thoughts of mortal men are fearful, and our devices are but uncertain. For a corruptible body presseth down the soul, and the earthly tabernacle weigheth down the mind that museth upon many things. And hardly do we guess aright at things that are upon the earth;[1] but the things that are in heaven who hath searched out? (Wisd. 9. 13–16). Who would not answer that it is impossible for man to search out the things in heaven? Nevertheless this, impossible though it is, becomes possible by the abundant grace of God; for he who was caught up into the third heaven no doubt searched out the things in the three heavens,[2] for he

---

[1] The Oxford edition adds καὶ τὰ ἐν χερσὶν εὑρίσκομεν μετὰ πόνου (A.V. "and with labour do we find the things that are before us"). But this is not found in the codex MS. Delarue also rejects it.

[2] Origen shared with St Paul the ordinary Greek scientific presuppositions. The heavens were considered to be a concentric series of revolving spheres with the earth at the centre. The innermost sphere was that in which the moon moved, and the outermost that in which the stars were fixed. A detailed description of this system is given by Cicero in "Somnium Scipionis" at the end of the last book of his *De Natura*, a work in which he is expounding Greek and especially Platonic thought. Cf. *De Princ.* II. xi. 6–7.
    The student must not fall into the error of thinking that the acceptance by

heard unspeakable words which it was not lawful for a man to utter (2 Cor. 12. 4). And who can say that it is possible for a man to know the mind of the Lord? (1 Cor. 2. 16). But this also God grants through Christ[1]... the will of their Lord who, when he teaches them his will, no longer wills to be Lord, but changes into a friend to those whose Lord he was hitherto. But even as no man knoweth the things of a man save the spirit of man which is in him, even so the things of God knoweth no man, but the Spirit of God (1 Cor. 2. 11). But if no man knoweth the things of God, but the Spirit of God, it is impossible for man to know the things of God. Yet mark this well, how it becomes possible: Now we received, he says, not the spirit of the world, but the Spirit which is of God; that we might know the things that are freely given to us of God. Which things also we speak, not in the words which man's wisdom teacheth, but which the Holy Ghost teacheth (1 Cor. 2. 12, 13).

---

ancient writers of outmoded scientific doctrines completely invalidates their thought. In no age do the greatest minds allow themselves to be shackled by the thought-forms of their day. Thus the particular conception under consideration played little part in St Paul's thought.

[1] ἀλλὰ καὶ τοῦτο ὁ θεὸς διὰ Χριστοῦ χαρίζεται. The codex MS. here has a lacuna of over three lines, followed by the words τὸ θέλημα τοῦ κυρίου ἑαυτῶν οὐκέτι ὅτε διδάσκει αὐτοὺς τὸ θέλημα τοῦ κυρίου εἶναι θέλοντος ἀλλὰ εἰς φίλον μεταβάλλοντος τούτοις ὧν κύριος πρότερον ἦν. Both the Oxford editor and Anglus supply a quotation of John 15. 15 preceded by εἶπε γάρ. Ox. ed. continues λέγει ὅτι οὐκ οἶδε..., "He says that he knows not...". Anglus continues Δούλοις οὖσιν αὐτοῖς γνωρίζει..., "To those who are themselves servants he makes known...". In neither case is the following ἑαυτῶν properly accounted for.

Koetschau suggests διὰ Χριστοῦ χαρίζεται λέγοντος ὅτι, followed by John 15. 14, 15 and then some such words as ἀγνοοῦσιν οὖν οἱ ἀκούειν ταῦτα λέγοντος Χριστοῦ βουλόμενοι... "But this also God grants through Christ who says: Ye are my friends, if ye do whatsoever I command you. Henceforth I call you not servants; for the servant knoweth not what his lord doeth: but I have called you friends; for all things that I have heard of my Father I have made known unto you. So then, those who are willing to listen to Christ speaking thus are no longer ignorant of the will of their Lord, when he teaches them the will of him who wills to be Lord, but changes into a friend to those whose Lord he was hitherto."

This, however, is not entirely satisfactory, for the οὐκέτι which according to Koetschau must be taken with ἀγνοοῦσιν is really required with θέλοντος. Οἴδασιν instead of ἀγνοοῦσιν would give the required sense: "So then, those who are willing to listen... know the will of their Lord who when he teaches them his will no longer wills to be Lord, but changes..."

ON PRAYER

God's grace needed in handling the subject of prayer

II.—1. But no doubt, my most devout and zealous Ambrosius,[1] and Tatiana,[2] most disciplined and of most manly virtue, whose womanly nature has now been left behind (a condition to boast of)[3] as was that of Sarah (Gen. 18. 11), you are wondering why, when the subject set before us is prayer, in my introduction these things have been said about what is impossible to men becoming possible by the grace of God. One of the impossible things, in so far as our weakness is concerned,[4] I am persuaded, is to explain the whole subject of prayer accurately and reverently, both concerning the manner in which we ought to pray and what we ought to say to God in our prayer, and also what occasions are more suitable for prayer than

---

[1] Ambrosius was one of Origen's converts from Gnosticism. He was a rich man, who became devoted to Origen. He supplied Origen's stenographers and copyists. Origen affectionately calls him his taskmaster, ἐργοδιώκτης. The adjective φιλοπονώτατε, translated here "zealous", which literally means "great lover of toil", may be a playful reference to Ambrosius' demands upon Origen's energy.

[2] Tatiana is not known. It has been suggested that she was Ambrosius' wife. In the *Epistle to Africanus*, however, Ambrosius' wife is called Marcella. But Tatiana may be a second name. On the other hand she may have been Ambrosius' sister. The question is discussed in the *Monitum* which precedes the *Libellus de Oratione* in Migne, *P.G.* xi.

[3] ἀφ' ἧς ἐκλελοιπέναι τὰ γυναικεῖα . . . εὔχομαι. Anglus' note (Migne, *P.G.* xi. 1633-4) is as follows: "By these words Origen seems to indicate that Tatiana was at that time of advanced age, being one in whom, as in Sarah, the menstrual periods had ceased. But surely he does not 'boast' at this (for why should he praise a woman whom he calls κοσμιωτάτη for something which is common to all old women?). Rather, using the words figuratively, he is asserting her chastity, in whom, although perhaps not yet extinct, the γυναικεῖα πάθη, i.e. the wayward desires to which women are prone, have been put to sleep and ceased, just as τὰ γυναικεῖα ἔμμηνα in Sarah's aged body. He 'boasts', therefore, that she is such as the Apostle describes in 1 Tim. 2. 9."

One might think that Origen should have made his meaning clearer. But Tatiana knew how old she was, and so doubtless did Origen. The precise sense in which he was using τὰ γυναικεῖα would therefore have been clear to those to whom he was dedicating the work.

There is evidently a play on the words ἀνδρειοτάτη and τὰ γυναικεῖα. The probable meaning of Origen's words is that Tatiana had taken a vow of chastity, so that what had occurred in Sarah because of her advanced age had also occurred in Tatiana of her own devout volition. And τὰ γυναικεῖα being inactive within her, she may appropriately be addressed as ἀνδρειοτάτη.

[4] I.e. if it is left to human weakness to attempt the task.

others [1] ... who was afraid, through the abundance of the revelations, lest any man should think of him above that which he seeth or heareth of him (2 Cor. 12. 6, 7), confesses that he knows not how to pray as he ought. For, he says, we know not what we should pray for as we ought (Rom. 8. 26).

Knowledge of both the proper method and the proper subject-matter of prayer necessary

But it is necessary not only to pray, but also to pray as we ought, and to pray for what we ought. For although [2] we be able to understand what we ought to pray for, this is not sufficient, unless we also add the words "as we ought". And what profit is there for us in praying "as we ought", if we do not know how to pray for what we ought?

Examples from Scripture of the subject-matter of prayer

2. One of these two things, namely praying for what we ought, consists in the words of our prayer; the other, praying as we ought, consists in the disposition of him who prays. To illustrate this, the following passages [3] show what we ought to pray for: Ask for the great things, and the small things shall be added unto you; [4] and, Ask for heavenly things and earthly things shall be added unto you (cf. Matt. 6. 33); and, Pray for them which despitefully use you (Matt. 5. 44); and, Pray ye therefore the Lord of the harvest, that he will send forth labourers into his harvest (Matt. 9. 38); and, Pray that ye enter not into temptation (Luke 22. 40); and, Pray ye that your flight be not in the winter, neither on the sabbath day (Matt. 24. 20); and,

---

[1] There is a lacuna in the codex MS. at this point. Before the words which follow the Oxford editor supplies οἴδαμεν τὸν Παῦλον, "We know that Paul ... confesses", etc. Koetschau suggests εἰκὸς οὖν καὶ Παῦλον ...

[2] The Greek is ἵνα γὰρ ... Bentley suggests ἐὰν γὰρ ...

[3] Notice how Origen rests his teaching on the Bible. He does not elaborate any theoretical scheme of the subject-matter of prayer or of the proper disposition of him who prays, but goes to the Bible for concrete examples. Origen's reliance on the Bible is apparent throughout the treatise.

[4] Origen refers to this saying of Jesus again in *Contra Celsum* vii. 726. Clement of Alexandria also quotes it (*Strom.* 1. 24). The note of Delarue on the passage in *Contra Celsum* suggests that it is either from the Gospel of the Nazarenes or an interpolation into the text of Matt. 6. 33 in a codex to which Origen had access.

When ye pray, use not vain repetitions (Matt. 6. 7), and other passages like these.

Examples illustrating how we ought to pray

The following illustrates how we ought to pray: I will therefore that men pray everywhere, lifting up holy hands, without wrath and doubting. In like manner also, that women adorn themselves in modest apparel,[1] with shamefacedness and sobriety; not with broided hair, or gold, or pearls, or costly array; but (which becometh women professing godliness) with good works (1 Tim. 2. 8–10). The following also teaches us how to pray as we ought: Therefore if thou bring thy gift to the altar, and there rememberest[2] that thy brother hath ought against thee; leave there thy gift before the altar, and go, first be reconciled to thy brother, and then come and offer thy gift (Matt. 5. 23, 24). For what greater gift can be presented to God by a rational creature than a sweet-smelling word of prayer, offered by one who is conscious that he possesses no evil savour by reason of any sin? The following also is an instance of how to pray as we ought: Defraud ye not one the other, except it be with consent for a time, that ye may give yourselves to prayer; and come together again, that Satan rejoice not over you[3] for your incontinency (1 Cor. 7. 5). For a man is prevented from praying as he ought, unless the act which is the mystery of marriage, and about which it is fitting to preserve silence, be performed with great sense of solemnity, without haste and without too much emphasis on the physical passions; for the consent (Gr. συμφωνία, harmony) which is spoken of in this passage causes the discord of passion to disappear, disperses the power of incontinence, and prevents the malicious rejoicing of Satan.[4] In addition to these passages, the following also teaches us how to pray as we ought: If ye stand praying, forgive, if ye have ought against any (Mark 11. 25); and the verse from Paul, Every man praying or

---

[1] ἐν καταστολῇ κοσμίῳ. So Oxf. ed. Codex MS. and Delarue have κοσμίως.

[2] κἀκεῖ μνησθῇς. So Oxf. ed. Codex MS. and Delarue μνησθείς.

[3] ἐπιχαρῇ. Note the variation from the πειράζῃ of the N.T. MSS. Whenever he quotes this verse Origen always omits the words "fasting and" before "prayer".

[4] Clement of Alexandria (*Strom.* III. 12) has a similar exegesis of this passage. Note the delicacy of Origen's treatment of it. Here is sound Christian teaching on the marriage relation.

prophesying, having his head covered, dishonoureth his head. But every woman that prayeth or prophesieth with her head uncovered dishonoureth her head (1 Cor. 11. 4, 5), also sets forth how we ought to pray.

The Holy Spirit helps those who know their own weakness in prayer

3. But Paul, knowing all these examples, could indeed have set forth many more [1] than these out of the Law and Prophets, and out of the Gospel which fulfilled them, with a variety of interpretation upon each; and perceiving how much, even after all these hints, we still fall short of knowing how to pray for what we ought "as we ought", he speaks out of a mind devoted not only to moderation but also to truth, when he says: We know not what we should pray for as we ought (Rom. 8. 26); and to the saying he makes the following addition, whence [2] that wherein he falls short may be supplied to the man who, while he knows not how to pray as he ought, yet tries to make himself worthy of having what is lacking supplied in him; for he says, The Spirit itself maketh intercession for us to God [3] with groanings which cannot be uttered. And he that searcheth the hearts knoweth what is the mind of the Spirit, because he maketh intercession for the saints according to (the will of) God (Rom. 8. 26, 27). And the Spirit that cries in the hearts of the blessed, Abba, Father (Gal. 4. 6), knowing in his anxious care [4] that the groans uttered in the earthly tabernacle are calculated to weigh down those who have fallen or transgressed, maketh intercession for us to God with groanings which cannot be uttered, out of his great love for men and pity taking upon himself our groanings; and in the wisdom which is his, seeing our soul bowed down to the dust (Psalm 44. 25, A.V.), and shut up in the body of our humiliation (Phil. 3. 21), he maketh intercession for us to God, uttering no ordinary groanings, but certain groanings which cannot be uttered, like those unspeakable words which it is not lawful for a man to utter (2 Cor. 12. 4). And this same Spirit, not content with

---

[1] I.e. passages upon the subject of how to pray.

[2] προστίθησιν, ὅθεν ἀναπληροῦται. It is, or course, not from St Paul's addition that a man's deficiencies in prayer are made up, but by the Spirit. Origen here expresses himself loosely. We may paraphrase, "he makes the following addition in which he tells of the Source whence...".

[3] τῷ θεῷ. Anglus notes that Origen adds these words when referring to this text four times in this section, and again in xiv. 5.

[4] ἐπιμελῶς, lit. "anxiously".

merely making intercession to God, intensifies his intercession and he *more than* maketh intercession,[1] and this, in my opinion he does for those who are *more than* conquerors, such as was Paul who says: Nay, in all these things we are more than conquerors (Rom. 8. 37). And it is probable that he makes simple intercession, not for those who are great enough to be more than conquerors, and not, on the other hand again, for such as are conquered, but for those who are simply conquerors.

The Spirit's aid is always necessary in prayer

4. But similar to the above verse, We know not what we should pray for as we ought; but the Spirit maketh intercession for us to God [2]

---

[1] Origen here plays upon the double meaning of the prefix in ὑπερεντυγχάνει. The prefix ὑπερ- may add the meaning "on behalf of" to the verb, or it may have the force of exaggerating the action of the verb; cf. the English "over-" in overeat, overdo. In St Paul's use of the word the prefix has the former meaning, but Origen suggests that it has the intensifying force. He thus distinguishes two levels in the Spirit's intercession. For those who are more than conquerors, he vehemently or "more than" makes intercession. For those who are simply conquerors, he simply makes intercession. In this piece of exegesis we are reminded that Origen is always eager, wherever possible, to gain an exact literal sense.

Since we shall have occasion to note Origen's interpretation of Scripture from time to time, it will be convenient here to give a brief description of his method (which he expounds fully in *De Principiis* iv. ii–iii. Holy Scripture consists, says Origen, as does man, of body, soul, and spirit. It has a threefold meaning, literal, moral, and mystical or spiritual, corresponding to the body, soul, and spirit in man. Every word of Scripture has meaning in one at least of these three ways. The bulk of it has a literal meaning, which Origen is always at pains to discover. The literal, which is the obvious, meaning is sufficient to meet the needs of the ordinary simple believer. Those passages which because of their contradictions or incongruities cannot be supposed to have a literal meaning are nevertheless allowed to stand in Holy Scripture in order to prompt the reader to seek for a yet deeper meaning (*De Princ.* iv. ii. 9). The moral, or soul, meaning Origen does not greatly employ. He gives as an example of it (*De Princ.* iv. ii. 6) St Paul's quotation of "Thou shalt not muzzle the ox that treadeth out the corn" in 1 Cor. 9. 9, which, the Apostle argues, is meant to apply to the preacher of the gospel. Origen seems to mean that it is the moral, or soul, meaning of a passage which yields a practical lesson. The mystical or spiritual interpretation is the allegorical, and in Origen's eyes the most important. By it practically the whole of Scripture is made to reveal the deep truths of redemption. The spiritual interpretation of the Scriptures is the proper work of the Christian teacher. We shall note examples of it in the body of this treatise.

[2] See note 3, p. 84.

with groanings which cannot be uttered, is the following: I will pray with the Spirit, and I will pray with the understanding also: I will sing with the Spirit, and I will sing with the understanding also (1 Cor. 14. 15). For neither can our understanding pray unless the Spirit [1] prays first, as it were in its hearing; just as neither can it sing psalms with rhythm and melody, in time and harmony, and praise the Father in Christ, unless the Spirit who searcheth all things, yea the deep things of God (1 Cor. 2. 10), first praises and hymns him whose depths [2] he hath searched out and comprehended as he is able. I think that it was perceiving that human weakness is incapable of praying in the manner in which men ought to pray and realizing this particularly when he heard the wise and mighty words uttered [3] by the Saviour in his prayer to the Father, that one of Jesus' disciples said to the Lord when he ceased from prayer, Lord, teach us to pray, as John also taught his disciples (Luke 11. 1). The whole context of the passage is as follows: And it came to pass, that as he was praying in a certain place, when he ceased, one of his disciples said unto him, Lord, teach us to pray, as John also taught his disciples to pray.[4]

The prayers of saints before Christ were inspired by the Holy Spirit

Then are we to suppose that a man nourished in the teachings of the law, and by listening to the words of the prophets, and who attended synagogues regularly, was altogether ignorant of how to

---

[1] Origen interprets the πνεῦμα of 1 Cor. 14. 15 as of the Holy Spirit. Notice again Origen's pressing of the literal sense. He here makes his point out of the fact that St Paul mentions praying and singing with the Spirit before praying and singing with the understanding.

[2] πρότερον αἰνέσῃ καὶ ὑμνήσῃ τοῦτον, οὗ τὰ βάθη ... Codex MS. has αἰνέσει καὶ ὑμνήσει τοῦ νοῦ τὰ βάθη. So Delarue in his text, but he cites with approval Bentley's correction, αἰνέσῃ καὶ ὑμνήσῃ τὸν οὗ τὰ βάθη ...

[3] ὅτε ... λόγων ἤκουεν ἀπαγγελλομένων.
λόγων, ἢ καὶ εὐεπαγγελλομένων is the reading given in Delarue's text. This is the Oxford editor's conjecture for ἢ καὶ ἐν ἐπαγγ. But Delarue in his footnote approves Bentley's restoration of the obviously corrupt text: λόγων ἤκουεν ἐπαγγελλομένων.
Anglus has λόγων ἤκουεν ἀπαγγ., and is followed by Koetschau. Delarue in his appended note to Anglus (Migne, *P.G.* xi. 1635) seems not to have noticed that Anglus reads ἀπαγγ. and not ἐπαγγ. as Bentley.

[4] In the codex MS. there is a hiatus of two or three lines, although the following ἆρα γὰρ ἄνθρωπος carries on the trend of the passage without apparent loss of sense.

pray, until he saw the Lord praying "in a certain place"? But to say this is absurd. For he used to pray after the manner of the Jews, but he perceived that he needed a greater knowledge to approach the passage concerning prayer.[1] What then did John teach his disciples about prayer when they came to him from Jerusalem and all Judaea and the region round about to be baptized (Matt. 3. 5), if there were not certain truths about prayer which he saw, inasmuch as he was more than a prophet (Matt. 11. 9), truths which it is probable that he secretly handed over, not indeed to all who were being baptized, but to those who were being instructed for Baptism?[2]

5. Such prayers, which are truly spiritual since the Spirit prays too in the heart of the saints, are recorded, and are full of ineffable and wonderful teaching. For in the First Book of Kings (1 Samuel, A.V.) there is recorded in part the prayer of Hannah (for when she continued praying before the Lord, speaking in her heart (1 Sam. 1. 12, 13), the whole[3] of it was not written),[4] and in the Psalms the sixteenth Psalm is entitled, A Prayer of David (Psalm 17, A.V.); and the eighty-ninth, A Prayer of Moses the man of God (Psalm 90, A.V.); and the hundred and first, A Prayer of the Afflicted when he is overwhelmed, and poureth out his complaint before the Lord (Psalm 102, A.V.). These prayers, since they were truly prayers made and spoken in the Spirit, are also full of the precepts of God's wisdom, so that one might say of words that are uttered in them, "Who is wise, and he

---

[1] εἰς τὸν περὶ τῆς εὐχῆς τόπον. This rather lame phrase reads like a gloss, but there is no MS. authority for so treating it. To translate τόπον as "place" gives no easier sense.

[2] τοῖς πρὸς τὸ βαπτίζεσθαι μαθητευομένοις. This implies that John only gave instruction to a few of those whom he baptized. Seeing this difficulty Bentley corrected to πρὸς τῷ βαπτ., "those who received instruction in addition to their Baptism". All the baptized would have had the preliminary instruction; but some of them, desiring to become disciples of John, were given further teaching. The conjecture is attractive. Anglus adopts it.

[3] ὅλη γὰρ ... The MS. has τῇ γὰρ ... Anglus suggests αὐτὴ γὰρ (i.e. Hannah).

[4] οὐκ † ἐχάρη γραφῇ. Koetschau places an obelus here in his text. He suggests οὐκ ἐγράφη, to be taken with ὅλη, "the whole of her prayer was not written" (i.e. in 1 Sam.). Bentley suggests either εὐχὴ οὐκ ἀνεγράφη or οὐκ ἔχρη γραφῆς. The uncertainty of the text makes it difficult to grasp Origen's meaning. Bentley's second suggestion would imply that Origen is making a distinction between prayers of the spirit, or from the heart, and prayers in which books of devotion are used. Delarue gives the codex MS. reading οὐκ ἐχάρη γραφῇ and cites Bentley's emendations.

shall understand these things? prudent, and he shall know them?" (Hos. 14. 9).

Origen prays for divine assistance in elucidating the subject of prayer

6. Since, then, to discuss prayer is a task such as to need the Father to shed light upon it, and the Word himself, the firstborn, to teach, and the Spirit to work within us that we may understand and speak worthily of such a subject, praying as a man (for it is not indeed to myself that I attribute my capacity for prayer) [1] I entreat the Spirit, before I come to my discussion of prayer, that it may be granted to me to discourse fully, and after the Spirit, and that the prayers written in the Gospels may be made clear to us. Let us begin then our discussion on prayer.[2]

The word εὐχή in the Scriptures sometimes means "prayer", sometimes "vow" [3]

III.—1. I first find the word εὐχή used, so far as I have noticed, when Jacob became a fugitive from his brother Esau's anger, and fled to Mesopotamia at the advice of Isaac and Rebecca. The passage is as follows: "And Jacob vowed a vow (ηὔξατο εὐχήν), saying, If the Lord God be with me, and keep me in this way that I go, and give me bread to eat and raiment to put on, and lead me back to my father's house in safety, then shall the Lord be my God: and this stone, which I have set for a pillar, shall be God's house: and of all that thou shalt give me I will surely give the tenth unto thee" (Gen. 28. 20–22).[4]

---

[1] (οὐ γάρ που ... τὴν προσευχὴν). Delarue continues the parenthesis to ... τυχεῖν τῆς εὐχῆς. This would give us: "For I do not indeed claim for myself that I am capable of the prayer of the Spirit before I have discovered the meaning of prayer." But the translation is difficult and the sense dubious. Bentley alters που to πω and omits τοῦ πνεύματος: "I do not yet claim for myself that I am capable of prayer until I have ..." Koetschau's punctuation gives greater point. The parenthesis is explanatory of εὐξάμενος ὡς ἄνθρωπος τοῦ πνεύματος ἀξιῶ.

[2] There is a hiatus of about one and a third lines here. Nothing, however, is lacking in the sense. The hiatus in the codex may merely mark the end of the section.

[3] Notice Origen's method, essentially scientific and surprisingly modern, of elucidating the meanings of εὐχή and προσευχή by specific instances.

[4] There is a hiatus of about two lines in the codex MS. at this point, but again nothing is lacking in the sense. Anglus suggests that Origen had here another example of a similar use of εὐχή. The καί following (ἔνθα καὶ σημειωτέον) bears this out perhaps.

III. 3   ON PRAYER

2. Here too it is to be noticed that the word εὐχή is taken (for in many places it is different in meaning from προσευχή) as of one who promises with a vow (εὐχή) to do certain things if he obtains certain other things from God. But the word is employed also in our customary sense,[1] as in Exodus we find the following after the plague of frogs, being the second in order of the ten plagues: [2] Pharaoh called for Moses and Aaron, and said unto them, Intreat (εὔξασθε) the Lord for me, and let him take away the frogs from me, and from my people; and I will let the people go, that they may do sacrifice [3] unto the Lord (Ex. 8. 8). But if Pharaoh's use of the word εὔξασθε does not easily persuade anyone that the customary meaning (prayer) is also signified by εὐχή as well as the former meaning (vow),[4] let him mark also what follows; it is this: And Moses said unto Pharaoh, Appoint for me when I shall intreat (εὔξομαι) for thee, and for thy servants, and for thy people, to destroy the frogs from thee and thy people and your houses. Only in the river shall they remain (Ex. 8. 9).

3. But we notice that in the case of the lice, the third plague, neither does Pharaoh ask that prayer be made, nor does Moses pray. And in the case of the plague of flies, which was the fourth, he says, Intreat (εὔξασθε) for me to the Lord, therefore. Whereupon also Moses said, I will go out from thee, and I will intreat (εὔξομαι) God, and the plague of flies shall depart from Pharaoh, and from his servants, and from his people, to-morrow (Ex. 8. 28, 29); and a little later: And Moses went out from Pharaoh, and intreated (ηὔξατο) God (Ex. 8. 30). Again, while in the fifth and sixth plagues neither did Pharaoh ask that prayer should be made, nor did Moses pray, in the seventh Pharaoh sent, and called for Moses and Aaron, and said unto them, I have sinned this time: the Lord is righteous, and I and my people are wicked. Intreat (εὔξασθε) the Lord, therefore, and let God's thunderings and hail and fire cease (Ex. 9. 27, 28); and a little later: Moses went out of the city from Pharaoh, and spread abroad

---

[1] ἐπὶ τοῖς κατὰ συνήθειαν ἡμῶν λεγομένοις. Koetschau follows the codex here. The Oxford editor alters to ἐπὶ τοῦ ... λεγομένου. Anglus suggests ἐπὶ τῆς ... λεγομένης (scil. εὐχῆς) ("employed also of prayer in our customary sense"). Delarue follows the Oxford edition.

[2] There is another lacuna here, of two lines. But there is no obvious hiatus in the sense.

[3] θύσωσι. Delarue has θύσουσι, following the Oxford editor.

[4] Ex. 8. 8 does introduce the idea of a vow, in so far as Pharaoh (through Moses) attempts to make a bargain with God. But Origen is making the point that in this verse the word εὔξασθε itself has the usual meaning of "pray".

his hands unto the Lord: and the thunders ceased (Ex. 9. 33). Why "and intreated" is not said as on the former occasions, but "spread abroad his hands unto the Lord", is to be inquired into more opportunely upon another occasion. In the eighth plague also Pharaoh says, And intreat (προσεύξασθε) the Lord your God, and let him take away from me this death. And Moses went out from Pharaoh and intreated (ηὔξατο) God (Ex. 10. 17, 18).

4. We have said that the word εὐχή is in many places, as in the Jacob passage, employed not in its usual sense (of prayer). There is another instance in Leviticus: The Lord spake unto Moses, saying, Speak unto the children of Israel, and say unto them, Whosoever vows a vow (εὔξηται εὐχήν) to give the price of his life unto the Lord, the price of the male from twenty years old even unto sixty years old—his price shall be fifty shekels of silver by the Temple weight (Lev. 27. 1–3). And in Numbers: And the Lord spake unto Moses, saying, Speak unto the children of Israel, and say unto them, Whosoever, man or woman, vows a mighty vow (εὔξηται εὐχήν) to sanctify themselves in chastity unto the Lord, he shall be purified from wine and strong drink (Num. 6. 1–3), and what follows concerning him who is called a Nazirite; then a little later, And he shall sanctify [1] his head in that day, in which he is sanctified unto the Lord for the days of his vow (εὐχή) (Num. 6. 5); and again a little later, This is the law of him who has made a vow (εὐξαμένου), on the day in which he fulfils the day of his vow (εὐχή) (Num. 6. 13); and again a little later, And after that he who has made a vow (ὁ ηὐγμένος) shall drink wine. This is the law of him who makes a vow (εὐξαμένου), whosoever vows unto the Lord his gift for a vow, beside that that his hand shall find, according to the power of his vow that he vows according to the law of purification (Num. 6. 20, 21); and at the end of Numbers, And Moses spake unto the heads of the tribes of the children of Israel, saying, This is the thing which the Lord hath commanded. Whatsoever man vows a vow unto the Lord, or swears an oath with a bond [2] or makes a bond concerning his soul, he shall not profane his word; he shall do all things whatsoever proceedeth out of his mouth. And if a woman vow a vow unto the Lord, and bind herself by a bond, in her father's house in her youth, and her father

---

[1] ἁγιάσει. Delarue ἁγιάσῃ.
[2] Koetschau follows the codex MS. in reading ἢ ὀμόσῃ ὅρκον ὁρισμῷ ἢ ὁρίσηται. Delarue alters to conform to the LXX, ἢ ὀμόσῃ ὅρκον ἢ ὁρισμῷ ὁρίσηται.

hear her vows, and her bonds wherewith she hath bound herself against her own soul, and her father shall hold his peace: then all her vows shall stand, and all the bonds wherewith she hath bound herself against her own soul shall remain unto her (Num. 30. 1–4), and the law goes on to lay down certain other requirements in the case of such a woman. In the same sense (i.e. of the word εὐχή) it is written in Proverbs [1] ... It is a snare to a man to dedicate any of his possessions hastily; for after he has made his vow (εὔξασθαι), he begins to repent it (Prov. 20. 25); and in Ecclesiastes, Better is it that thou shouldest not vow, than that thou shouldest vow (εὔξασθαι) and not pay (Eccles. 5. 5); and in the Acts of the Apostles, We have four men which have a vow (εὐχήν) on [2] them (Acts 21. 23).

Προσευχή may have the meaning "vow" as well as "prayer"

IV.—1. I did not think it at all irrelevant first to determine the scriptural meaning of the word εὐχή, signifying as it does two things; we must do the same with the word προσευχή. For this word, in addition to the common and customary sense which it frequently denotes (i.e. prayer), is employed also for εὐχή in the sense we customarily give to it (i.e. vow), in the story of Hannah [3] in the First Book of Kings (A.V., 1 Sam.): And Eli the priest sat upon a

---

[1] After γέγραπται the codex has a lacuna of about two lines. The Oxford editor inserts the one word παγίς, "snare", from Prov. 20. 25, putting it in brackets, and both Delarue and Koetschau follow him in this in their text. Koetschau, following Anglus, in his note suggests that the lacuna be filled from Prov. 7. 14 and 19. 13 (LXX): "'I have a peace offering; to-day I pay my vows', and 'A foolish son is a shame to his father; his vows are unchaste because of the courtesan's hire', and 'It is a snare, etc.'."

[2] ἀφ' ἑαυτῶν. So the Oxford editor. Delarue prefers the ἐφ' ἑαυτῶν of the codex MS.

[3] τέτακται καὶ ἐπὶ τῆς κατὰ τὸ σύνηθες ἡμῖν σημαινόμενον [τῆς] εὐχῆς ἐν τοῖς περὶ τῆς Ἄννης λεγομένοις. Koetschau would omit the τῆς before εὐχῆς. Anglus maintains that the "sense we customarily give to" εὐχή is "prayer". He therefore emends: τέτακται καὶ ἐπὶ τοῦ μὴ κατὰ τὸ σύνηθες ἡμῖν σημαινομένου τῆς εὐχῆς, i.e. the word προσευχή, in addition to its customary sense of "prayer", in 1 Sam. 1. 9–11 is employed also for the sense of εὐχή which is *not* customary with us, i.e. "vow".

Delarue points out that whilst in general the meaning of εὐχή is "prayer", in the Hannah passage the word εὐχή is customarily taken to mean "vow". If he is right, we should translate: "For this word, in addition to the common and customary sense which it frequently denotes (i.e. prayer) is employed also for the sense we commonly give to εὐχή in the story of Hannah (i.e. vow)."

seat by the doorposts of the temple of the Lord. And she was in bitterness of soul and she vowed (προσηύξατο) unto the Lord, and wept sore. And she vowed a vow (ηὔξατο εὐχήν), and said, O Lord of Hosts, if thou wilt indeed look on the affliction of thine handmaid, and remember me, and not forget thine handmaid, and wilt give unto thine handmaid a man child, then I will give him unto the Lord as a gift all the days of his life, and there shall no razor come upon his head (1 Sam. 1. 9–11).

2. However, it is possible with regard to this passage, giving attention to the words προσηύξατο πρὸς κύριον, καὶ ηὔξατο εὐχήν, to say with some show of probability, that if she did the two things, that is "*prayed* unto the Lord" and "vowed a vow", probably the word προσηύξατο is used in the same sense of what we usually call εὐχή (i.e. prayer) [1]; but ηὔξατο εὐχήν in the sense laid down in Leviticus and Numbers (i.e. vow). For the phrase, I will give him unto the Lord as a gift all the days of his life and there shall no razor come upon his head, is not properly "prayer" (προσευχή), but the kind of vow (εὐχή) which Jephthah made in the following terms, And Jephthah vowed a vow (ηὔξατο εὐχήν) unto the Lord, and said, If thou shalt without fail deliver the children of Ammon into mine hand, then it shall be that whosoever cometh forth of the doors of my house to meet me, when I return in peace from the children of Ammon, shall surely be the Lord's, and I will offer him up for a burnt offering (Judges 11. 30, 31).

Some deny the power of prayer, yet believe in God

V.—1. After this, if we ought, as you bade us, to explain the arguments first of those who think that nothing is achieved by prayer, and for this reason say that to pray is unnecessary, we will not refuse

---

But ἐν τοῖς περὶ τῆς Ἄννης λεγομένοις must be taken with τέτακται rather than with κατὰ τὸ σύνηθες ἡμῖν σημαινόμενον.

The translation I give makes good sense. Origen is arguing that προσευχή is used in the sense of "vow" in 1 Sam. 1. 9–11, and he goes on to urge that in this passage προσηύξατο means "vowed" and is synonymous with ηὔξατο εὐχήν. My exegesis means that we must assume that Origen does here say that the customary meaning of εὐχή is "vow", which is in contradiction to what he says in III. 2 and IV. 2. But in this passage he is labouring hard to make his point about the two meanings of εὐχή and προσευχή, and the difficulty of doing so in the case of προσευχή has evidently led him into ambiguity.

[1] Notice the inconsistency with Section 1.

to do this also, according to our ability, using the word "prayer" now in a more general and simpler way . . .¹ The argument indeed is such a poor one, and so lacking in eminent supporters, that it is quite impossible to discover any who will not admit prayer among those who accept providence at all, and who establish a God over the universe. For it is the teaching either of those who are altogether atheists, and deny the existence of God, or else of those who admit God, so far as the name is concerned, but deprive him of his providence. Yet already, the opposing power, desiring to invest the name of Christ and the teaching of the Son of God with most impious doctrines, has even been able to persuade some that they ought not to pray.² The supporters of this opinion are those who do away with the things of sense altogether,³ have no use for Baptism or the Eucharist, and falsely

---

¹ κοινότερον νῦν καὶ ἁπλούστερον τοῦ τῆς εὐχῆς ὀνόματος ἡμῖν λεγομένου . . . The sentence is incomplete, and it is impossible to say what Origen intended. Codex MS. has a hiatus here of two lines. The Oxford editor inserts τινὲς μὲν παντελῶς τὴν προσευχὴν ἀναιροῦσι, "there are some who do away with prayer altogether". Koetschau supplies: εἰσὶ γὰρ οἳ οὐδὲ οὕτως σημαινομένην τὴν εὐχὴν παραδέχονται ἀλλὰ καταγελάσαντες τῶν εὐχομένων πᾶσαν εὐχὴν ὁπώσποτε λεγομένην παντελῶς ἀναιρεῖσθαι βούλονται, "for there are those who do not admit prayer in this sense, but laugh to scorn those who pray, and want to do away altogether with prayer in whatever sense the word is used".

² Anglus identifies the heretics here mentioned with the followers of a Prodicus who is mentioned in Clem. Alex., *Strom.* VII. 7. Delarue gives the passage: "I recollect the doctrines about there being no necessity to pray, introduced by . . . the followers of the heresy of Prodicus. That they may not then be uplifted with conceit . . . let them learn that it was embraced before by the philosophers called Cyrenaics."

It is to be noted that Ambrosius had asked Origen to answer those who said that prayer was unnecessary, but yet claimed to be Christians, and it is to this task that Origen applies himself and not to answering the arguments of atheists. The controversy had evidently included discussion of the meaning of εὐχή. The heretics, it seems, had asserted that the word did not mean what simple Christians thought. It is for this reason that Origen has devoted so much space to the meaning of εὐχή and προσευχή in Scripture.

Origen is the first writer (at least of those whose works have come down to us) to deal with these objections to the practice of prayer. It is a mark of his intellectual honesty that he so readily takes up the challenge.

³ Anglus suggests the names of heretical sects to whom Origen may here be referring, Docetae, Ascodrutae, Archontici, Marcionitae, etc. Speaking generally, it is to Gnosticism that Origen refers, which, in some of its forms, denied the reality of matter (τὰ αἰσθητά), and hence robbed the Sacraments of meaning.

accuse the Scriptures of not meaning prayer by that word, but of teaching something else with a different meaning.

Their arguments: (a) Prayer rendered unnecessary by God's foreknowledge, and his fatherly love

2. The following might be the arguments of those who reject prayer (those, I mean, who yet set God over the universe and say that there is a providence; for it is not proposed here to inquire into what is said by those who do away with God or providence altogether):

God knows all things before they come into being and there is nothing that becomes known to him from the fact of its beginning for the first time when it begins, as though it were not previously known. What need then is there to send up prayer to him who knows what we need even before we pray? For the heavenly Father knoweth what things we have need of before we ask him (Matt. 6. 8). And it is fitting that he, being Father and Maker of all, who loves all the things that are, and abhors nothing which he has made (Wisd. 11. 24), should order in safety all that has to do with each one, even without prayer, like a father who provides for his little children, and does not wait for them to ask, either because they are quite unable to ask, or because through ignorance they often want to receive the opposite of what is of use and help to them. And we men fall short of God more than those who are quite children fall short of the mind of those who begot them.[1]

(b) God's predestination renders prayer useless

3. And it is in accordance with reason [2] to suppose that God not only foreknows what shall be, but also foreordains it, and that nothing comes to pass contrary to what has been foreordained by him. So then just as, if anyone were to pray for the sun to rise, he would be deemed

---

[1] It is interesting to note that this argument against prayer, so often heard from twentieth-century rationalists, was known in Origen's day. The modern rationalist uses it to ridicule prayer, and puts the argument conditionally: "If there is a God," he says, "he must know beforehand what you need. What, then, is the good of praying?" But it must not be forgotten that there are also devout believers in God who have intellectual difficulty over this question. It is the latter whom Origen has particularly in mind as he proceeds to answer the objection.

[2] εἰκὸς δέ. So Anglus. Codex MS. has no δέ. Nor Delarue.

foolish for thinking that what would happen without his prayer comes to pass through his prayer, in the same way a man would be out of his wits who thought that those things which assuredly would happen even if he did not pray, come to pass because of his prayer. And again, just as he excels in all madness who thinks, because he is annoyed and scorched by the sun when it is in the summer solstice, that he will by prayer transfer the sun to the spring signs so that he can enjoy air which is temperate, so if anybody were to think that because he prayed he would not have to endure the circumstances which necessarily happen to mankind, he too would excel in all madness.[1]

(c) Prayer is vain whether for the righteous or for sinners, since all have been predestined

4. If, moreover, sinners are *estranged* from the womb (Psalm 58. 3), and the righteous is *separated* from his mother's belly [2] (Gal. 1. 15), and if,[3] they being not yet born neither having done any good or evil, that the purpose of God according to election might stand, not of works, but of him that calleth, it is said, The elder shall serve the younger (Rom. 9. 11, 12), then in vain do we ask for remission of sins, or to receive the Spirit of strength that we may be able to do all things through Christ which strengtheneth us (Phil. 4. 13). For if we are sinners, then we are estranged from the womb; and if we are separated [4] from our mother's belly, then what is best will befall us even though we do not pray. For what prayer did Jacob offer before he was born, that it was foretold that he should be stronger than Esau, and that his brother should serve him (Gen. 25. 23)? And in what way did Esau sin that he was hated before he was born (Rom. 9. 12, 13)? And why does Moses pray, as is found in the eighty-ninth

---

[1] πᾶσαν ἂν ὑπερβάλοι μελαγχολίαν. Codex MS. and Delarue have no ἄν.

[2] The point here is that Scripture speaks of sinners as being *estranged* from the womb, whilst the righteous are said to be *separated*.

[3] Koetschau adopts Bentley's conjecture and adds καί to join together the quotations from Galatians and Romans. The εἰ with which the sentence begins governs the verbs of all three quotations (Psalms, Galatians, Romans): if all these three assertions are true, then in vain ...

[4] I.e. if we are righteous, since it is the righteous who are *separated* (Gal. 1. 15), while sinners are *estranged* from the womb (Psalm 58. 3). An instance of over-subtle treatment of Holy Scripture. But Origen is presenting the argument of an opponent.

Psalm,[1] if God is his refuge before the mountains were settled, and the earth and the world were formed (A.V., Psalm 90. 2)?[2]

5. But concerning all those that are to be saved, it is written in the Epistle to the Ephesians that the Father chose them in him, in Christ that is, before the foundation of the world, that they should be holy and without blame before him, in love having predestinated them unto adoption by Christ to himself (Eph. 1. 4, 5). So, then, either a man is chosen from among those who are "before the foundation of the world",[3] and it is impossible for him to fall from his election, wherefore he has no need of prayer; or else he has not been chosen, nor foreordained, and he prays in vain since he will not be heard even if he prays ten thousand times. For whom God foreknew, he also did predestinate to be conformed to the image of his Son's glory;[4] and whom he did predestinate, them he also called; and whom he called, them he also justified; and whom he justified, them he also glorified (Rom. 8. 29, 30). For why does Josiah toil, or why when he prays is he anxious concerning whether he will ever be heard or not, when he was named in prophecy many generations before, and it was not only foreknown what he should do, but also foretold in the hearing of many?[5] And why does Judas pray so that his prayer even becomes a sin, when it was announced beforehand of him, from the time of David, that he should lose his office, another taking it in his place

---

[1] ὀγδοηκοστῷ ἐνάτῳ. The citation is from Psalm 89 (90 in A.V.), but codex MS. has ὀγδοηκοστῷ ἑβδόμῳ. Koetschau follows the Oxford editor and Anglus in correcting. Delarue keeps ἑβδόμῳ. He suggests that the numbering of the Psalter used by Origen was different.

[2] There is a hiatus of about 1½ lines at this point in the codex MS.

[3] ἤτοι οὖν τις ἐκ τῶν „πρὸ καταβολῆς κόσμου" ἐστὶν ἐξειλεγμένος. The alteration of ἐξειλεγμένος to ἐξειλεγμένων, as Bentley suggests, would give better sense: "either a man is of those who are chosen before . . .". Koetschau approves.

Anglus suggests that ἐκ τῶν should read ἐν Χριστῷ, "either a man is chosen in Christ before . . .". Koetschau says "without probability".

[4] τῆς εἰκόνος τῆς δόξης. Anglus notes that in the *Commentary on Matthew*, tom. XII, quoting Romans 8. 29, Origen again adds the words τῆς δόξης, and in tom. XIII he has συμμόρφους τῆς δόξης, with the omission of τῆς εἰκόνος. Anglus ascribes this to Origen's haste, for in his more careful exposition of the passage, in the *Commentary on Romans*, the normal reading appears. Τῆς δόξης is doubtless, as Anglus and Koetschau suggest, a recollection of Philippians 3. 21.

[5] 2 Kings 22. 11–13, 18 ff.; 23. 3 ff. record Josiah's "toil" and anxiety. 2 Kings 23. 15–20 record his fulfilment of the prophecy in 1 Kings 13. 2, "many generations before".

(Psalm 109. 8; Acts 1. 20)?[1] Hence it is not congruous, since God is immutable and understands all things beforehand, and abides in the things he has before decreed, to pray thinking to turn aside his will through prayer, or to intercede as though with one who has not settled things beforehand but waits for each man's prayer, that on account of the prayer he may arrange what is fitting for the man who prays, ordering at that time what is approved as good, as though it had not previously been envisaged by him.

The problem summarized

6. At this juncture let me set down in the actual words the propositions which you set out in your letter to me. They are as follows: first, if God foreknows the future, and if this must needs come to pass, prayer is vain; secondly, if all things come to pass by the will of God, and his counsels are fixed, and none of the things he wills can be changed, prayer is vain. Now, as it seems to me, we must first take the following points as useful in resolving those arguments which make for unwillingness to pray.

Origen's reply:
Some things are moved by outside agency, but rational beings through themselves

VI.—1. Of those things which are in motion,[2] some have their source of movement outside themselves, as for example lifeless things which are held in being solely by their own constitution,[3] as well as those things which are moved by their nature[4] and inner life,[5] when they are moved not by virtue of what they are, but by being

---

[1] No prayer of Judas is recorded in the New Testament. Origen, it seems, assumes that being of the Twelve, Judas did pray.

[2] Compare a very similar passage in *De Princ.* III. i. 2, in which, as here, Origen goes on to argue for the reality of free will in man. Cf. also Clem. Alex., *Strom.* II. 20.

[3] ὑπὸ ἕξεως. The word ἕξις is usually applied to rational beings, and denotes a more or less permanent "habit", i.e. a condition or tendency which is *held* (*habitus* from *habeo*: cf. ἕξις from ἔχω, "to hold"). By analogy ἕξις can be used of the more or less permanent condition in which inanimate things like stones exist.

[4] φύσις.

[5] ψυχή, often translated "soul", but here referring to the life-principle of any living thing.

treated like those things which are held in being solely by their own constitution.[1] For stones [2] hewn out of a mine and timber which has lost the power of growth, being held in being solely by their own constitution, have their motive power from outside themselves; but the bodies of animals also, and plants which can be carried, when they are transplanted by somebody are transplanted not *qua* living creatures and plants, but like stones and timber which has lost the power of growth. And even if these things are moved by reason of the fact that all corruptible bodies are in a state of flux, they possess consequently that kind of movement which consists in corruption.[3] But apart from these there is a second class of things which are in motion, namely those that are moved by the nature or life that is in them, and these are said to be moved "of themselves" [4] by those who use words with some degree of exactitude. There is a third kind of movement, namely that in the case of animals, which is named movement "from themselves".[5] And I consider that the movement of rational beings is movement "through themselves".[6] But if we take away from the animal its power of movement "from itself" [7] it cannot be considered any longer to be an animal, but will be like a plant which is moved by nature only, or a stone which is carried by some outside agency. And

---

[1] I.e. animate things when treated as though inanimate, and moved bodily from one place to another, have their source of movement outside themselves.

[2] The codex MS. has λίθος. So Delarue. Koetschau follows Anglus in reading λίθοι.

[3] κἂν κινῆται καὶ ταῦτα τῷ ῥευστὰ εἶναι πάντα τὰ σώματα φθίνοντα, παρακολουθητικὴν ἔχει τὴν ἐν τῷ φθίνειν κίνησιν.
Codex MS., κἂν κινῆτε . . . φθίνονται . . . κίνησιν, which Delarue gives. All editors have experienced difficulty in interpreting this sentence.
The meaning of the passage seems to be that if no external agent causes movement in the classes of things mentioned above, but their only "movement" is that of natural corruption, even so they may rightly be said to have their source of "movement" outside themselves, namely in the principle of corruption. It is to be noticed that κίνησις not only means movement in space, but also includes the idea of change.

[4] ἐξ αὐτῶν.

[5] ἀφ' αὐτῶν. Codex MS. ἀπ'αὐτοῦ. Bentley and Delarue have ἀπ'αὐτῶν.

[6] δι'αὐτῶν. The distinction between these three prepositions employed to denote the distinction between classes of movement is difficult to convey in English. The movement of plants is movement ἐξ; that of animals, movement ἀπό; that of rational beings, movement διά.

[7] τὴν ἀφ'αὐτοῦ κίνησιν. Codex MS., ἀπ'αὐτοῦ. Bentley and Delarue, ἀπ'αὐτῶν. Anglus, ἀφ'αὐτοῦ.

Common experience proves that man possesses free will

2. Therefore those who do not allow that anything is in our power, necessarily admit something which is obviously foolish:[2] first that we are not living creatures, and secondly also that we are not rational, but that, as though dependent on an external agent and in no wise self-moving, we might be said to do by means of that agent those things which we think we do ourselves. Furthermore, let a man consider his own experience and see if he can honestly say that he himself does not will, he himself does not eat, he himself does not walk, he himself does not agree to and accept certain opinions, he himself does not dissent from others as false. Therefore, just as there are certain opinions to which it is impossible for a man to agree,[3] even if he go over the arguments ten thousand times, multiplying and employing persuasive words, so with regard to practical human affairs it is impossible for anyone to agree that we have no free will at all. For who would admit that nothing can be grasped by the mind, or who lives in such a way as to suspend judgement about everything, whatsoever it is? And who does not punish his servant when he catches sight of a slave doing wrong? And who is there who does not accuse a son who does not render what is fitting to his parents, or does not blame and censure the adulteress as one who has done a shameful thing? For truth forces and compels us, even if one multiplies ten thousand arguments, eagerly to give praise and blame, taking it for granted that free will is preserved, and that it deserves either our praise or our blame.[4]

---

[1] The foregoing analysis of the classes of things which are in motion or suffer change is made in order to bring out clearly the fact that rational beings are essentially different from the rest. Origen then proceeds to point out that the difference consists in their possession of free will.

[2] The somewhat thin argument at this point would not satisfy a modern determinist. He holds precisely that "those things which we think we do ourselves" we do because of outside agencies at work upon us. Origen is on surer ground when, a few lines below, he appeals to man's universal experience of possessing free will.

[3] διατεθῆναι ἄνθρωπον. So Oxford ed. Codex MS. and Delarue, διατεθεῖσθαι.

[4] Notice Origen's forcible presentation of this argument from experience against determinism. There is a practical and not merely logical *reductio ad absurdum* in the fact that even the determinist behaves as though free will existed.

While man's will is free, God foreknows its movements

3. If, then, our free will is intact, with its numerous inclinations to virtue or vice, and again to what is becoming or to what is unbecoming, it is necessarily known to God, together with all else, before it come to pass, from the creation and foundation of the world, what this will be. And in all the things which God prearranges in accordance with what [1] he has seen concerning each action of our free will, what is necessary to meet it out of his providence appropriately to each movement of our free will has also been prearranged, and moreover what shall happen in accordance with the succession [2] of things to come—not that God's foreknowledge is the cause of all that is to come and all that is to be done of our free will according to our desire; for if it could be supposed that God did not know what was to come, we should not on that account lose [3] the power of doing and willing these things.[4] Rather, it is from his foreknowledge that the free will of each of us is ordered with a view to the arrangement of everything in a way useful for the settled condition of the world.

God's foreknowledge enables him to foresee man's prayers, and answer them in accordance with man's deserts

4. If, then, each man's free will is known to him, and on this account it is in accordance with reason that what is appropriate for every contingency is foreseen by him and arranged of his providence,[5] and that he comprehends beforehand what a man prays for, and what disposition a man has who thus shows his faith and what he wishes to be done for him—comprehending this beforehand, I say, he will then

---

[1] ἀκολούθως οἷς. Koetschau accepts Bentley's emendation here. Codex MS. has ἀκολ. ὡς.

[2] κατὰ τὸν εἱρμὸν . . .

[3] ἀπολοῦμεν. Koetschau accepts Bentley's suggestion for the ἀπειλοῦμεν of codex MS.

[4] Anglus comments that Origen here asserts that man possesses an innate faculty of acting freely which is unaffected whether God knows the future or not.

[5] καὶ διὰ τοῦτο προεωραμένον αὐτῷ διατάττεσθαι ἀπὸ τῆς προνοίας τὸ κατ' ἀξίαν παντὶ τῷ εὐλόγῳ. Codex MS. has διατάττεται. Delarue puts a comma after αὐτῷ, and reads διατάττεται ἀπὸ τῆς προνοίας τὸ κατ' ἀξίαν παντὶ τὸ εὔλογον. The Greek is difficult, and the English translation here presents the probable sense.

in his disposition of things make arrangements accordingly,[1] in some such way as follows: for example, This man who prays wisely [2] will I hear, for the sake of the very prayer he makes; but this man will I not hear, either because he will be unworthy of being heard, or because he prays [3] for things which it is not profitable for him who prays to receive nor fitting for me to give; and in accordance with this prayer of such and such a man, God says, as it were, I will not answer him, but in accordance with that prayer I will answer. (And if anybody is disturbed on the ground that compulsion is thus brought upon events, because God, who foreknows the future, cannot lie,[4] we must say to him that God inevitably knows that a particular man does not inevitably and unswervingly will the better,[5] or will so desire the worse that he becomes incapable of a change towards improvement.) And again, we may think of God as saying,[6] Such and such things will I do to this man who shall pray, for it is fitting that I should do so since his prayer will be blameless, nor will he behave himself carelessly in the matter of prayer; and to this man who will pray at some length I will give such and such things exceeding abundantly above what he asks or thinks (Eph. 3. 20), for it is fitting that I should overcome him with kindness and supply more than he could ask; and to this man

---

[1] Origen's argument is that since God has created man with free will and capable of spiritual communion with himself, it is reasonable to suppose that these spiritual movements have a part in the determining of events. Man's prayers (or his failure to pray) are among the factors that God takes into account from eternity.
   There is a modern exposition of this argument in C. S. Lewis, *Miracles* (Bles, 1947), Appendix B on "Special Providences". C. S. Lewis is able to give greater cogency to the argument by employing the conception of the simultaneity of eternity: "To God (though not to me) I and the prayer I make in 1945 were just as much present at the creation of the world as they are now and will be a million years hence. God's creative act is timeless and timelessly adapted to the 'free' elements within it: but this timeless adaptation meets our consciousness as a sequence of prayer and answer."

[2] συνετῶς. Delarue conjectures συνεχῶς, "continuously".

[3] εὔξασθαι. Bentley and Anglus suggest the future infinitive εὔξεσθαι, which Delarue prefers.

[4] Origen is evidently not quite sure that his argument has completely resolved the contradiction between God's foreknowledge and man's free will. It is the fact that his argument is confined within the category of time which introduces this weakness.

[5] I.e. God's certain knowledge includes knowledge of the fact that man is not determined.

[6] The words "we may think of God as saying" are not in the Greek.

who will be of such and such a sort, I will send this ministering angel to begin to work with him for his salvation from such a time, and to be with him until such a time; and to that man I will send that angel, more honourable, so to speak, than the other, because that man is going to be better than the other, but from such and such a man, who, after giving himself to the words that are excellent, will fail and slip backwards to more material things, I will remove this good helper;[1] and when he has departed, this power worse indeed than he,[2] as is meet, having found an opportunity to attack by reason of his indifference, will be at hand to prompt him to such and such sins, seeing that he has offered himself in readiness for sin.

Examples of God's foreknowledge of men : Josiah, Judas, Paul

5. It is therefore as though he who foreordains all things should say, Amon will beget Josiah, who will not emulate the sins of his father, but having found this road which leads to virtue by the help of these men who shall be with him, will prove to be honourable and good, and will overthrow the altar which Jeroboam sinned in building (*vide* 2 Kings 23. 15). And I know that Judas, when my Son dwells among the race of men, will at first be honourable and good, but afterwards will turn and fall into human sins for which it will be right for him to suffer such and such things. (The Son of God possesses this foreknowledge perhaps with regard to all things, and certainly with regard to Judas and other mysteries, having seen with his understanding of the unfolding[3] of things to come both Judas and the sins which he would commit: so that with comprehension of these things he could say through David, even before Judas was born, Hold not thy peace, O God, at my praise, and so on (Psalm 109. 1).)[4] And knowing the future, and what efforts Paul would make towards godliness, he says, In my own counsels,[5] before creating the world, even while I apply

---

[1] I.e. a guardian angel.
[2] Possibly a reminiscence of the Parable of the Unclean Spirit (Luke 11. 24–26).
[3] ἐξελιγμοῦ. This is Bentley's conjecture for the ἐξελεγμοῦ of codex MS.
[4] This Psalm was interpreted as a prophecy of the fate of Judas in the early days of Christianity. Cf. Acts 1. 20.
[5] ἐν ἐμαυτῷ. Anglus considers this should read ἐν ἐμῷ υἱῷ, or ἐν ἐμοῦ τῷ Χριστῷ, in consonance with the language of Scripture which speaks of God choosing a man in Christ. He refers the passage to Ephesians 1. 4, where "in him" means "in Christ".

myself to begin the fashioning of the world, will I choose him, and to such and such powers which work together for the salvation of men will I commit him at the moment of his begetting, separating him from his mother's womb, and permitting him at the beginning in his youth to persecute with a zeal mingled with ignorance under the pretence of godliness those who have professed faith in my Christ, and to guard the garments of those who stone my servant and martyr Stephen, so that, after the wantonness of youth, having taken his opportunity, and being changed [1] for the better, he may not boast before me, but say, I am not meet to be called an apostle, because I persecuted the Church of God (1 Cor. 15. 9); and perceiving my future kindness towards him after the sins done in his youth in the name of godliness, he may say, But by the grace of God I am what I am (1 Cor. 15. 10); and being restrained by conscience because of what he did against Christ while he was still a young man, he shall not be exalted above measure through the abundance of the revelations which shall be made manifest to him by my kindness (*vide* 2 Cor. 12. 7).

Since there is a kind of free will—under God's providence—in the heavenly bodies, it is as reasonable to pray about them as for things which—under God's providence—are within the power of men's free will

VII. And in answer to the objection about prayer for the rising of the sun, we must make the following reply. There is also a kind of free will of the sun,[2] even when with the moon it praises God, for it says, Praise ye him, sun and moon (Psalm 148. 3). It is clear also that there is a kind of free will in the moon, and consequently in all the stars; for it says, Praise him, all ye stars and light (Psalm 148. 3). Therefore, just as we have said God uses the free will of all upon the earth, and has arranged them as is needful for the advantage of those upon the earth, so we must understand him to use the free will of sun,

---

[1] μεταβαλόμενος: so Anglus; codex MS. has μεταβαλλόμενος, and so Delarue.

[2] For this doctrine, so strange to the modern reader, cf. *Contra Celsum* v. 585 and VIII. 791: "We honour the sun therefore as the fair work of God, which keeps the laws of God, and which obeys the command 'Praise the Lord, sun and moon'." Cf. also *De Princ.* I. vii for Origen's belief that the sun, moon, and stars are living creatures. The doctrine was widely held among the ancients (Plato, *Timaeus* 40B; Cicero, *De Natura Deorum* II. 15, 39).

moon, and stars, fixed and steadfast, stable and wise, as it is, and to have arranged the whole order of heaven, and the pathway and movement of the stars, in harmony with the whole universe. And if I do not pray in vain in a matter which concerns another's free will, much less shall I do so in a matter which concerns the free will of the stars in heaven, which pursue their course in a manner which conduces to the safety of the universe.[1] And furthermore it is possible to maintain with regard to those who live on the earth that there are certain impressions proceeding from our environment which call forth what is weak in us, or else what is prone to the better, so that we do or say either this or that. But with regard to celestial things, what kind of impression can enter in and remove and change from that pathway which is advantageous to the world all those celestial beings which possess a soul [2] fashioned by reason, and within their own control, and which employ a body so ethereal and exceedingly pure?[3]

There are certain moral prerequisites of effective prayer

VIII.—1. Again, it is not out of place to use the following example to encourage men to pray and to discourage them from neglecting

---

[1] Origen considers that the stars by their ordered movement contribute to the safety of the universe. Their work is called in *De Princ.* i. vii. 5 "a splendid work of service".

[2] See *De Princ.* i. vii. 4, where Origen discusses the soul and body of the sun, moon, and stars.

[3] ποία δύναται ἐγγενομένη φαντασία ἐκστῆσαι καὶ μετακινῆσαι ἀπὸ τῆς ὠφελίμου τῷ κόσμῳ πορείας ἕκαστον τῶν τοιαύτην ψυχὴν ὑπὸ λόγου κατηρτισμένην καὶ παρὰ τὴν αὐτῶν αἰτίαν ἐχόντων καὶ τοιούτῳ σώματι αἰθερίῳ καὶ καθαρωτάτῳ χρωμένων;

Delarue punctuates πορείας; ἕκαστον and interprets ἕκαστον . . . χρωμένων as an absolute, explanatory of the difficulty implied in the previous question.

ὑπὸ λόγου Anglus interprets as ὑπὸ δημιουργοῦ, the λόγος through whom all things were made.

παρὰ τὴν αὐτῶν αἰτίαν. Codex MS. has περί. Anglus corrects to παρὰ τὴν αὐτῶν αἰτίαν, and cites several other instances of this phrase in Origen. He makes it equivalent to ἐκ τοῦ ἐν αὐτοῖς αὐτεξουσίου. But it is not easy to translate the phrase in this context, and Delarue in his comment on Anglus' note confesses to difficulty with it. Αἰτία, "cause", "source of movement", could have the meaning of "control".

The argument in the last two sentences of this paragraph seems to be that the heavenly bodies are not distracted, as are human beings, by the pressure of their environment, and may therefore be regarded as more amenable than men to the effects of prayer.

their prayers. Just as it is impossible to procreate children without a woman and the accompanying act which is instrumental in procreation, so no man could obtain such and such things, unless he had prayed in the following way, with the following disposition, in the following belief, and if he had not lived, prior to his prayer, in the following manner of life. Thus, he must not make vain repetitions (Matt. 6. 7), nor must he ask for small things, nor pray for earthly things, nor come to his prayer with anger or with confused thoughts, and neither is it possible without purity to contrive the leisure which prayer requires (cf. 1 Cor. 7. 5), nor can he who prays obtain remission of his sins, unless he from his heart has forgiven his brother who has trespassed, and who asks to receive pardon.

The supreme importance of the recollection of God

2. I think that he who prays as he ought, or who is eager to do so according to his ability, can receive help in many ways. First he is greatly helped who is intent in his mind on his prayer, through his very intentness in prayer adapting himself to the presence of God,[1] and to speech with him who is present [2] as with one who both looks upon him and is present.[3] For as certain impressions and memories of certain things to do with objects of which memories have arisen [4] spoil the thoughts which have been created by these impressions, so we must believe that it is useful to have a recollection of the God in whom we believe, and who knows the movements in the inmost shrine of the soul, the soul meanwhile composing itself to be pleasing to him who examines hearts and searches reins (Psalm 7. 9), as being present, and beholding, and taking the initiative in coming to every man's mind. For although we were to suppose that no further help

---

[1] θεῷ παριστάναι. Delarue, παρεστάναι.
[2] παρόντι. Delarue omits.
[3] παρόντι. Anglus alters to ἀκούοντι in order to avoid the repetition.
[4] ὥσπερ γὰρ αἱ τοιαίδε φαντασίαι καὶ ὑπομνήσεις τῶνδέ τινων περὶ τὰ, ὧν γεγόνασιν αἱ ὑπομνήσεις ... The Greek here is cumbrous and difficult to translate. The general sense seems to be that an impression or memory may introduce distracting as well as useful thoughts. For example, I may remember a beautiful strain of music on which it would be well for me to ponder. But the thought of the music may remind me that I first heard it in circumstances upon which it would not be good for me to dwell. The remedy is to concentrate on the music itself. So in prayer we must concentrate our attention on God himself.

apart from this could come to the man who settles his thoughts upon prayer, we must realize that he who composes himself thus with devotion in his time of prayer obtains no ordinary result. From how many sins this keeps us, when it is done often, and to how many righteous deeds it leads, they know by experience who have given themselves continuously to prayer. For if the remembrance and recollection of a man of reputation who has derived benefit by his wisdom encourages us to emulate him, and frequently hinders our worse impulses, how much more does the remembrance of God, the Father of all, when it is accompanied by prayer unto him, help those who are persuaded that they are present with and speak to God who is himself present and hears them! [1]

St Paul's advice about the disposition of the mind in prayer

IX.—1. What has been said is to be justified from divine Scripture in the following way. He who prays must lift up holy hands (1 Tim. 2. 8) by forgiving each of those who have trespassed against him, banishing the feeling of anger from his soul, and bearing wrath to no man. And again, so that his mind be not disturbed by other thoughts, he must forget all those things that are extraneous to his prayer during the time that he prays (and such a state is assuredly most blessed),[2] as Paul teaches in his First Epistle to Timothy, when he says, I will therefore that men pray everywhere, lifting up holy hands,[3] without wrath and doubting (1 Tim. 2. 8). But in addition to this it is good for a woman, especially at her prayers, to be sedate and decorous in both soul and body, above all when she prays, reverencing God, and banishing from her mind [4] every licentious and womanish re-

---

[1] The intensity of Origen's thought in the foregoing section is noteworthy. Notice especially that although he believes in the objective efficacy of prayer he is here arguing that even if prayer could accomplish nothing objectively its value would still be great for what it achieves in a man's soul.

[2] κατὰ τὸν καιρόν, ἐν ᾧ τις εὔχεται, (τοιοῦτον δὲ εἶναι πῶς οὐκ ἔστι μακαριώτατον;) ὡς διδάσκει Παῦλος . . .
Koetschau puts τοιοῦτον δὲ . . . μακαριώτατον; in parenthesis. Delarue puts a full stop after εὔχεται, and makes τοιοῦτον δέ start a sentence. Against this punctuation is the fact that the words of Paul quoted do not make any such assertion about the blessedness of the composed mind.

[3] ὁσίους χεῖρας. Codex MS. has ὁσίας, and so Delarue. Oxford edition, ὁσίους, as in the Greek text of 1 Tim.

[4] ἀπὸ τοῦ ἡγεμονικοῦ. Τὸ ἡγεμονικόν is the Stoic word for the part of the soul which directs, i.e. the reason.

collection, being adorned not with broided hair and gold, or pearls, or costly array, but with those things with which it is fitting that a woman who professes godliness should be adorned (and I wonder if anybody would doubt that one who proved herself such in her prayer was evidently blessed from her possession of such a disposition alone),[1] as Paul taught in the same epistle, when he says, In like manner also, that women adorn themselves in modest [2] apparel, with shamefacedness and sobriety; not with broided hair, and gold, or pearls, or costly array; but (which becometh women professing godliness) with good works (1 Tim. 2. 9, 10).

David also counsels preparation of the mind for prayer

2. Again, the prophet David says that the holy man who prays possesses many other things; and we can conveniently set these out, so that the disposition and state of preparation for prayer of him who has committed himself to God may be clearly seen by us to be of the greatest assistance, even if it be considered by itself. He says, then, Unto thee do I lift up mine eyes, O thou that dwellest in heaven (Psalm 123. 1), and, Unto thee do I lift up my soul, O God (Psalm 25. 1). For the eyes of the intellect being raised above concern with earthly things, and above satisfaction with any impression arising from the more physical, and being lifted up to such a degree that they despise begotten things and, besides the mere contemplation of God, hold reverent and modest converse with him who hears them, (such men) assuredly give the greatest possible benefit to their very eyes,[3] which with open face behold as in a glass the glory of the Lord, and are

---

[1] Koetschau places θαυμάζω δὲ . . . παραστήσασαν in parenthesis. Delarue starts a new sentence with θαυμάζω δέ, but again his punctuation is disproved by the fact that the words of Paul which are quoted make no statement about the blessedness of such a disposition in prayer. Cf. the thought of VIII. 2 and see Note 1, p. 106.

[2] κοσμίῳ. Codex MS., κοσμίως, and so Delarue. Oxford edition has κοσμίῳ.

[3] ὤνησαν αὐτοὺς τοὺς ὀφθαλμούς. So codex MS. But the Greek of this sentence is very difficult. The subject of ὤνησαν can only be an unexpressed "such men" (i.e. as have the eyes of their intellect raised). Bentley deletes τοὺς ὀφθαλμούς and changes αὐτούς into ἑαυτούς, thus making οἱ ὀφθαλμοὶ τοῦ διανοητικοῦ, the eyes of the intellect, the subject of ὤνησαν.
N.B. "Eyes" here means the "eyes of the intellect", that is, the intellect itself, which can rightly be said to hold converse with God, and to be changed into his image.

changed into the same image from glory to glory (2 Cor. 3. 18). For they then become partakers of the effluence of a more divine mind, as is clear from the words, The light of thy countenance is signed upon us, O Lord (Psalm 4. 6; cf. LXX). And the soul which is lifted up, which follows after the Spirit, and is separated from the body, and which not only follows after the Spirit, but is actually in the Spirit (as is indicated by the words, Unto thee do I lift up my soul), assuredly such a soul which lays aside its being becomes spiritual [1] (cf. Rom. 8. 9; 2 Cor. 2. 14, 15).

Forgiveness of enemies necessary before prayer

3. And if to forget injuries is the greatest act of righteousness, so that the whole law is comprehended therein, according to Jeremiah the prophet, who says, I did not command your fathers concerning these things when they came forth out of the land of Egypt, but this thing commanded I them (Jer. 7. 22, 23), Let none bear malice against a neighbour in his heart (Zech. 7. 10),[2] and if,[3] when we leave off from bearing malice [4] and come to our prayer, we keep the commandment of the Saviour who said, If ye stand praying, forgive, if ye have ought against any (Mark 11. 25), it is [5] clear that we who stand thus at prayer have already gained the fairest rewards.

[1] Cf. *De Princ.* III. iv. 2: "if, however, it (*anima*, soul) joins itself to the spirit, it causes a man to be 'in the spirit' and on this account to be called spiritual. It is this that the apostle seems to indicate when he says, 'Ye are not in the flesh, but in the spirit' (Rom. 8. 9)" (Butterworth's translation).

In this whole section Origen comes very near the intellectual mysticism of Clement of Alexandria (see p. 68). But Origen never allows himself long to forget the needs of the "average" Christian, and the practical Christian duties, to which he quickly returns in section 3.

[2] Anglus points out that Origen here has conflated two passages, one from Jeremiah, and the other from Zechariah, and has attributed the whole to Jeremiah. He notes that elsewhere in Origen and in other early Fathers words of Zechariah are attributed to Jeremiah.

[3] The force of the "if" (εἰ) at the beginning of the sentence continues. The apodosis of the sentence is "it is clear that we who stand . . .".

[4] ἀπὸ μνησικακίας δέ. So codex MS., the verb being supplied. Bentley suggests ἀπ'ἀμνησικακίας, the meaning of which would be "when we come to our prayer out of a spirit of forgiveness".

[5] δῆλον ὅτι. Bentley's suggestion. Delarue has δηλονότι following codex MS. and Oxford ed.

Again we have the thought of the value of prayer to the soul, even apart from what it may achieve objectively.

The spirit of rebellion or sullenness against God must be eschewed

X.—1. And we have said this, taking it for granted that even if nothing else should accrue to us when we pray, even so we gain the fairest rewards, if we have understood how we ought to pray, and succeed in so doing. But it is clear that he who prays thus, giving his attention to the power of him who hears the prayer,[1] will while he still speaks hear the words, Here I am (Isa. 58. 9), if before praying he has put aside all his displeasure against Providence. For this is indicated by the words, If thou take from thee the yoke, the putting forth of the hand, and the word of murmuring (Isa. 58. 9), and he who is well pleased with what befalls him is made free from every yoke, and does not stretch forth his hand against God who ordains what he wills for our exercise; nor again does he murmur in the secrecy of his thoughts where there is no voice that can be heard of men, with the murmuring which they make who, like wicked servants, finding fault with their master's orders, but not openly, do not dare with voice and whole heart to curse Providence for the things which happen, but seem as though they wish to hide their displeasure at these things even from the Lord of all. I think this is the meaning of the passage in Job: In all these things which happened Job sinned not with his lips before God (Job. 2. 10); whereas with reference to the temptation which preceded it is written,[2] In all these things which happened Job sinned not before God (Job 1. 22). The text which forbids this to be done in Deuteronomy says, Beware that there be not a hidden word in thy heart, and transgression,[3] saying, The seventh year is at hand, and so on (Deut. 15. 9).

---

[1] τῇ ἐνεργείᾳ τοῦ ἐπακούοντος ἐνορῶν. Anglus thinks ἐν οὐρανῷ should be read for ἐνορῶν, thus making Origen refer to 1 Kings 8. 30, "hear thou in heaven thy dwelling place". This would give us, "while he still speaks will, by the power of him who hears in heaven, hear the words . . .".

[2] ἐπὶ τοῦ πρὸ αὐτοῦ πειρασμοῦ ἀναγεγραμμένου. So codex MS. But it is not clear to what αὐτοῦ refers. Anglus suggests ἐπὶ τοῦ πρώτου, since Origen is noting the fact that Job is said to have refrained from sin *with his lips* after his second temptation as related in Job 2; whereas after the first temptation it is said that "he sinned not" without further qualification. Koetschau suggests ἐπὶ τοῦ πρὸ τούτου πειρασμοῦ, "in the temptation before this". Notice once more the great attention to the details of the literal meaning.

[3] Delarue's punctuation here would require the translation "Beware that the hidden word in thy heart become not transgression".

The prayer of the Word of God assists him who prays after due preparation and with perseverance

2. He, then, who, so greatly assisted, prays thus, becomes more fit to be mingled with the Spirit of the Lord which filleth the whole world (Wisd. 1. 7) and him who filleth all the earth and heaven, and who through the prophet says, Do not I fill heaven and earth? saith the Lord (Jer. 23. 24). Moreover, through his purity of heart, of which we have spoken before, he will become a sharer in the prayer of the Word of God who stands in the midst even of those who know him not,[1] who neglects the prayer of nobody, and who prays to the Father together with him whose mediator he is. For the High Priest of our offerings and our advocate with the Father (1 John 2. 1) is the Son of God, who prays for those who pray, and beseeches with those who beseech, but who would not pray as for his friends if they did not pray constantly through him, and would not be an advocate with God as on behalf of those who are already his own, if they did not obey his teaching that men ought always to pray, and not to faint. For, the Gospel says, he spake a parable that men ought always to pray, and not to faint: There was in a certain city a judge, etc. (Luke 18. 1, 2); and prior to this it says: And he said unto them, Which of you shall have a friend, and shall go unto him at midnight and say unto him, Friend, lend me three loaves; for a friend of mine in his journey is come to me, and I have nothing to set before him? (Luke 11. 5, 6). And a little later, I say unto you, Though he will not rise and give him, because he is his friend, yet because of his importunity he will rise and give him as many as he needeth (Luke 11. 8). And of those who believe the trusty words of Jesus, who will not be encouraged to pray resolutely when he says, Ask, and it shall be given you; for every one that asketh receiveth (Luke 11. 9, 10)? For the good Father, when we ask him, gives the living bread to those who have received the spirit of adoption (Rom. 8. 15) from the Father (and not the stone which the Adversary wants to be made into bread for Jesus and his disciples); and the Father gives the good gift, raining it from heaven upon those that ask him [2] (Luke 11. 13).

---

[1] Anglus sees here a reference to John 1. 26, "there standeth one among you, whom ye know not".

[2] ὕων ἐξ οὐρανοῦ τοῖς αἰτοῦσιν αὐτόν. So codex MS. If ὕων is correct, it is a reference to Exodus 16. 4: "I will rain bread from heaven for you", where ὕω is the verb used in LXX.

Angels and saints also assist men's prayers

XI.—1. But not only does the High Priest pray together with those whose prayer is genuine, but so also do the angels who rejoice in heaven over one sinner that repenteth, more than over ninety and nine just persons which need no repentance (Luke 15. 7), and likewise the souls of the saints who have fallen asleep.[1] This is shown to be true by the fact that Raphael offered reasonable service to God for Tobit and Sara; for after they had prayed, the prayer of them both, says the Scripture, was heard before the majesty of the great Raphael, and he was sent [2] to heal them both (Tobit 3. 16, 17), and Raphael himself, revealing his ministry towards them both as an angel according to the commandment of God, says, And now, when thou didst pray, thou and Sara thy daughter-in-law, I did bring the remembrance of your prayer before the Holy One (Tobit 12. 12), and a little later, I am Raphael, one of the seven angels which present the prayers of the saints,[3] and which go in and out before the glory of the Holy One (Tobit 12. 15). So, then, according to the word of Raphael, Prayer is good with fasting and alms and righteousness (Tobit 12. 8). It is also shown to be true by the fact that Jeremiah,[4] as it says in Maccabees, appeared, so resplendent with his gray hairs and his glory that the excellency which surrounded him was wondrous and most magnificent, and held forth his right hand and gave to Judas a sword of gold, to whom another saint who had fallen asleep bore witness, saying, This is he who prayeth much for the people, and for the holy city, Jeremiah the prophet of God (2 Macc. 15. 13–15).

For the saints' love for their brethren on earth continues

2. For again, it is absurd, when knowledge is made manifest to those who are worthy through a glass and darkly in this life present, but

---

[1] Origen held a strong doctrine of angelic ministration towards man and of the Communion of Saints. Cf. *De Princ.* III. ii. 4; *Comm. on Matthew* XXVII. 30; *Comm. on John* XIII. 57; *Hom. in Num.* XXVI. 6; *Exhortation to Martyrdom* XXX. 38. See also VI. 4 and XXXI. 5 of this treatise.

[2] τοῦ μεγάλου 'Ραφαὴλ, καὶ ἀπεστάλη. So the codex MS. Delarue conjectures τοῦ μεγάλου· καὶ 'Ραφαὴλ ἀπεστάλη. Cf. A.V.

[3] τὰς προσευχὰς τῶν ἁγίων. Koetschau adds these words, which are missing from the codex MS. They are present in LXX. Cf. A.V.

[4] Anglus remarks that Origen, having said that the angels and the saints pray together with those who pray on earth, gives first an example of the former in Raphael, and here an example of a departed saint praying for those on earth in Jeremiah.

then revealed face to face (1 Cor. 13. 12), not to take the analogy also of the other virtues; for assuredly those things that are prepared [1] beforehand in this life are then made perfect. Now the one supreme virtue [2] according to the divine word is love towards neighbour, which we must surely consider to belong to the saints who have fallen asleep towards those who still struggle in this life, much more than to those who are still subject to human weakness and yet help the weaker brethren in their struggle; for the text, Whether one member suffer, all the members suffer with it, and one member be honoured, all the members rejoice with it (1 Cor. 12. 26), does not apply only to those who love the brethren here below; for it is consonant also with their love, who are outside this present life, to say, The care of all the churches. Who is weak, and I am not weak? who is offended and I burn not? [3] (2 Cor. 11. 28, 29); moreover Christ confesses that he is weak like all the saints in their weakness, likewise also that he is in prison, is naked and a stranger, hungry and thirsty (Matt. 25. 35, 36). For who that reads the Gospel does not know that Christ, by the transference of the things which happen to those who believe in him to himself, reckons those things as his own sufferings?

The angels are really thus ministering to Christ

3. And if the angels of God came to Jesus and ministered unto him (Matt. 4. 11), and if it is not meet that we should think that this ministry of angels to Jesus was for a short time only, during his bodily sojourn among men, and while he himself was still in the midst of those who believed in him, not as one that sitteth at meat, but as he that serveth (Luke 22. 27), how many angels are likely to serve Jesus when he wills to gather together the children of Israel one by one (Isa. 27. 12; John 11. 52) and to assemble them of the dispersion, and when he saves those who fear him and call upon him (Acts 2. 21; Rom. 10. 13), and likely also to work with him, more than do the Apostles, for the increase and multiplying of the Church, so that certain angels are said by John in the Apocalypse to be set over the

---

[1] προπαρεσκευασμένων. Codex MS., προπαρασκευασαμένων, which Delarue reads. The perfect passive is, however, necessary. Koetschau follows Anglus.

[2] μία δὲ κυριωτάτη τῶν ἀρετῶν. Delarue has κυριωτάτων, following Oxford ed.

[3] Origen's argument for the truth of the Communion of Saints is compelling.

churches (Rev. 1. 20; 2. 1, etc.)? For not for nothing do the angels of God ascend and descend upon the Son of man (John 1. 51), being seen by the eyes which are enlightened with the light of knowledge.

Human analogies for the assistance given by angels to those who pray

4. And therefore during the actual time of prayer, being reminded by him who prays of the things he needs, they bring to pass what they can, as having received a general commission to do so. We may use the following illustration [1] of this argument in order to grasp [2] our meaning. Suppose some physician who has a care for righteousness is present with a sick man who prays for health, and that he knows the right way to cure him of the sickness concerning which the sick man lifts up his prayer, it is surely clear that he will be moved to heal him who has prayed, perhaps understanding, and rightly so, that this very thing was in the mind of God when he heard the prayer of him who prayed that he might have release from his sickness. Or suppose that one who possesses in abundance life's necessities and is generous, hears the prayer of one who is poor and lifts up his intercession to God for his needs. Surely it is clear that he also will fulfil the prayer of the poor man, being a minister of the will of the Father who has brought together at the time of the prayer, into the same place with him who is to pray, him who is able to give, who because of the rectitude [3] of his will cannot neglect him who needs these things.

5. Therefore just as, when these things happen, they are not to be thought to happen by chance, since he who has numbered all the hairs of the saints (Matt. 10. 30) brings together into harmony [4] at the time of the prayer him who is to be a minister to and to answer him who is in need of the kindness that he can do, and also him who has

---

[1] Notice how Origen here, as often, gives an illustration from human affairs to make clear the doctrine he is expounding.

[2] πρὸς τὸ παραδέξασθαι τὸ νενοημένον ἡμῖν. So codex MS. Oxford edition has παραδείξασθαι, which Delarue prefers to παραδέξασθαι. Παραδέχομαι is used of receiving or admitting an argument, and could be translated "grasp". But in view of the fact that the virtual subject of the sentence is in the first person (indicated by the ἡμῖν), I consider that the sense is unsuitable and that παραδείξασθαι is more likely to be correct: "in order to show our meaning".

[3] διὰ τὸ δεξιόν ... Codex MS. has διά τε τὸ δεξιὸν ... Oxford ed. omits τε; Delarue keeps it.

[4] ἁρμονίως. Delarue prefers ἁρμοδίως with Bentley.

asked with faith,[1] so we must understand that the presence of the angels who guard us and serve God is sometimes gathered together for a man who prays, that they may conspire together for the things which he who prays has asked. Yea, and each man's angel, even of those who are little ones in the Church, always beholding the face of the Father which is in heaven (Matt. 18. 10) and gazing on the divinity of him who created us, prays with us and acts with us in whatever way is possible as regards the things we pray for.

Prayer is a defence against the attacks of evil spirits

XII.—1. In addition to this, I think that the words of the prayers of the saints, being full of power,[2] especially when in their prayer they pray with the spirit and with the understanding (1 Cor. 14. 15), by the light, so to speak,[3] which rises [4] from the mind of him who prays, and proceeds from his mouth, dissolve by the power of God the spiritual poison which is instilled by the hostile powers [5] into the mind of those who neglect prayer, and who do not observe the words of Paul, following the exhortations of Jesus, Pray without ceasing (1 Thess. 5. 17). For like a dart from the soul of him who prays with knowledge and reason or faith, it will go forth from the saint, wounding to destruction and death the spirits that are hostile to God and that desire to encircle us with the bonds of sin.

There is a sense in which the whole of life may be prayer; yet there should be stated times of prayer, not less than thrice daily

2. The man who links together his prayer with deeds of duty and fits seemly actions with his prayer is the man who prays without

---

[1] τὸν ὑπηρέτην ἐσόμενον τῷ δεομένῳ τῆς εὐποιΐας τῆς ἀπ' αὐτοῦ εἰσακούοντα, τῷ πιστῶς δεδεημένῳ. Anglus suggests τοῦ πιστοῦ δεδεημένου. Delarue, τοῦ πιστῶς δεδεημένου. Delarue punctuates with a comma after αὐτοῦ, "hearkening to him who has asked with faith". With Koetschau's punctuation we must take τῷ πιστῶς δεδεημένῳ as the dative of indirect object after συναγαγόντος, "brings together".

[2] πρὸς δὲ τούτοις δυνάμεως πεπληρωμένους νομίζω τοὺς λόγους. Delarue reads πεπληρωμένοις with Bentley: "In addition to these things (i.e. the considerations mentioned in the previous section) which are full of power". But this is awkward.

[3] ἐοικότι. Omitted by Delarue.

[4] Koetschau sees in this obscure phrase a reference to Psalm 97. 11 and Isa. 58. 10.

[5] Origen strongly believed in the reality of spiritual forces of wickedness which attack the souls of men. See *De Princ.* III. iii. 2–6.

ceasing, for his virtuous deeds or the commandments he has fulfilled are taken up as a part of his prayer. For only in this way can we take the saying "Pray without ceasing" as being possible, if we can say that the whole life of the saint is one mighty integrated prayer.[1] Of such prayer, part is what is usually called "prayer", and ought not to be performed less than three times each day. This is clear from the practice of Daniel, who, when great danger threatened him, prayed three times a day (Dan. 6. 10). And Peter, going up to the housetop to pray about [2] the sixth hour, at which time also he saw the vessel let down from heaven, let down by the four corners (Acts 10. 9, 11), gives an example of the middle of the three times of prayer spoken of by David before him: In the morning thou shalt hear my prayer; in the morning will I stand beside thee, and will look unto thee (Psalm 5. 3).[3] The last of the three is indicated in the words, "the lifting up of my hands as an evening sacrifice" (Psalm 141. 2). But not even the time of night shall we rightly pass without such prayer, for David says, At midnight I rose to give thanks unto thee because of thy righteous judgements (Psalm 119. 62), and Paul, as related in the Acts of the Apostles, at midnight together with Silas at Philippi prayed and sang praises unto God, so that the prisoners also heard them (Acts 16. 25).

---

[1] Cf. Clem. Alex., *Strom.* VII. 7.
[2] περί. Not in codex MS., but in the Oxford edition. Delarue omits it.
[3] Anglus sees difficulty in the codex MS. reading here, because Origen identifies the Psalmist's prayer "in the morning" with the midday prayer of Peter. Anglus assumes that the phrase "in the morning" must refer to the first and not the middle of the three times which Origen enjoins. But as Origen points out, the first of the three times of prayer was during the night. Origen is justified in identifying the Psalmist's "in the morning" with prayer at the sixth hour.

C. W. Dugmore in *The Influence of the Synagogue upon the Divine Office*, Chapter IV, cites Origen as here speaking of prayer in the morning, at noon, and in the evening. Later in the same chapter he suggests that since one of the three times of daily prayer mentioned here by Origen is the sixth hour, or noon, he doubtless intended the other two to be the third and ninth hours. But this cannot be assumed. In this passage Origen first of all counsels prayer three times a day. He quotes Peter's prayer at the sixth hour (Acts 10. 9) as an example of the middle of the three times, and this sixth hour of prayer, he says, is what David was speaking of in the words "In the morning thou shalt hear my prayer, etc." (Psalm 5. 3). Then the last of the three times of prayer is in the evening (Psalm 141. 2). The remaining time of prayer is in the night (Psalm 119. 62 and Acts 16. 25). To assume that Origen intended to suggest prayer at 9.0 a.m., noon, and 3.0 p.m. for the three stated times is to

Jesus' own example of effective prayer

XIII.—1. And if Jesus prays, and does not pray in vain, attaining what he asks for through his prayer (and perhaps he would not have received it apart from prayer), which of us may neglect to pray? For Mark says that in the morning, rising up a great while before day, he went out, and departed into a solitary place, and there prayed (Mark 1. 35); and Luke says, And it came to pass, that, as he was praying in a certain place, when he ceased, one of his disciples said unto him (Luke 11. 1); and in another place, And he continued all night in prayer to God (Luke 6. 12); and John records his prayer, saying, These words spake Jesus, and lifted up his eyes to heaven, and said, Father, the hour is come; glorify thy Son, that thy Son also may glorify thee (John 17. 1); and the verse recorded by the same Evangelist as spoken by the Lord, I knew that thou hearest me always (John 11. 42), shows that he who always prays is always heard.

Examples of effective prayer from the Scriptures

2. But what need is there to make a list of those who, because they have prayed in the right way, have obtained great benefits from God, since each can choose for himself more examples from the Scriptures?[1] For Hannah ministered[2] to the birth of Samuel, who was reckoned together with Moses (Jer. 15. 1), because when she was barren she had faith and prayed to the Lord (1 Sam. 1. 10 ff.); and Hezekiah,

---

make him in this section counsel prayer *four* times a day, for otherwise the night prayers cannot be brought into his scheme.

It seems more likely that Delarue is right, and that Origen counsels prayers three times in the day, each of which is mentioned in this passage—prayers at night, at noon, and in the evening.

The Church in the West undoubtedly taught prayer at the third, sixth, and ninth hours in the early part of the third century. The evidence of the *Apostolic Tradition* of Hippolytus and of Tertullian is conclusive on this point. But the passage under review gives no evidence that this was a practice Origen desired to become general. Prayer at the third, sixth, and ninth hours was, however, known at Alexandria. See pp. 37–8 above.

[1] παρὸν ἑκάστῳ ἑαυτῷ ἀπὸ τῶν γραφῶν ἀναλέξασθαι πλείονα. Codex MS. is ambiguous here through abbreviation. Bentley reads παρὸν ἑκάστῳ τὰ ἑαυτῷ ἀπὸ τῶν . . ., which Delarue approves, while in his text he reads παρὸν ἑκάστῳ τῶν ἑαυτῶν ἀπὸ τῶν . . .

[2] ὑπηρέτησε τῇ γενέσει, a quaint expression, which might be rendered "was the handmaid of the birth"; cf. Luke 1. 48, though the Greek there is δούλη.

when he was still childless, and had learned from Isaiah that he was about to die, prayed, and was admitted into the genealogy of the Saviour [1] (2 Kings 20. 1 ff.; cf. Matt. 1. 9, 10); and when the people was about to be destroyed under a single decree because of the plotting of Haman, the prayer with fasting of Mordecai and Esther was heard, and gave birth to the day of Mordecai,[2] a day of rejoicing for the people, in addition to the feasts instituted by Moses (Esther 3. 6; 4. 16; 9. 26). Judith too, having offered holy prayer, overcomes Holofernes with the help of God, and a single Hebrew woman brought shame to the house of Nebuchadnezzar (Judith 13. 4–9); and Ananias,[3] Azarias, and Misael were heard, and were counted worthy to receive a whispering dewy wind which did not suffer the flame of fire to have its effect (Dan. 3. 50, LXX). The lions also in the den in Babylon have their mouths stopped because of Daniel's prayers (Dan. 6. 22); and Jonah, by no means despairing of being heard out of the belly of the monster that swallowed him, comes forth from the monster's belly to fulfil what was wanting of the prophecy to the Ninevites (Jonah 2).

We ourselves can give examples of the benefits of prayer [4]

3. And how many benefits are there which each of us can speak of, if he remembers with gratitude kindnesses received, and will lift up praises to God for them? For souls which had long been barren,[5] experiencing unfruitfulness in their own intellects and barrenness in their mind, have become pregnant by the Holy Spirit through constant prayer, and have brought forth words of salvation, filled with the principles of truth. And how many enemies are destroyed, when on many occasions the hosts of the power of the adversary war against us [6] and try to destroy our faith in God? For we take heart because some trust in chariots, and some in horses, but we, calling upon the name of the Lord (Psalm 20. 7), realize that truly an horse is a vain thing for safety (Psalm 33. 17). Yea, and even the captain of the host

[1] Anglus notes that the Hebrew has no mention of Hezekiah's begetting a son soon after his prayer. The reference is to Isaiah 38. 19 in LXX, ἀπὸ γὰρ τῆς σήμερον παιδία ποιήσω.
[2] τὴν Μαρδοχαϊκὴν ἡμέραν.
[3] Ἀνανίας δέ. Codex MS., τε; so Delarue.
[4] Origen turns from biblical examples to examples from personal experience. Notice his thoroughness in pressing the argument.
[5] As Hannah was literally barren.
[6] As Haman and Holofernes literally sought to destroy the Jewish faith.

of the adversary, namely deceitful and persuasive speech, which makes many tremble, even of those who are thought to have faith, is often smitten by him who puts his trust in praising God. For "Judith" means by interpretation "praise". What need is there to recount how many there are who have fallen into temptations often hard to overcome, and burning hotter than any flame,[1] and have yet suffered nothing of them, but have come through them unharmed in every way, receiving no hurt, not even so much as by the smell of the enemy's fire?[2] Yea, and[3] how many wild beasts, raging against us,[4] evil spirits and savage men, have men met, and by their prayers often stopped their mouths, since they have not been able to fasten their teeth upon those members of ours which have become Christ's? For oft-times for the saints one by one has the Lord broken the great teeth of the lions, and they have been brought to nought as water which runs continually (Psalm 58. 6, 7). And we know that fugitives from God's commandments, swallowed up by the death which aforetime prevailed against them,[5] have often been saved by repentance from this great calamity, for they have not despaired of the possibility of salvation even when already held in the belly of death; for death prevailed and swallowed them up, and again, God wiped away every tear from every face (Isa. 25. 8).[6]

The spiritual benefits which are typified by the answers to the prayers of Hannah etc. (Vide XIII. 2 above)

4. I consider that it was necessary that I should say these things[7] after enumerating those who have been helped by prayer, endeavouring as I do to turn those who desire the spiritual life which is in Christ

[1] As Ananias and his companions were literally cast into flames.
[2] οὐδὲ τὸ τυχὸν ὀσμῆς τοῦ πολεμίου πυρὸς βλάβην ἐσχηκότες, τί δεῖ καὶ λέγειν; Delarue punctuates differently, putting a full stop after βλάβην ἐσχηκότες, and taking τί δεῖ καὶ λέγειν with what follows.
[3] ἀλλὰ καὶ... Delarue reads ἄλλα for ἀλλά, and omits ἐν after καί. Thus, τί δεῖ καὶ λέγειν ἄλλα καὶ ὅσοις ..., "What need is there to speak of other instances, and how many...?"
[4] As wild beasts literally raged against Daniel.
[5] As Jonah was literally swallowed up by the monster.
[6] In this section Origen gives a spiritual meaning to the material benefits gained in the instances of effective prayer mentioned in XIII. 2. This does not imply any doubt in his mind as to the literal truth of those stories.
[7] ταῦτα δέ μοι ἀναγκαιότατα ... εἰρῆσθαι νομίζω. Delarue has ἀναγκαιότατον. Codex MS. is ambiguous owing to abbreviation. Ταῦτα

XIII. 4 ON PRAYER

away from praying for small and earthly things, and exhorting those who read this treatise to the mysteries of which the things I have already mentioned were the types. For every prayer for the spiritual and mysterious gifts which are set before us will always be brought to fulfilment by him who does not war after the flesh (2 Cor. 10. 3), but through the Spirit mortifies the deeds of the body (Rom. 8. 13); for those things which, if we inquire closely, are presented to us by way of mystical interpretation are preferred to the literal benefit which has evidently come to those who have prayed.[1] For we must practise that it be not barren and unfruitful in us,[2] listening to the spiritual law with out spiritual ears, so that, laying aside our barren and unfruitful state, we may be answered, as were Hannah and Hezekiah, and may be delivered from the wicked spiritual enemies that plot against us, as were Mordecai and Esther and Judith. And since the iron furnace is Egypt[3] (Deut. 4. 20; Jer. 11. 4), which is the symbol of the whole earth, let everyone who is uncontaminated by[4] the evil of human life, and is not inflamed by sin, nor has a heart full of fire like a baking pot,[5] give thanks no less than they who experienced the dew in the fire. Moreover let him who was answered when he prayed and said, Deliver not the soul that confesseth thee unto the wild beasts (Psalm 74. 19; cf. LXX, Psalm 73. 19), and who took no hurt

---

refers to the previous section, XIII. 3, the enumeration of those who have been helped by prayer being in XIII. 2. According to the mystical or spiritual interpretation these examples of prayer answered by material benefits are seen to typify the spiritual gifts of God in answer to those who pray aright.

[1] προκρινομένων τῶν ἀπὸ τῆς ἀναγωγῆς μετ' ἐξετάσεως παρισταμένων τῆς ἐμφαινομένης κατὰ τὴν λέξιν γεγονέναι τοῖς προσευξαμένοις εὐεργεσίας. Difficult Greek; τῶν παρισταμένων is the subject of a genitive absolute, and τῆς εὐεργεσίας is a genitive of comparison.

[2] μὴ ἐγγενέσθαι ἄγονον ἢ στεῖραν. Bentley conjectures ψυχήν after στεῖραν, and Delarue approves. Otherwise the feminine adjectives can only be referred to the word εὐχή, the subject of the previous sentence: "we must practise that our prayer be not barren".

[3] In the Old Testament "furnace" is used as a metaphor of suffering. Hence it is applied to Egypt where the Israelites suffered the rigours of slavery. Origen here applies it to the whole earth as a "vale of suffering".

[4] ὁ ἐκπεφευγώς, literally "who has escaped the evil of human life"; but not, of course, in the sense of never having been born.

[5] ὡς κλίβανον. A κλίβανος was "a covered earthen vessel, a pot or pan, wider at bottom than at top, wherein bread was baked by putting hot embers round it, thus producing a more equable heat than in the regular oven (ἰπνός)" (Liddell and Scott). Thus Origen's simile is not very apt. The "baking pot" was not "full of fire"; the fire was all round it.

O.T.P.—5·

from the asp and the basilisk because by Christ's aid he trod upon them, and who trampled underfoot the lion and the dragon (Psalm 91. 13), and has used the glorious power given by Jesus of treading on serpents and scorpions, and over all the power of the enemy (Luke 10. 19), and was in no way harmed by these great monsters, give thanks more than did Daniel, inasmuch as he is delivered from wild beasts at once more fearful and more noxious.

Moreover let him who knows what monster is typified by that which swallowed Jonah, and understands that it is the one spoken of by Job in the words, Let him curse it that curses that day, who is ready to engage the great monster (Job. 3. 8, LXX), repent and pray, if at any time he be "in the belly of the monster" because of some disobedience, and he shall come out thence; and having come out, if he abide in obedience to the commands of God, he shall have power by the goodness of the Spirit to prophesy even to the Ninevites of the present day who are perishing, and to become an occasion of salvation to them, neither being displeased at the goodness of God, nor seeking to hinder him out of severity towards those who repent.[1]

God's answer to the prayers for rain of Samuel and Elijah typifies his watering of the Christian soul

5. And the mighty thing that Samuel is said to have done by prayer, it is also possible in a spiritual sense for everyone who is truly devoted [2] to God now to perform, being worthy of having his prayer answered. For it is written, Now therefore stand and see this great thing, which the Lord doeth before your eyes. Is it not wheat harvest to-day? I will call unto the Lord, and he shall send thunder and rain; then a little later it says, And Samuel called unto the Lord, and the Lord sent thunder and rain that day (1 Sam. 12. 16–18). For to every saint and to every true disciple of Jesus, the Lord says, Lift up your eyes, and look on the fields; for they are white already to harvest. And

---

[1] μηδὲ ζητῶν ἐπιμένειν αὐτὸν πρὸς τοὺς μετανοοῦντας τῇ ἀποτομίᾳ. So Codex MS. and Delarue; but translation is not easy. Ἐπιμένειν must here have an unusual transitive sense, "stay" or "hinder"; αὐτόν must refer to God. Anglus' suggestion that τῇ πρὸς τοὺς μετανοοῦντας ἀποτομίᾳ should be read is very attractive.

[2] ἕκαστον τῶν ἀνακειμένων γνησίως τῷ θεῷ. Ἀνακεῖμαι must here have its older sense of "to be devoted to". The common N.T. sense of "to sit at meat" is not appropriate here, unless Origen's imagery is very bold indeed.

ON PRAYER

he that reapeth receiveth wages, and gathereth fruit unto life eternal (John 4. 35, 36). In this time of harvest indeed the Lord doeth a great thing before the eyes of those who hearken to the prophets; for when he who is governed by the Holy Spirit calls upon the Lord, God gives from heaven thunder and rain that waters the soul, that he who before lived in wickedness may greatly fear the Lord and the minister of God's kindness, shown as he is to be worthy of awe and reverence through his prayers which are answered. Elijah also, when the heaven had been shut up unto the wicked for three years and six months, afterwards opens it by a divinely inspired word [1] (James 5. 17, 18; 1 Kings 17; 18); and this same thing is constantly accomplished by anyone who, though before deprived of it through sin,[2] receives through his prayer the rain of the soul.

We should pray for great and heavenly benefits and leave our small and earthly needs to God's wisdom

XIV.—1. Now that we have given this interpretation to the benefits which have come to the saints through prayer, let us consider [3] the words, Ask for the great things, and the small things shall be added unto you; and, ask for heavenly things, and earthly things shall be added unto you.[4] Now all those things which are symbols and types are "small" and "earthly" by comparison with the true and spiritual realities. And with reason does the divine word, in exhorting us to imitate the prayers of the saints, in order that we may ask these prayers in accordance with the reality of those things which they attained in type,[5] declare that the heavenly and great things are revealed through

---

[1] θείῳ λόγῳ, lit. "by a divine word". Origen's meaning is "by prayer". Cf. James 5. 18.

[2] τῶν διὰ τὴν ἁμαρτίαν πρότερον αὐτοῦ ἐστερημένων. The genitive is to be taken with παντί τῳ, lit. "by anyone of those who . . .". Αὐτοῦ is the genitive of deprivation which is usual with στερῶ. Bentley reads τὸν . . . ἐστερημένον. This would agree with ὑετόν, rain, and αὐτοῦ would then be genitive of person deprived, "the rain of the soul, which had before been taken away from him". But στερῶ in the sense of "to take away" with acc. *rei* and gen. *personae* is rare; and there seems little need to dispute the reading of the MS.

[3] κατανοήσωμεν. Bentley and Delarue suggest κατανοήσομεν.

[4] See II. 2 and XIII. 4.

[5] ἵν' αἰτῶμεν αὐτὰς κατὰ τὸ ἀληθὲς ὧν ἐκεῖνοι ἐπετέλουν τυπικῶν. A difficult passage which has consequently been variously emended. Bentley, ἵν' αἰτῶμεν αὐτοὶ . . . ἐπέτυχον τυπικῶς. This neatly obviates both the

the things which have to do with what is earthly and small, saying in effect, Ye who desire to be spiritual, ask in your prayers for heavenly and great things,¹ in order that having attained them ye may inherit the kingdom of heaven, since the objects of your prayer are "heavenly things", and may enjoy also the greatest of good things, since the objects of your prayer are the "great things"; and in order that the Father may supply for you, according to the measure of your needs, the "earthly and small things" of which ye stand in need because of your bodily necessities.

Four kinds of prayer mentioned by St Paul (1 Tim. 2. 1)

2. Now since the Apostle in his First Epistle to Timothy used four words for four things which resemble prayer, it will be useful to have his words in front of us and to see whether we can rightly understand each of the four if its meaning is properly conceived. This is what he says: I exhort therefore, that, first of all, supplications, prayers, intercessions, and giving of thanks be made for all men (1 Tim. 2. 1), and so on. Now I consider that "supplication" is the prayer of a man who lacks something, sent up with entreaty for the obtaining of it; "prayer" is that sent up with greater magnanimity ² by a man for greater gifts and accompanied by words of praise; ³ "intercession" is a request to God on behalf of certain persons made by one who has a greater boldness; and "giving thanks" is an acknowledgement with prayer upon receiving ⁴ good things from God, when the acknowledgement of the greatness, or what seems greatness in the eyes of him who has received it, of the kindness conferred upon him is received by God in exchange.⁵

difficult αὐτὰς and the τυπικῶν. So also Delarue. Anglus, ἵν' ἐπιτελῶμεν αὐτὰς ... τυπικῶν. He considers αἰτῶμεν αὐτὰς (sc. εὐχάς) to be very improbable Greek. Koetschau himself suggests ἵν' εἴπωμεν.

¹ ὑμεῖς οἱ πνευματικοὶ εἶναι βουλόμενοι διὰ τῶν προσευχῶν αἰτήσατε <" τὰ ἐπουράνια " καὶ " μεγάλα ">. The addition of the bracketed words as object of αἰτήσατε is suggested by Koetschau, following Anglus, who, however, has τὰ μεγάλα καὶ ἐπουράνια. Delarue inserts πνευματικά after βουλόμενοι. So Bentley.

² μεγαλοφυέστερον, more nobly, and so, less selfishly.

³ The distinction between δέησις, "supplication", and προσευχή, "prayer", is somewhat forced.

⁴ ἐπὶ τῷ τετευχέναι. Delarue τετυχέναι.

⁵ ἀντειλημμένου τοῦ ἀνθομολογουμένου τοῦ μεγέθους ἢ τῷ εὐεργετηθέντι μεγέθους φαινομένου τῆς εἰς αὐτὸν γεγενημένης εὐεργεσίας. The

XIV. 4   ON PRAYER   123

(a) Supplication: δέησις

3. As examples[1] of the first, there is the word of Gabriel to Zacharias, who had no doubt prayed for the birth of John; he said, Fear not, Zacharias: for thy supplication (δέησις) is heard; and thy wife Elisabeth shall bear thee a son, and thou shalt call his name John (Luke 1. 13); and what is written in Exodus where it speaks of the making of the calf, as follows, And Moses made supplication before the Lord his God, and said, Why doth thy wrath wax hot[2] against thy people, which thou hast brought forth out of the land of Egypt with great power? (Ex. 32. 11), and in Deuteronomy, And I made supplication before the Lord the second time, as at the first, forty days and forty nights (I did neither eat bread, nor drink water), because of all your sins which ye sinned (Deut. 9. 18); and in the Book of Esther, Mardocheus thought upon all the works of the Lord, and made supplication unto God, and said, O Lord, Lord, the King Almighty (Esther 13. 8, 9), and Esther herself made supplication unto the Lord God of Israel and said, O Lord, our King (Esther 14. 3).

(b) Prayer: προσευχή

4. There is an example of the second in Daniel: And Azarias stood and prayed thus, and, opening his mouth in the midst of the fire, said (Dan. 3. 25, LXX);[3] and in Tobit, And I prayed with sorrow, saying, O Lord, thou art just, and all thy works and all thy ways are mercy and truth, and thou judgest truly and justly for ever (Tobit 3. 1, 2). But since they of the circumcision have marked the passage in Daniel with an obelus, as not being in the Hebrew, and reject the Book of Tobit as not being canonical, I will add the prayer of Hannah from the First Book of Kings: And she prayed unto the Lord, and wept sore. And she vowed a vow, and said, O Lord of hosts, if thou wilt indeed

text seems in good order, but translation is difficult. Ἀνθομολογουμένου is here passive in meaning; τοῦ ἀνθ. τοῦ μεγέθους is the subject of ἀντειλημμένου, with which is understood "by God". The genitive τῆς ... εὐεργεσίας depends on the first μεγέθους, the clause ᾗ τῷ ... φαινομένου being parenthetical.

[1] With customary thoroughness Origen gives examples.
[2] ἵνα τί θυμοῖ ὀργῇ, following the Oxf. ed.; literally "why dost thou wax wroth with anger". Codex MS. and Delarue, ἱνατί θυμῇ. Anglus, θυμοῦ.
[3] For this passage consult H. B. Swete, *The Old Testament in Greek*, Vol. iii, p. 515, and introductory volume, p. 260 f.

look on the affliction of thine handmaid (1 Sam. 1. 10, 11), and so on; and in Habakkuk: *A prayer of Habakkuk the prophet with a canticle. O Lord, I have heard thy speech, and was afraid; O Lord I have considered thy works, and was astonished; in the midst of the two living creatures thou shalt be known, when the years draw nigh thou shalt be recognized* (Hab. 3. 1, 2, LXX). And this clearly shows, in accordance with my definition of prayer, that it is sent up by him who prays "accompanied by words of praise". There is also an example in Jonah: *Jonah prayed unto the Lord his God out of the fish's belly, and said, I cried by reason of mine affliction unto the Lord, and he heard me; out of the belly of hell thou heardest my crying, my voice. Thou didst cast me into the depths of the heart of the sea; and the floods compassed me about* (Jonah 2. 1–3).[1]

(*c*) *Intercession*: ἔντευξις

5. There is an example of the third given by the Apostle, who rightly attributes "prayer" to us, but "intercession" to the Spirit, for he is more powerful, and has boldness towards him with whom he intercedes. *For we know not,* he says, *what we should pray for as we ought; but the Spirit itself*[2] *maketh intercession for us to God with groanings which cannot be uttered. And he that searcheth the hearts knoweth what is the mind of the Spirit, because he maketh intercession for the saints according to the will of God* (Rom. 8. 26, 27). For the Spirit strongly intercedes and makes intercession,[3] but we pray. What was said by Joshua about the sun standing still over Gibeon seems to me to be intercession:[4] *Then spake Joshua to the Lord in the day when God delivered the Amorite into the hand of Israel, when he crushed them upon Gibeon, and they were crushed from before the face of the children of Israel. And Joshua said, Let the sun stand over*

---

[1] But there are no accompanying words of praise here. Origen does not wholly give substance to the distinction he has made between δέησις and προσευχή.

[2] αὐτὸ τὸ πνεῦμα. Delarue omits τό.

[3] ὑπερεντυγχάνει γὰρ καὶ ἐντυγχάνει. Adequate translation is difficult, as there is a light play on the word ὑπερεντυγχάνει, the prefix ὑπερ having both the meaning of the preposition, "on behalf of", and an intensive force "strongly". Cf. II. 3 *ad fin.*

[4] But this example does not bear out Origen's suggestion that it is the Spirit alone who can be truly said to intercede. There is no hint in the passage that Joshua was "in the Spirit".

Gibeon, and the moon over the valley of Elom (Josh. 10. 12). And I think that Samson, in the Book of Judges, was interceding when he said, Let my soul die with the foreigners, when he bowed himself with might; and the house fell upon the lords, and upon all the people that were therein (Judges 16. 30). Although it is not stated that Joshua and Samson made intercession but that they *said*, nevertheless what they said seems to be intercession,[1] which I consider to be different from prayer, if we are to understand the words properly.

(*d*) *Thanksgiving*: εὐχαριστία

An example of thanksgiving is the utterance of our Lord, when he said, I thank thee (ἐξομολογοῦμαι), O Father, Lord of heaven and earth, that thou hast hid these things from the wise and prudent, and hast revealed them unto babes (Luke 10. 21); for the word ἐξομολογοῦμαι is the equivalent of εὐχαριστῶ, "I thank".

Since supplication, intercession, and thanksgiving may even be offered to men, much more may they be offered to Christ

6. Supplication, then, and intercession and giving of thanks it is not unfitting to offer even to men who are saints,[2] but two of these (I refer indeed to intercession [3] and giving of thanks) not only to saints, but indeed to other men besides,[4] while supplication may only be

---

[1] Anglus in a note on this passage disagrees with Origen. Origen evidently classes Joshua's and Samson's pleading as "intercession" because of their greater boldness (see the definition in xiv. 2). But Anglus thinks that Samson should rather be said to "pray" than to "intercede", since his request is on his own behalf. One must agree. Origen is not at his best in this chapter, in which he is seeking to impose on the four words descriptive of prayer in 1 Tim. 2. 1 a sharp distinction which they were not intended to convey.

[2] οὐκ ἄτοπον καὶ ἀνθρώποις ⟨ἁγίοις⟩ προσενεγκεῖν. Codex MS. has ἀνθρώποις προσενεγκεῖν: Koetschau follows Anglus, who adds ἁγίοις, considering the sense of the passage to demand it. But see note 4. Bentley and Delarue substitute ἁγίοις for ἀνθρώποις.

[3] λέγω δὴ ἔντευξιν. Delarue has δέ for δή.

[4] οὐ μόνον ἁγίοις ἀλλὰ δὴ καὶ ⟨ἄλλοις⟩ ἀνθρώποις. Codex MS. has καὶ ἀνθρώποις. We have here translated Koetschau's text with the insertions. These, however, are unnecessary, and the passage has more point without them. Omitting them we should translate "Supplication, then, and intercession and giving of thanks it is not unfitting to offer even to men, but two of these (I refer indeed to intercession and giving of thanks) not only to saints, but indeed even to men in general, while supplication (δέησις) may

offered to saints, provided a Paul or a Peter may be found,[1] that they may help us, making us worthy of attaining the power given to them of remitting sins (John 20. 23); except indeed, even if a man be not a saint, and we wrong him, it is permissible for us, when we perceive our sin against him, to supplicate such a man to grant us pardon for wronging him. Now if these prayers are rightly offered to men who are saints, how much more ought we to give thanks to Christ who has shown us such great kindness by the will of the Father! But we must also make intercession to him, like Stephen, when he said, Lord, lay not this sin to their charge (Acts 7. 60). And we shall be imitators of the father of the lunatic if we say, Lord, I make supplication unto thee, have mercy upon my son (Luke 9. 38) or on me, or on whomsoever it may be.[2]

But properly, prayer is to be addressed to God the Father alone

XV.—1. But if we give heed to what prayer properly is, surely prayer is to be addressed to no man born of woman, not even to Christ himself,[3] but to the God and Father of all alone, to whom even our

only be offered to saints, provided a Paul or a Peter may be found, ..." There is thus a general statement that on the human level we use δέησις, ἔντευξις, and εὐχαριστία. This is followed by a more precise statement that ἔντευξις and εὐχαριστία may be addressed to any man, but δέησις (which here seems to be used in the special sense of supplication for forgiveness of sins against God) can only be offered to those who have divine authority to remit sins.

It is to be noted that this passage nowhere refers to *departed* saints. "Saint" here has its frequent N.T. meaning of "Christian".

[1] I.e. somebody who has the apostolic power of declaring sins forgiven, a priest of the Church. Note that Origen assumes that Paul as well as Peter was commissioned to forgive sins.

[2] The argument of this difficult passage seems to be that if there is a true though limited sense in which we may address supplication, intercession, and thanksgiving to men, they must, *a fortiori*, be offered to Christ. But see the next section (xv. 1).

[3] Anglus has a lengthy note on this passage. He cites references to this startling phrase by later Fathers. He then champions Origen's orthodoxy, and puts a strong case. Prayer properly so called (κυρίως) is offered to the Father through the mediation of Christ. If this is taken as a definition of prayer, it is obvious that such *cannot* be offered to Christ. But prayer in a wider sense of the word, and by what is really, in view of the strict definition of the word "prayer", a misuse of language (καταχρηστικῶς), may be offered to Christ as our High Priest and Advocate with the Father. Anglus quotes *Contra Celsum* v. 580, and viii. 751 and 761 to the same effect, that prayer properly

Saviour himself prayed, as we have recorded above, and to whom he teaches us to pray. For hearing the request, Teach us to pray (Luke 11. 1), he does not teach them to pray to himself but to the Father, in the words, Our Father which art in heaven, etc. (Matt. 6. 9). For if, as is shown elsewhere, the Son is distinct from the Father in being and person (κατ' οὐσίαν καὶ ὑποκείμενον),[1] then either we must pray to the Son and not to the Father, or to both, or to the Father alone. Everybody will agree that it would be most absurd and contrary to clear evidence to say that we must pray to the Son and not to the Father; and if we must pray to both, it is clear that we should proffer is to be addressed to the Father through the Son. He then goes on to say that this does not mean that Origen denied that prayer ought to be addressed to Christ *as God and Son of God*, and quotes passages in which Origen declares that prayer may be offered to Christ alone (*Contra Celsum* v. 586), or to Christ together with the Father (ibid. VIII. 750).

To put Anglus' argument shortly, it is that prayer properly speaking is offered to the Father through Christ. Hence it cannot be offered to Christ as Mediator. But it may be offered to Christ as God. But this is over-subtlety. If we are to keep strictly to Anglus' definition of prayer, it is difficult to understand how it may even be offered to Christ as God. The attempt to justify Origen's language in this passage by means of close definition of what he means by "prayer" and of the significance he gives to the word "Christ" fails. It will be nearer the truth if we admit that Origen is not always consistent, and that his devotion to Christ led him both himself to pray boldly to Christ, and to encourage others to do so, even though when he comes to write a treatise on the subject he is unable to justify the practice theologically. He also addresses the Holy Spirit in prayer (see Bigg, *Christian Platonists of Alexandria*, 1913 ed., p. 214).

[1] "As is shown elsewhere". See *Comm. on John* x. 21 (Brooke, Vol. I, p. 231), where Origen speaks of opponents who misinterpret scriptural passages: οἷον τὸ ἐκ τούτων παρίστασθαι μὴ διαφέρειν τῷ ἀριθμῷ τὸν υἱὸν τοῦ πατρός, ἀλλ' ἐν οὐ μόνον οὐσίᾳ ἀλλὰ καὶ ὑποκειμένῳ τυγχάνοντας ἀμφοτέρους, κατά τινας ἐπινοίας διαφόρους, οὐ κατὰ ὑπόστασιν λέγεσθαι πατέρα καὶ υἱόν.

The phrase "the Son is distinct from the Father in being (οὐσία) and person" is startling to those who read it from the standpoint of later orthodox Trinitarian terminology, in which the Son is said to be of one substance (οὐσία) with the Father, and the Trinity to be one οὐσία and three ὑποστάσεις. But it must be remembered that the technical language of theology was still unsettled in Origen's day. Nevertheless Origen does frequently use the two words οὐσία and ὑπόστασις in the way in which later orthodoxy used them. Bigg, *Christian Platonists of Alexandria*, Lecture V (p. 202), says "The word for Person in Origen is commonly *Hypostasis*, that for the Divine Nature is less determinate but is frequently *Ousia*", and in a useful footnote gives references to substantiate his statement. The passage from *Comm. on*

our requests [1] using the plural number, saying when we pray, "Grant ye", and "Shew ye kindness", and "Supply ye", and "Save ye", and similar expressions; this in itself is incongruous, nor can anybody show that it is found in the Scriptures as said by any. There remains, then, to pray to God the Father of all alone, but not apart from the High Priest who was appointed by the Father with an oath, according to the words, He hath sworn, and will not repent, Thou art a priest for ever after the order of Melchizedek (Psalm 110. 4).

Yet this prayer to the Father must be through Christ and in his name

2. Therefore the saints, when they give thanks to God in their prayers, confess their thanks to him through Christ Jesus. And just as

John x. 21, quoted above, gives an instance of οὐσία used by Origen to mean "substance" in the orthodox sense. The οὐ μόνον ... ἀλλὰ καί forbids the equation of οὐσία with ὑποκείμενον, "Person".

But Bigg notes Origen's use of οὐσία for Person in *Comm. on John* II. 6 with the qualifying adjective ἰδία, and without qualification, ibid. I. 30 and II. 18. It is not special pleading, therefore, to argue that in the present passage οὐσία also means Person, and that ὑποκείμενον is a synonym.

We are further supported by the fact that in Greek philosophic thought, from the time of Aristotle at least, οὐσία had two meanings. If we ask the question "What is the οὐσία of Socrates?" or "What makes Socrates what he is?", we can answer (a) "that which makes him unlike everybody else", his Socraticness. In this sense οὐσία is practically equivalent to the ὑπόστασις of Cappadocian orthodoxy. This is what Aristotle called "primary substance" (*Categoriae* 2a. 11). We can also answer (b) "that which makes him like everybody else", his humanity. In this sense οὐσία is practically equivalent to the οὐσία of Cappadocian orthodoxy. This is what Aristotle called "secondary substance". That Origen here and there used οὐσία in the sense of the Aristotelian "primary substance" need occasion no surprise.

The later credal significance of words is not therefore to be read into the sentence "the Son is distinct from the Father in being and person". Οὐσία, "being", is here used by Origen very much as we use the phrase "his whole being", i.e. practically as the equivalent of "person".

That Origen was very far from asserting a distinction in essence between the Father and the Son is verified by a perusal of *De Principiis* I. ii. In Origen's day the question of the Homoousion had not yet been raised, still less settled, and we should not expect, therefore, to find in him a concise statement of the doctrine of the Trinity in Cappadocian terminology. Failure to realize this accounts largely for Origen's condemnation as unorthodox.

Ὑποκείμενον is also used for "person" in *Hom. in Jerem.* VIII. 2 as well as in *Comm. on John* x. 21, quoted above.

[1] δῆλον ὅτι κἂν ἀξιώσεις προσενέγκοιμεν. But codex MS. has δῆλον ὅτι καὶ ἀξιώσεις προσενεγκοῦμεν. So Delarue.

it is not right for one who is exact in his prayers to pray to one who himself prays, but only to the Father whom our Lord Jesus taught us to call upon in our prayers, so we must not offer any prayer to the Father apart from him, as he himself clearly shows when he says, Verily, verily, I say unto you, If ye shall ask the Father anything, he will give it you in my name. Hitherto have ye asked nothing in my name: ask, and ye shall receive, that your joy may be full (John 16. 23, 24). For he did not say "Ask me", nor "Ask the Father" simply, but "If ye shall ask the Father anything, he will give it you in my name". For until Jesus taught [1] this nobody asked the Father "in the name of the Son"; and Jesus' words were true, Hitherto have ye asked nothing in my name; true also is the saying, Ask, and ye shall receive, that your joy may be full (John 16. 24).[2]

3. And if anybody, thinking we ought to pray to Christ himself, being troubled by the meaning of the word "worship", brings against us the passage, Let all the angels of God worship him (Deut. 32. 43, LXX; cf. Heb. 1. 6), which is admittedly spoken of Christ in Deuteronomy, we must say to him that the Church, which is named Jerusalem by the prophet, is also said to be "worshipped" by kings and queens who are its nursing fathers and nursing mothers, in the following quotation,[3] Behold, I lift up mine hand to the Gentiles, and will set up my standard to the isles: and they shall bring thy sons in their bosom, and they shall lift up thy daughters upon their shoulders. And kings shall be thy nursing fathers and their queens thy nursing mothers; they shall worship thee [4] upon the face of the earth, and lick up the dust of thy feet; and thou shalt know that I am the Lord: and thou shalt not be ashamed (Isa. 49. 22, 23).

[1] ἐδίδαξε. So Anglus. Codex MS., διδάξει. Bentley and Delarue, διδάξῃ.
[2] The principle enunciated by Origen in this section is one to which the Christian Church has generally adhered in its liturgical formulae. See, for instance, the Collects of the Book of Common Prayer.
[3] Anglus' note on this passage points out that Origen means that worship is not properly (κυρίως) to be paid to Christ, but only by an extended use of the word (καταχρηστικῶς). Cf. the distinction Anglus draws between προσεύχεσθαι κυρίως and προσεύχεσθαι καταχρηστικῶς referred to in Note 3 on p. 126. But Anglus cites passages where Origen clearly teaches that Christ is to be worshipped equally with the Father.
[4] προσκυνήσουσί ⟨σοι⟩. Codex MS., προσκυνήσουσι. Delarue adds σε.

Prayer through Christ

4. And surely it is in keeping with his words, Why callest thou me good? there is none good but one, that is, God the Father [1] (Mark 10. 18), that he might have said, Why dost thou pray to me? To the Father alone must prayer be made, to whom I also pray. This you learn from Holy Scripture. For you ought not to pray to a High Priest who was established on your behalf by the Father and who received the office of Advocate from [2] the Father, but rather *through* a High Priest and Advocate who can be touched with the feeling of your infirmities, being in all points tempted like as you are, yet, because of the Father who endowed me, tempted without sin (Heb. 4. 15). Learn, then, what a great gift ye have received from my Father, through your regeneration in me, in that ye have received the spirit of adoption (Rom. 8. 15), that ye may bear the name of sons of God (Rom. 8. 14) and my brethren. For ye have read the words addressed by me to the Father about you, by the mouth of David: I will declare thy name unto my brethren: in the midst of the congregation will I praise thee (Psalm 22. 22). It is not meet that those who are deemed worthy of their one Father [3] should pray to a brother. For to the Father alone must your prayers be lifted up with me, and through me.

An exhortation to confident prayer to the Father

XVI.—1. Hearing, then, Jesus declare these things, let us pray to God through him; let us all say the same thing and not be divided in our method of prayer. Are we not divided if some of us pray to the Father and some to the Son, inasmuch as they who pray to the Son, whether with or without the Father, commit a foolish sin [4] in great simplicity because of their lack of discernment and criticism? Let us

---

[1] ὁ θεός, ὁ πατήρ. Origen also adds ὁ πατήρ in quoting this text in *Contra Celsum* v. 586; *Comm. on John* 1. 40, 11. 7 (Brooke, Vol. I, p. 48 and p. 75). Epiphanius (*Haeres.* 42) attributes the addition to Marcion in his edition of St Luke's Gospel. Anglus, however, considers the words a paraphrastic addition on the part of Origen and other Fathers who use the text. Delarue notes that the author of *Dialogi de Trinitate*, quoted by Athanasius, specifically says καίτοι οὐκ εἴρηται Οὐδεὶς ἀγαθὸς εἰ μὴ εἷς ὁ πατήρ· ἀλλ' Οὐδεὶς ἀγαθὸς εἰ μὴ εἷς ὁ θεός.

[2] ἀπό. So Anglus. Codex MS. and Delarue, ὑπό.

[3] ἑνὸς αὐτῶν πατρός. Codex MS. ambiguous. Bentley, αὐτῷ. Delarue, αὐτοῦ.

[4] ἰδιωτικὴν ἁμαρτίαν. Codex MS., ἰδιωτῶν ἁμαρτ., and so Delarue.

pray, then, as to God, let us make intercession as to the Father, let us make supplication as to the Lord, and let us give thanks as to God, Father and Lord, a Lord who is not in any way Lord of a slave, for the Father may rightly be thought of as Lord of the Son and Lord of those who by him became sons. And as he is not the God of the dead, but of the living (Matt. 22. 32), so he is not Lord of slaves of no birth, but of those who at first receive ennoblement with fear because of their immaturity [1] but afterwards serve in love a bondage which is happier than the bondage which is in fear. For there are in the soul the characteristic marks both of God's slaves and of his sons, manifest to him alone who looks upon the heart.

Prayer should be for heavenly and great gifts: God may add the earthly and small things

2. So, then, everyone that asks of God earthly and small things disobeys him that bids us ask for heavenly and great things of God, who knows not how to bestow anything earthly or small.[2] And if anybody brings forward as an objection the bodily gifts granted to the saints through prayer,[3] and the words of the Gospel which teaches that earthly and small things are added to us, we must give him the answer that just as we must not say, when somebody gives us a body of some sort, that so-and-so has given us the shadow of the body (for in giving us the body he did not intend to bestow two separate things, a body and a shadow, but the intention of the giver is to give a body, and that we receive also its shadow is a fact that accompanies the giving of the body),[4] so in the same way, if, with our mind lifted higher, we consider the gifts which are given to us of set purpose by God, we shall admit that the bodily gifts are the most fitting accompaniments of the great

---

[1] τῶν κατὰ μὲν τὰς ἀρχὰς φόβῳ διὰ τὴν νηπιότητα ἐξευγενιζομένων. Ἐξευγενίζω = εὐγενίζω (both of which verbs are exceedingly rare) means "to ennoble". Here it must be used as the equivalent of "to free" (of slaves). Origen seems to draw a contrast between the lack of assurance and timidity of the newly converted Christian, and his later experience of the full freedom of life in ἀγάπη.
[2] "Ask for the great things, and the small things shall be added unto you; ask for heavenly things and earthly things shall be added unto you" might well be said to be the main theme of the whole treatise. Cf. XIV. 1.
[3] I.e. if anybody argues that Scripture in recording the giving of material gifts in answer to petition seems to encourage prayer for such things.
[4] Note again Origen's use of striking illustration.

and heavenly spiritual gifts, and are given to each of the saints to profit withal (1 Cor. 12. 7), or according to the proportion of faith (Rom. 12. 6), or as the giver wills; and he wills wisely, even if we are unable to name a cause or reason worthy of the giver for each of the gifts.

This principle illustrated by the Old Testament stories of Hannah, Hezekiah, etc.

3. Thus the soul of Hannah,[1] changing from a sort of barrenness, bore fruit more than did her body which was pregnant with Samuel; and Hezekiah begat divine children of the mind rather than of the body, when they were begotten of his bodily seed;[2] and Esther and Mordecai and the people were delivered from spiritual plots much more than from Haman and those who conspired with him; (and Judith) cut off the might of the prince who desired to destroy her soul even more than the might of the famous Holophernes.[3] And who would not agree [4] that the spiritual blessing which comes upon all the saints, spoken of by Isaac to Jacob in the words, God give thee of the dew of heaven (Gen. 27. 28), was given to Ananias and his companions more abundantly than the physical dew which overcame the flame of Nebuchadnezzar (LXX, Dan. 3. 50)? And the lions whose mouths were stopped by the prophet Daniel were invisible lions, unable to achieve anything against his soul, rather than the perceptible

---

[1] Origen returns to his previous Old Testament examples of prayer (see XIII. 2), and shows how in each case the material benefit granted was but the "shadow" of some spiritual benefit.

[2] ἤπερ σώματος, ἐκ τοῦ σωματικοῦ σπέρματος αὐτῶν γεγεννημένων. Bentley reads ἤπερ τὸ ἐκ τοῦ σωματικοῦ σπέρματος αὐτῷ γεγεννημένον, "rather than that which was begotten by him of his bodily seed". Delarue has ἤπερ τῶν ἐκ τοῦ σωμ. σπερμ. αὐτοῦ γεγεννημένων, "rather than those who were begotten of his bodily seed". Anglus suggests ἤπερ τὰ ἐκ τοῦ σωμ. σπερμ. αὐτοῦ γεγεννημένα. Codex MS. is ambiguous.

[3] Codex MS. has καὶ τῶν συμπνεόντων ... τοῦ διαφθεῖραι τὴν ψυχὴν αὐτῆς θέλοντος ἄρχοντος τὴν δύναμιν διακεκόφει ἢ ἐκείνου τοῦ Ὀλοφέρνου. Koetschau suggests the insertion after συμπνεόντων of αὐτῷ· καὶ μᾶλλον Ἰουδήθ. Anglus suggests αὐτῷ· καὶ μᾶλλον after συμπνεόντων and Ἰουδίθ after ἄρχοντος. Delarue inserts καὶ Ἰουδὴθ μᾶλλον after συμπνεόντων.

[4] τίς δ'οὐκ ἂν ὁμολογῆσαι τῷ Ἀνανίᾳ. Codex MS. has τίς δ'οὐκ ἂν ὁμολογήσαιτο Ἀνανίᾳ. So Delarue.

lions to which all we who read this Scripture have taken it to refer.[1] And who has escaped from the belly of the monster [2] overpowered by Jesus our Saviour, the monster which swallows up every fugitive from God, in the same way as did Jonah when like one of the saints he became possessed of the Holy Spirit?

Earthly and small gifts may be compared to shadows which may or may not accompany a body

XVII.—1. Now it is not to be wondered at if all those [3] who in the same way receive, so to speak, bodies which produce such shadows are not given a shadow of the same kind, while to others in the same way a shadow is given.[4] For to those who study the problems of the sundial [5] and the relation of shadows to the body which gives light, this is clearly shown to happen according as the bodies vary; [6] for in some cases [7] the sundial indices have no shadow at all at certain times; in others the shadow is, so to speak, short, and in others the shadow is

---

[1] Origen does not here express disbelief in the literal truth of the story of Daniel in the lions' den. His point is that the allegorical interpretation of the story brings out the far more significant truth of the overcoming of spiritual enemies by God's grace given in answer to faithful prayer. The same is true of the other O.T. instances of prayer.

[2] Anglus notes that "the monster" is here used allegorically of the Devil.

[3] εἰ μὲν πᾶσιν. Codex MS., εἰ μὴ πᾶσιν. So Delarue. Anglus first suggests μέν.

[4] ἡ ὁμοία οὐ δίδοται σκιά, τισὶ δ'ὁμοίως δίδοται σκιά. Codex MS., ἢ ὅμοιον οὐ δίδοται σκιά, τισὶ δ'ὁμοίως δίδοται σκιά. Bentley, ἡ ὁμοία οὐ δίδοται σκιά, τισὶ δ'ὅλως οὐ δίδοται σκιά. Anglus, ὁμοίως οὐ δίδοται σκιά, τισὶ δ'ὁμοίως δίδοται σκιά. Delarue adopts Bentley's emendation. The sense is difficult. The omission of τισὶ δ'ὁμοίως δίδοται σκιά would give clearer meaning: "all those who ... receive ... bodies which produce such shadows are not given a shadow of the same kind". This is an evident fact and is sufficient to provide the illustration Origen here wants.

[5] τὰ γνωμονικὰ προβλήματα. The γνώμων is the index of the sundial. See Liddell and Scott *sub* γνώμων.

[6] κατὰ τὰ σώματα. Anglus suggests κατὰ τὰ κλίματα, because shadows vary according to the inclination (κλίμα) at which the sun's rays strike the object. This is the salient point rather than variation in the size, shape, and position of the bodies which cast the shadow. But as is often the case when ancient writers deal with scientific subjects, the whole passage is difficult to interpret.

[7] If κατὰ τὰ κλίματα is read above, we should translate "for at some inclinations".

longer, compared with others. Since the purpose of him who grants the aforementioned gifts bestows them [1] in certain ineffable and secret proportions as is meet for those who receive them, and as is meet for the times, it is no great wonder then if, when the gifts are given, sometimes no "shadows" at all accompany those who receive them, and sometimes there are "shadows" not of all, but only of a few,[2] and at other times the "shadows" are smaller in comparison with the rest, while larger "shadows" accompany others. So, then, just as neither the presence nor the absence of the shadow of bodies gives pleasure to or grieves one who seeks the sun's rays, since he has what he most wants whensoever, having the light shining upon him, he is either deprived of the shadow or possessed of a longer or shorter one;[3] so also if we possess spiritual things and are enlightened by God unto the complete possession of true goods we shall not meanly quibble about the worthless "shadow". For all material and bodily things, whatsoever they may be, have within them the principle of the fleeting and feeble shadow and can in no wise be compared with the saving and holy gifts of the God of all.[4] For what comparison is there between bodily riches and the riches which consist in all utterance and in all knowledge (1 Cor. 1. 5)? And who, unless he were mad, would compare health of flesh and bones with a healthy mind, a robust soul, and power of reasoning in accordance therewith? All of these things, if they are duly ordered by the Word of God, make bodily experience as it were an unimportant pin-prick, or whatever else we like to consider smaller than a pin-prick.

---

[1] χαριζομένης, the subject of which is προθέσεως. Delarue has χαριζομένου, following the Oxford edition.

[2] οὐ πάντων ἀλλὰ ὀλίγων. These words are probably to be referred to God's gifts. The point of Origen's elaborate analogy here is that just as we are given bodies, and the shadow thereof varies or even disappears at times, so God's spiritual gifts to us may or may not be accompanied by material gifts. Hence the likeliest interpretation of this phrase is that "sometimes there are shadows (i.e. material gifts), not of all but only of a few of God's spiritual gifts to us".

[3] ἐπὰν πεφωτισμένος ἤτοι ἐστερημένος ῃ (sic) τῆς σκιᾶς ἢ πλεῖον ἢ ἔλαττον ἔχῃ τῆς σκιᾶς. So codex MS. Bentley suggests πεφωτισμένος ᾖ, εἴτ' ἐστερημένος, etc., and is followed by Delarue. Anglus, πεφωτισμένος ᾖ, ἤτοι . . . Whatever reading is followed it is difficult to avoid the conclusion either that Origen's observation is at fault or that his language is obscure. A man who has no shadow is not in the path of the sun's rays.

[4] Origen's Platonism is very apparent in this passage.

The true worth of the heavenly and great gifts for which men should pray, compared with the shadowy nature of earthly things

2. And he who recognizes the beauty of the bride whom the Bridegroom who is the Word of God loves, that is to say, the soul which flourishes with a beauty surpassing that of heaven and earth, will be ashamed to dignify with the same word "beauty" the physical beauty of wife or child or husband. For the flesh is not capable of true beauty, being altogether a thing of shame.¹ For all flesh is as grass, and the glory thereof, which is seen in what is called the beauty of women and children, has been compared to a flower by the words of the prophet who says, All flesh is grass and all the goodliness thereof is as the flower of grass. The grass withereth and the flower falleth: but the word of the Lord abideth for ever (Isa. 40. 6–8). And who will still call true nobility that which commonly goes by the name among men, when once he has understood the nobility of the sons of God? And if the mind has beheld the kingdom of Christ which cannot be moved,² it will surely despise every earthly kingdom as not worth reckoning. And seeing clearly, in so far as the human mind is capable of so doing while remaining bound to the body, and in so far as it is possible, the angelic host, and the captains of the armies of the Lord among them, and archangels and thrones and dominations and principalities and supercelestial powers (Col. 1. 16), and realizing that it can attain to equal honour with them as a gift from the Father, it will surely, even though it be feebler than a shadow,³ despise as most

---

¹ αἶσχος. The word also connotes ugliness; "shameful ugliness" would be an accurate rendering.
² βασιλείαν δὲ Χριστοῦ ἀσάλευτον θεωρήσας. Codex MS., βασιλ. (*sic*) δὲ Χριστοῦ βασιλευόντων θεωρ. Oxf. ed., βασιλέα δὲ Χριστὸν βασιλευόντων θεωρ. (cf. 1 Tim. 6. 15). Anglus, βασιλείαν δὲ Χριστοῦ βασιλευόντος. Koetschau, like Delarue, adopts Bentley's emendation here.
³ κἂν σκιᾶς ἀδρανέστερος ᾖ, καὶ τούτων . . . καταφρονῶν. Codex MS., καὶ σκιᾶς ἀδρανέστερος ἢ καὶ τούτων. Anglus, καὶ σκιᾶς ἀδρανεστέρων τούτων.
Koetschau here accepts Delarue's emendation. But to speak of the "human mind" which is the subject of the sentence as "feebler than a shadow" seems to lack point in the context. Origen is speaking of the mind which perceives the difference between shadowy and insubstantial earthly honours, and the real and eternal goods. Anglus' emendation appears to give better sense although it is a more drastic alteration of the text of the codex: ". . . it will surely (for they are even feebler than a shadow) despise as most shadowy and not worth reckoning by comparison those things which are . . ."

shadowy and not worth reckoning by comparison those things which are a cause of wonder to the foolish, even if all these gifts have been bestowed upon it, and will let them go, rather than fail to attain to the true principalities and divine powers. We must pray then, pray for those things which are chiefly and truly great [1] and heavenly. And what is concerned with the shadows which accompany the antecedent gift of God we must leave to God, who knows what things we have need of for our mortal body's sake before we ask him (Matt. 6. 8).

The Lord's Prayer

XVIII.—1. Having sufficiently gone into the question of prayer in what we have already said, according to the grace given to us, as we have received the capacity, by God [2] through his Christ—and in the Holy Spirit too, I trust; and you who read this treatise will judge whether it is so—we shall now pass on to the next task; and our intention is to consider the prayer outlined [3] by the Lord and the power which fills it.

The versions of Matthew and Luke

2. First of all we must notice that Matthew and Luke are thought by many to have recorded the same prayer in outline to the end that we should thus pray. This is the reading of Matthew: Our Father, which art in heaven, Hallowed be thy name. Thy kingdom come. Thy will be done in earth, as it is in heaven. Give us this day our daily bread. And forgive us our debts, as we forgive our debtors. And lead us not into temptation, but deliver us from evil (Matt. 6. 9–13). And the words of Luke are as follows: Father, Hallowed be thy name. Thy kingdom come. Give us day by day our daily bread. And forgive us our sins; for we also forgive every one that is indebted to us. And lead us not into temptation (Luke 11. 2–4).

---

[1] προηγουμένως καὶ ἀληθῶς μεγάλων. Delarue, προηγουμένων, following codex MS.

[2] ὑπὸ θεοῦ. So codex MS. Bentley and Delarue read ἀπὸ θεοῦ, taking the phrase with "as we have received the capacity".

[3] ὑπογραφεῖσαν. The use of the verb ὑπογράφω suggests that Origen regards the Lord's Prayer as an outlined scheme of prayer.

These two versions probably given by our Lord on different occasions, but they have much in common

3. To those who suspect this to be the case [1] we must say that in the first place although the words have certain points of similarity to each other, nevertheless in other points they appear to differ, as we shall show when we examine them; and secondly, that it is not possible that the same prayer was spoken both on the mountain where "seeing the multitudes, he went up" on the occasion upon which, "when he was set, his disciples came unto him: and he opened his mouth, and taught them" (Matt. 5. 1, 2)—for this prayer is found recorded in Matthew in the passage which announces the beatitudes and the commandments which follow them—and that it was also spoken, "as he was praying in a certain place, when he ceased", to one of his disciples who asked to be taught to pray as John also taught his disciples (Luke 11. 1). For how can the same words have been spoken without any prior question and on a special occasion,[2] and also be proclaimed in response to the request of a disciple? But perhaps it might be argued that the two prayers have the same meaning, the same words being spoken on the one occasion in the course of a lengthy speech [3] and on the other in response to another of the disciples who

[1] I.e. that St Matthew and St Luke record the same prayer.

[2] ἀποτακτικῶς, an adverb derived from ἀποτάσσω, "to set apart". So codex MS. Bentley, followed by Delarue, reads ἀποτατικῶς, from ἀποτείνω, "to extend"; this would be rendered "in the course of a lengthy speech". Anglus' conjecture, ἐπιτακτικῶς, could be translated "by way of command" (i.e. a direct injunction by our Lord, rather than the response to a question). Ἀποτακτικῶς is a rare adverb. Liddell and Scott give no examples. The more frequent adjective ἀπότακτος means "set apart for a special use, specially appointed" (Liddell and Scott). The precise meaning of the adverb here is difficult to determine. But see the next note.

[3] ἐν ἀποτατικῷ λόγῳ. So codex MS. Oxford ed. has ἀποτακτικῷ. Anglus, ἐπιτακτικῷ.

I find it difficult to believe that Origen could have used two such rare words with so closely similar spellings in such a small space. I suggest ἀποτατικῶς should be read above, and ἀποτατικῷ here. Derived from ἀποτείνω, "to extend", the adverb and adjective would bear the meaning "in an extended manner"; and this would describe Matthew's account of the Lord's Prayer, which comes in the course of an extended discourse, as contrasted with Luke's account of it as given by our Lord in response to a particular question. This conjecture is supported by the consideration that ἀποτακτικῶς does not really suit the occasion which Matthew records, but actually would apply better to Luke's version, wherein the prayer is taught to the disciples by themselves "in a set-apart manner".

asked him, and who was probably not present when he spoke what Matthew records, or who did not remember what had been said so long before. But perhaps it is better to consider the prayers as being different, while having certain parts in common.[1] When we searched in Mark, in case a similar prayer with the same meaning was recorded there and escaped our notice, we found not a trace of it therein.

The Saviour's words about the importance of due preparation for prayer

XIX.—1. Now since, as we have said above,[2] it is first necessary for him who prays to be settled and composed in a certain way, and so to pray, let us consider the words spoken by our Saviour about it just before the prayer which is in Matthew; they are as follows: When ye pray, ye shall not be as the hypocrites are: for they love to pray standing in the synagogues and in the corners of the streets, that they may be seen of men. Verily I say unto you that they have their reward. But thou, when thou prayest, enter into thy closet, and when thou hast shut thy door, pray to thy Father which is in secret: and thy Father which seeth thee in secret shall reward thee. But when ye pray, use not vain repetitions, as the heathen do; for they think that they shall be heard for their much speaking. Be not ye therefore like unto them: for your Father knoweth what things ye have need of before ye ask him. After this manner therefore pray ye (Matt. 6. 5–9).

Humility in prayer. Ostentation already has its reward

2. Our Saviour, then, in many places seems to attack the love of glory as a deadly disease; and this he does here, forbidding the doing of hypocrites' work at the time of prayer; for it is hypocrites' work to

---

[1] Thus three possibilities are enumerated by Origen: (*a*) Matthew and Luke describe the same occasion. Against this are the different details which each records, Matthew "on the mountain" and without any prior question, Luke "in a certain place" and in answer to a question. (*b*) Matthew and Luke describe two occasions, but the prayer is the same in each case. (*c*) Matthew and Luke describe two occasions, and the prayers, too, are different, but with certain similarities. Origen himself seems to hold the third opinion, but in his subsequent commentary he does not bring out many points of difference between Matthew and Luke. That one or other document gives a mistaken account of the setting of the prayer is a modern critical suggestion which would not have occurred to Origen.

[2] See VIII, IX, X.

want to be conceited before men about one's piety or liberality.¹ We must bear in mind the words, How can ye believe, which receive honour of men, and seek not the honour that cometh from God only? (John 5. 44), and must despise every honour among men, even if it be thought to be the reward of nobility, and seek the proper and true glory which comes from him alone who glorifies one who is worthy of glory as befits himself beyond the worth of the man to whom the glory is given. Even the very thing, then, which might have been thought to be noble, and is considered praiseworthy, becomes sullied when we do it that we may have glory of men, or that we may be seen of men (Matt. 6. 2, 5). Wherefore no reward from God follows upon this for us. For every word of Jesus is true, and (if it is right to say so, being pressed) becomes more true whenever he speaks with his customary oath.² And he says concerning those who appear to do good to their neighbour for the glory of men, or concerning those who pray in the synagogues and in the corners of the streets that they may be seen of men, Verily I say unto you, They have their reward (Matt. 6. 5). For as the rich man in Luke had his good things in his mortal lifetime, and because he had them was no longer capable of receiving them after this present life, so likewise he who has his reward if he gives something to somebody or in his prayers,³ inasmuch as he has not sowed to the spirit but to the flesh, shall reap corruption and shall not reap life everlasting (Gal. 6. 8). And sow to the flesh he does who performs his alms in the synagogue and in the streets that he may have glory of men, with the sounding of a trumpet before him,⁴ or who loves to pray standing in the synagogues and in the corners of the streets, that being seen of men he may be thought pious and holy by those who have seen him.

---

¹ ἢ τῷ κοινωνικῷ. Codex MS., ἢ τῷ κοινωνεῖν, which Delarue keeps. Anglus has ἢ θεῷ κοινωνεῖν, or ἢ τῷ θεῷ κ., "one's communion with God".

² τοῦ συνήθους αὐτοῦ ὅρκου. So codex MS. Delarue, following Bentley, and Anglus prefer αὐτῷ. The "oath" is the word ἀμήν, translated in the English versions "verily".

³ εἴ τι δώσει τινὶ ἢ ἐν εὐχαῖς. So codex MS. Oxford ed., εἴτε δώσει. Bentley emends to εἴτ᾽ἐν δόσει ("either in giving or in his prayers"), which both Anglus and Delarue accept. But the text gives good sense; εἴ τι δώσει τινί refers to Matt. 6. 1, and ἐν εὐχαῖς refers to Matt. 6. 5.

⁴ μετὰ σαλπισμοῦ τοῦ ἔμπροσθεν ἑαυτοῦ. Bentley, followed by Delarue, has σαλπισμοῦ του . . .

Prayer in the corners of the streets (i.e. when still addicted to pleasures) to be avoided

3. Moreover every man who travels along the broad and spacious way which leads to destruction, the way which is not straight and direct, but all crooked and full of corners (for its straightness is for the most part broken up), stands therein not well, praying in the corners of the streets, through his love of pleasure [1] being not in one, but in many streets; wherein those who die like men (Psalm 82. 7) because they have fallen away from the divine nature are wont to glorify and count as happy those whom they consider to act impiously [2] in the streets. There are always many who seem when they pray to be lovers of pleasures more than lovers of God (2 Tim. 3. 4), drunken at their prayer in the middle of their drinking parties and at their carousals; these truly stand and pray "in the corners of the streets". For everyone who lives a life of pleasure loves the broad places and has declined from the narrow and confined way of Jesus Christ, which has neither the slightest turning nor any corner at all.[3]

[1] ἐν αὐτῇ ἕστηκεν οὐ καλῶς, ἐν ταῖς γωνίαις τῶν πλατειῶν προσευχόμενος, διὰ τῆς φιληδονίας . . . So Delarue in his text. But his notes indicate a liking for Bentley's emendation—ἐν αὐτῇ ἕστηκεν, οὐκ ἄλλως ἐν ταῖς γωνίαις τῶν πλατειῶν προσευχόμενος, ἢ διὰ τῆς φιλοδοξίας. But it is difficult to assume the corruption of φιλοδοξίας into φιληδονίας in a passage in which δόξα and cognate words, including φιλοδοξία, have been frequently used. See XIX. 2. Moreover φιληδονίας exactly suits the context. It is precisely "love of pleasure" which distracts a man's mind so that he may be said to be "in many streets". Anglus emends to ἐν ᾗ ἕστηκεν οὐ καλῶς ὁ ἐν ταῖς γωνίαις τῶν πλατειῶν προσευχόμενος διὰ τῆς φιληδονίας. . . .

Koetschau, while keeping the codex reading in his text, suggests in a footnote a combination of Bentley's and Anglus' readings: ἐν αὐτῇ ἕστηκεν οὐκ ἄλλως ἢ ὁ ἐν ταῖς γωνίαις τῶν πλατειῶν προσευχόμενος διὰ τῆς φιληδονίας . . ., "stands therein just like the man who prays in the corners of the streets . . .".

[2] ἀσεβεῖν. So codex MS. Bentley, Anglus, and Delarue read εὐσεβεῖν. It is difficult to understand how Koetschau makes good sense of ἀσεβεῖν. The meaning is surely that those who are alien from God glorify those whom *they* consider to act in a pious way (εὐσεβεῖν), though in reality these are acting impiously.

[3] This passage illustrates how in the hands of a master the allegorical method of interpreting Scripture can be of great homiletic value.

ON PRAYER

Prayer in church and not in the synagogue is required of the Christian

XX.—1. But if there is any difference between the Church and the Synagogue [1] [I mean the true Church not having spot, or wrinkle, or any such thing, but holy and without blemish (Eph. 5. 27), into which he that is born of a harlot enters not, nor the eunuch nor he that hath his privy member cut off (Deut. 23. 1), yea and no Egyptian or Edomite (except if sons are born to them they can be joined to the Church only after the third generation (Deut. 23. 7, 8)), nor the Moabite and Ammonite (unless the tenth generation be fulfilled and the age be brought to an end (Deut. 23. 3)); and I mean the synagogue which was built by the centurion,[2] who did this in the days before the coming of Jesus, when he had not yet received the witness that he had faith such as the Son of God had not found, no, not in Israel (Matt. 8. 10)]—if there is any difference, I say, he who takes delight indeed [3] in praying in the synagogues is not far from the corners of the streets. But the saint is not one of this kind; for he *loves* to pray rather than delights therein, and not in the synagogues but in the churches,[4] and not in the corners of the streets but in the straightness of the narrow and confined way, and moreover not that he may be seen of men, but that he may be beheld before the face of the Lord God. For he is a male who perceives the acceptable year of the Lord (Luke 4. 19) and keeps the commandment which says, Three times in a year shall all thy males appear before the Lord God (Deut. 16. 16).[5]

[1] At this point there begins a long parenthesis in which Origen explains what he means by "Church" and "Synagogue".

[2] ὑπὸ ἑκατοντάρχου. So Delarue. Codex MS. has ρχου. ρ is the symbol of 100. Oxford edition has χριστοῦ, doubtless owing to a confusion of ρχου with χρου.

Why Origen specifies the synagogue built by the centurion is not clear unless it is to emphasize that there is a difference between the Church and even a synagogue built by such an estimable man.

[3] ὁ φιλῶν δή ... This takes up the sentence after the long parenthesis. Codex MS. has δέ. Delarue would omit δέ or read δή.

[4] ἐν ἐκκλησίαις, i.e. Christian places of worship (whether private houses, or special buildings) are contrasted with Jewish places of worship.

[5] Origen is not here referring to any particular three occasions in the year when the Christian is bound to take part in public prayer, such as Christmas, Easter, and Whitsun. This is a later idea. He is here only asserting in a general way that the Christian worshipper fulfils the requirements of Deut. 16. 16.

Prayer in the secret chamber. The world of sense-perception must be excluded

2. But we must pay careful attention to the words "may be seen", since nothing that is merely seen is good,[1] inasmuch as it exists in opinion and not in reality,[2] and deceives the imagination [3] and does not give an exact and true representation. And just as the actors of dramas [4] in the theatres are not what they say they are, nor are really what they look like in the character mask which they put on, so also all those who counterfeit in outward appearance a display [5] of goodness are not righteous, but are acting the part of righteousness, and they act in a theatre of their own, namely the synagogues and the corners of the streets. But he who is not an actor, but has put aside all that is not his own,[6] practising to make himself pleasing [7] in a theatre greater by far than any of the theatres spoken of above, enters into his own chamber where his riches are stored up,[8] shutting away with himself his treasure of wisdom and knowledge (Col. 2. 3); he gives no assent at all to the outside world, nor gapes about at extraneous things, and, shutting up every door of the senses so that he may not be drawn away by them, and that the impression they receive [9] may not enter into his mind, he prays to the Father who neither leaves nor forsakes such

---

[1] καλόν. This common word is often difficult to translate. It has both a moral and an aesthetic meaning. To the Greek mind there is a quality of goodness in what is beautiful; and a quality of beauty in the morally good. In this context I consider "good" to be a better translation than "beautiful".

[2] Platonism is clear again here in this contrast between the phenomenal world which is the object of δόξα and the real world of forms which is the object of ἐπιστήμη.

[3] φαντασίαν. Below (see n. 5 below) the same word is used in the sense of "show" or "display". Here it refers to that faculty on which the φαντασία impresses itself.

[4] Note the lively simile.

[5] φαντασίαν. See n. 3.

[6] πᾶν τὸ ἀλλότριον, i.e. costume and disguise.

[7] ἑαυτὸν ἀρέσκειν εὐτρεπίζων. Codex MS., ἑαυτῷ, which gives intolerable sense. Anglus emends to ἑαυτόν. Delarue keeps ἑαυτῷ in his text, but in a comment on Anglus' note on the passage approves the latter's reading. He would therefore alter the Latin translation of Fleury from "*sibi ipsi placere studet*" to "*se ad placendum parat*".

[8] ἐπὶ τοῦ ἐναποτεθησαυρισμένου πλούτου. The preposition here has the same force as in its more frequent use with genitive of the person, "in the presence of".

[9] ἐκείνων ἡ φαντασία, i.e. the impressions of the senses.

a hidden sanctuary, but dwells therein, and his only-begotten Son with him. For I, he says, and the Father will come unto him, and make our abode with him (John 14. 23). It is clear that if, then, we thus pray, we shall make our intercession not only to the righteous God, but to a Father who does not abandon his sons, but is present in our hidden sanctuary, inspects it, and increases the treasure in our chamber, if only we will shut the door thereof.

Vain repetition (i.e. to ask for material things) is to be avoided

XXI.—1. But when we pray, let us not speak vain things,[1] but the things of God. We speak vain things when, without paying careful attention either to ourselves or the words we send up in prayer, we talk of corrupt deeds or words or thoughts which are mean and reprehensible, and alien from the purity of the Lord. He, however, who speaks vain things in his prayer is already in the condition of those who pray in the synagogues even to a more serious extent than those we have spoken of above [2] and is in a path of greater difficulty than the corners in the streets,[3] preserving not even a trace of the outward appearance of good. For according to the words of the Gospel it is the heathen alone who speak of vain things, for they do not even hold to an appearance of great or heavenly petitions, but every prayer they send up is for bodily and external things. Therefore he who asks inferior things of the Lord who dwells in the heavens and beyond the heights of the heavens is to be likened to the heathen who speaks vain things (Matt. 6. 7).

Prayer consisting in a multitude of vain repetitions lacks the unity which is necessary for attaining the things of God

2. Now the man who talks much speaks vain things, and the man who speaks vain things is one who talks much. For there is no unity in matter and bodies,[4] but everything which is thought to be one has

---

[1] βαττολογήσωμεν. This is the word which in Matt. 6. 7 is translated in the A.V. as "use vain repetitions".

[2] ἐν τῇ χείρονι τῶν προειρημένων ἡμῖν συναγωγικῇ ἐστι καταστάσει. Codex MS., ἐν τῷ χείρονι τῶν προειρημένων ἡμῖν συναγωγικῶν (συναγωγικός, Oxford). Delarue has ἐν τῇ χείρονι, which he refers to καταστάσει (as Koetschau) and συναγωγικῶν. "Spoken of above" refers to xx. 1.

[3] τε ⟨καὶ⟩ χαλεπωτέρᾳ τῶν ἐν ταῖς πλατείαις γωνιῶν ὁδῷ. Codex MS., τε χαλεπωτέρᾳ. Bentley and Delarue have ἤ or καὶ χαλεπωτέρᾳ.

[4] This is a common doctrine in ancient philosophy.

lost[1] its unity and is split and sundered and divided into many parts. For goodness is one, but many are the things of shame; truth is one, but there are many falsehoods; and true righteousness is one, but there are many habits of mind which simulate it; and the wisdom of God is one, but there are many kinds of wisdom of this world and of the princes of this world that come to nought (1 Cor. 2. 6); and the word of God is one, but there are many words which are alien from God. For this reason no man shall avoid sin in the multitude of words (Prov. 10. 19), and no man can be heard who thinks that he shall be heard for his much speaking (Matt. 6. 7). Wherefore, in our prayers we must not be like the heathen who speak vain things or indulge in much talking or whatever it is they do according to the likeness of a serpent (Psalm 58. 4). For the God of the saints, being a Father, knows what things his sons have need of, since such things are worthy of his fatherly knowledge. But if any man knows not God, he also knows not the things of God, and knows not what things he needs, for the things he thinks he needs are the wrong things.[2] But he who has contemplated the greater and more divine gifts of which he is in need, will obtain what he has contemplated, for they are known by God, and indeed have been known to the Father even before he asks. So, then, having said this about the preamble to the prayer in the Gospel according to Matthew, let us now consider what is taught by that prayer.

Commentary on the Lord's Prayer: "Our Father, which art in heaven". No Old Testament prayer so addressed

XXII.—1. Our Father, which art in heaven. It is worth a very careful search into the Old Testament, as men call it, to see if it is possible anywhere to find therein a prayer of anybody who addresses God as Father.[3] For up to the present, although I have searched according to my ability, I have not found one. I do not say that God

---

[1] ἀπολωλεκός. Codex MS., ἀπολελωκώς. Delarue, following Bentley, ἀπολωλεκότα (agreeing with πλείονα), "divided into many parts which have lost their unity".

[2] Cf. Clem. Alex., *Strom.* vi. 14. See p. 33 above. Origen's teaching here is very similar to Clement's doctrine of "Gnostic" prayer.

[3] Cf. *Comm. on John* xix. 1 (Brooke, Vol. II, p. 7): μυρίων γοῦν οὐσῶν εὐχῶν ἀναγεγραμμένων ἐν τοῖς ψαλμοῖς καὶ τοῖς προφήταις, ἀλλὰ καὶ τῷ νόμῳ, οὐ πάνυ τι εὕρομεν εὐξάμενόν τινα καὶ λέγοντα τῷ θεῷ· Πάτερ.

is not spoken of as a Father, or that those who are thought to believe in God are not called sons of God, but that I have not yet found in a prayer that boldness of speech (mentioned by the Saviour) in calling God "Father". But that God is spoken of as Father, and that those who have approached the word of God are spoken of as sons, can be seen in many passages as in Deuteronomy: God that begot thee thou hast forsaken, and hast forgotten God that nourished thee (Deut. 32. 18); and again: Has not he himself, thy father, bought thee, and made thee and established thee? (Deut. 32. 6); and again: Sons in whom is no faith (Deut. 32. 20); and in Isaiah: I have begotten and exalted sons, and they have rejected me (Isa. 1. 2); and in Malachi: A son shall honour his father, and a servant his master. And if I be a father, where is mine honour? and if I be a master, where is my fear? (Mal. 1. 6).

Those called "sons of God" in the Old Testament had not the full privileges of sonship

2. Moreover, even if God is called "Father", and those who are begotten by the word of faith in him are called sons, yet it is not possible to see among the ancients the full strength and stability of sonship. At all events the passages which we have adduced show that those who are called sons are under restraint; [1] for according to the Apostle, The heir, as long as he is a child, differeth nothing from a servant, though he be lord of all; but is under tutors and governors until the time appointed of the father (Gal. 4. 1, 2). But the fulness of time (Gal. 4. 4) has come with the advent of our Lord Jesus Christ, when those who are willing receive adoption, as Paul teaches in the words, For ye have not received a spirit of bondage to fear, but ye have received a Spirit of adoption, whereby we cry, Abba, Father (Rom. 8. 15). And in the Gospel according to John: But as many as received him, to them gave he power to become the sons of God, even to them that believe on his name (John 1. 12). And because of this spirit of adoption we learn in the Catholic Epistle of John, concerning those that are born of God, that: Whosoever is born of God doth not commit sin; for his seed remaineth in him: and he cannot sin, because he is born of God (1 John 3. 9).

[1] ὑπαιτίους; literally, "liable to be called to account".

The true sons of God are joint-heirs with Christ: they eschew sin and pursue good works

3. If, however, we understand what the words written by Luke mean: When ye pray, say Father (Luke 11. 2), we shall shrink from addressing this word to him unless we are true sons, lest, in addition to our other sins, we also become subject to the accusation of impiety. What I mean is this: Paul says in his First Epistle to the Corinthians, No man can say "Jesus is Lord" but by the Holy Spirit: and no man speaking by the Spirit of God says [1] "Jesus is anathema" [2] (1 Cor. 12. 3). Paul here calls the same Spirit Holy Spirit and Spirit of God. What is meant by the phrase "say 'Jesus is Lord' by the Holy Spirit" [3] is not altogether clear, since the expression is used by thousands of hypocrites, even more numerous unorthodox,[4] and sometimes also by demons, overcome by the power which is in the name. No one will venture to declare that any of these says "Jesus is Lord" by the Holy Spirit. Wherefore it cannot even be shown that they do say "Jesus is Lord",[5] since only they say the words "Jesus is Lord" of set purpose in serving the Word of God who also address no one beside him as "Lord" in anything that they do.[6] And if these are they who (truly) say "Jesus is Lord", it may be that every man who sins shouts aloud by his deeds "Jesus is anathema", since he anathematizes the divine Word through his offences. Therefore just as he who is of the one

---

[1] καὶ οὐδεὶς ἐν πνεύματι θεοῦ λαλῶν λέγει. Codex MS. has ἐν πν. ἁγίῳ, and so Delarue. Anglus corrects to ἐν πν. θεοῦ, remarking that the words immediately following make it clear that this is what Origen wrote.

[2] ἀνάθεμα Ἰησοῦς. Codex MS., Ἰησοῦν, which Delarue keeps.

[3] τί δὲ τὸ εἰπεῖν „ ἐν πνεύματι ἁγίῳ" κύριον Ἰησοῦν.

[4] Anglus conjectures that Origen here refers to Marcion, Basilides, and Valentinus, of whom he says: "They name the name of Jesus, but they do not possess Jesus, for they do not acknowledge him as Christ" (*Hom. in Jerem.* x).

[5] διόπερ οὐδ'ἂν δειχθεῖεν λέγειν κύριον Ἰησοῦν. Codex MS. and Delarue, δεχθεῖεν λέγειν. Koetschau follows E. Klostermann.

[6] μόνων τῶν ἀπὸ διαθέσεως λεγόντων ἐν τῷ δουλεύειν τῷ λόγῳ τοῦ θεοῦ καὶ μηδένα παρὰ τοῦτον ἐν τῷ ὅ τι ποτ'οὖν πράττειν ἀναγορευόντων κύριον τό· κύριος Ἰησοῦς.
Anglus suspects the omission of some words, e.g. καλῶς εἰπόντων, between κύριον and τό· κύριος Ἰησοῦς. This would make translation much easier.
Bentley and Delarue suggest κυρίως for κύριον. Koetschau points out, however, that κύριον is to be taken with ἀναγορευόντων and τό· κύριος Ἰησοῦς with λεγόντων. But the Greek is not easy.

sort says "Jesus is Lord" and he who is of the opposite disposition says "Jesus is anathema", so whosoever is born of God and doth not commit sin (1 John 3. 9), by sharing in God's seed which turns him away from every sin, says through his actions, "Our Father which art in heaven", the Spirit itself bearing witness with their spirit that they are children of God, and his heirs, and joint-heirs with Christ, since as they suffer with him they have good hope also that they will be glorified together with him (Rom. 8. 16, 17). But that such men may avoid saying "Our Father" half-heartedly, in addition to the works they do, the heart also, which is the fount and source of good works, believes unto righteousness, and in consonance with their good works the mouth makes confession unto salvation (Rom. 10. 10).

They are conformed to the only-begotten Word and from him take the "impression" of sonship

4. Therefore every work of theirs and word and thought, being conformed by the only-begotten Word unto himself, imitates the image of the invisible God and comes to be in the image of him who created (Col. 3. 10) and who maketh the sun to rise on the evil and on the good, and sendeth rain on the just and on the unjust [1] (Matt. 5. 45), so that there is in them the image of the heavenly (1 Cor. 15. 49), even of him who is the image of God. The saints, therefore, being an image of an image (that image being the Son), take the impression of sonship, not being conformed only to Christ's glorious body (Phil. 3. 21) but to him who is in the body.[2] They become conformed to him who is in a glorious body, being transformed by the renewing of the mind (Rom. 12. 2). And if it is they who are such, who in all things say "Our Father, which art in heaven", clearly he that committeth sin, as John says in the Catholic Epistle, is of the Devil; for the Devil sinneth from the beginning (1 John 3. 8). And as the seed of God [3] abiding in him who is begotten of God

---

[1] Those who are "conformed" to the Word of God must, therefore, also do good works. Origen does not rest content with the idea of a purely passive sonship.

[2] The point of this phrase is not very clear. Possibly Origen is again insisting that the saints, being conformed to one who is "in the body", the organ of work, must themselves continue to do good works.

[3] Origen here uses the thought, common in the Scriptures, of a father's seed being in his son. The idea is here used metaphorically. Origen does not believe in the seminal identity of man with God. See, for instance, xxiii. 5.

causes him who is conformed to the only-begotten Word to be unable to sin, so the seed of the Devil is in everyone that committeth sin, and as long as it remains in the soul it does not permit him who possesses it to be capable of doing anything aright. But since for this purpose the Son of God was manifested, that he might destroy the works of the Devil (1 John 3. 8), by the advent of the Word of God into our soul it is possible that, the works of the Devil being destroyed, the evil seed that is within us may be made to vanish, and we may become sons of God.

The whole of life to be lived in the spirit of sonship

5. Let us not, then, consider that we are taught to say these words at some fixed time of prayer. On the contrary, if we understand what we have previously discussed on the subject of "Pray without ceasing",[1] let our whole life as we pray without ceasing say "Our Father, which art in heaven", having its citizenship [2] in no wise upon the earth but in every way in the heavens (Phil. 3, 20) which are God's thrones, inasmuch as the kingdom of God is set up in all those who bear the image of the heavenly and for that reason have become heavenly.[3]

The words "in heaven" do not imply that the Father is locally circumscribed

XXIII.—1. But when [4] it is said that the Father of the saints is in heaven, we must not understand him to be circumscribed and to dwell in heaven in bodily fashion; for God contained in this way will then be found less than heaven if heaven contains him. We must believe that all things are contained and held together by him, by the ineffable power of his Godhead. And in general we must interpret those passages which, in so far as they are taken literally, are thought by the more simple to assert that God is in a place, in conformity with large and spiritual ideas about God. Such passages are the following in the

---

[1] εἰς τὸ "ἀδιαλείπτως" προσεύχεσθαι. So codex MS. Delarue reads προσεύχεσθε. (The reference is to XII. 2.)

[2] πολίτευμα. A.V., "conversation".

[3] A fine passage. Cf. XII. 2. Cf. also Clem. Alex., *Strom*. VII. 7. See p. 29 above.

[4] Ἐπὰν ⟨δὲ⟩. Koetschau with Anglus adds the δέ, which is not in codex MS.

Gospel according to John: [1] Now before the feast of the passover, when Jesus knew that his hour was come that he should depart out of this world unto the Father, having loved his own which were in the world, he loved them unto the end (John 13. 1); and a little later, Knowing that the Father had given all things into his hands, and that he was come from God, and went to God (John 13. 3); and later, Ye have heard that I said unto you, I go away, and come again unto you. If ye loved me, ye would rejoice, because I go unto the Father (John 14. 28); and again, somewhat later, But now I go my way to him that sent me, and none of you asketh me, Whither goest thou? (John 16. 5). For if these passages are to be understood as referring to place, clearly so must also the following: Jesus answered and said unto them, If a man love me, he will keep my word: and my Father will love him, and we will come unto him, and make our abode with him [2] (John 14. 23).

Passages which speak of the "coming" and "going" of the Word of God likewise not to be understood locally

2. But this last at any rate does not occur because a change of place is understood on the part of the Father and the Son in relation to him who loves the word of Jesus; nor, then, are the other passages to be interpreted as referring to place. But the Word of God, coming down to us, and while he is still among men humbling himself as touching his own proper dignity, is said to pass from this world to the Father, that we may also contemplate him there in his perfection, returning to his own proper fulness after the emptying with which he emptied himself among us (cf. Phil. 2. 8; Col. 1. 19), where we also with him as our guide shall be fulfilled and delivered from all emptiness.[3] Let the Word of God then leave the world and depart unto him that sent him and go unto the Father. And let us seek to understand in a mystical sense the words at the end of the Gospel according to John, Touch me not; for I am not yet ascended to my Father (John 20. 17), thinking of the ascension of the Son to the Father in a manner

---

[1] All the passages quoted refer to "place", speaking of Jesus as "going to" God.

[2] Origen's point is that this passage is not understood to refer to spatial movement. Nor, then, ought the former passages to be so taken.

[3] There is a play here on the words πληρῶ and κενῶ.

more befitting his divinity, with sanctified perspicuity, as an ascension of the mind rather than the body.[1]

Old Testament passages describing God as in a place are not to be taken literally

3. I consider that it was necessary to go into these points [2] in connection with the words "Our Father, which art in heaven", for the purpose of removing the low conception of God of those who think that he is in heaven as in a place, and of preventing anyone saying (since it is a consequence of this doctrine that God is a body) that God is in a corporeal place,[3] for upon this follow most impious doctrines, namely the belief that he is divisible, material, and corruptible; for every body is divisible, material, and corruptible.[4] Or let them tell us, not on the basis of unsubstantiated feelings,[5] but clearly asserting that they comprehend, how it is possible (in that case) for him to be of a nature other than material.[6] And since many words written before the advent of Christ in the body seem to assert that God is in a corporeal place I do not think it irrelevant to set out a few of them also in order to remove all hesitation from those who, because of their ignorance, confine the God who is over all things, as much as it is in their power to do so, in a small and circumscribed place. First of all in Genesis it says, Adam and Eve heard the voice of the Lord

---

[1] Again it must be insisted that this does not imply that Origen disbelieved in the literal truth of the Ascension. The fact that a passage of Scripture has a mystical interpretation does not necessarily mean that its literal sense is untrue.

[2] ταῦτα ἡγοῦμαι συνεξητακέναι. Anglus suggests ἀναγκαίως after ἡγοῦμαι, "not without probability", says Koetschau. Συνεξητακέναι is from συνεξετάζω. Origen here brings his argument back to the original question about the meaning of the words "in heaven" in the clause under consideration.

[3] καὶ μὴ ἐάν τινα ἐν σωματικῷ τόπῳ εἶναι τὸν θεὸν (ἐπεὶ τούτῳ ἀκόλουθόν ἐστι καὶ σῶμα αὐτὸν εἶναι) λέγειν. Delarue suggests οἴεσθαι after τινα. Anglus suggests φάσκειν after τόπῳ. But, as Koetschau remarks, λέγειν is to be taken with ἐν σωματικῷ τόπῳ εἶναι τὸν θεόν. His insertion of brackets makes this clear.

[4] See Aristotle, *Org.* I. I. Cf. also XXI. 2 of this treatise.

[5] μὴ κενοπαθοῦντες.

[6] πῶς οἷόν τε ἐστὶν ἑτέρας ⟨εἶναι⟩ φύσεως παρὰ τὴν ὑλικήν. Koetschau inserts εἶναι with Anglus. Delarue follows Bentley in reading πῶς οἷόν τε εἶναι. The words "in that case" (i.e. if God is in a corporeal place) seem to be demanded in English translation.

God walking in the garden in the cool of the day; and Adam and his wife hid themselves from the presence of the Lord God amongst the trees of the garden (Gen. 3. 8). We shall ask those who do not wish to enter into the treasures of Scripture, and do not even knock at all at its door,[1] whether they can prove that the Lord God who fills heaven and earth, and who uses the heaven as his throne, as they suppose in a bodily way, and the earth as the footstool of his feet (Matt. 5. 34, 35; Isa. 61. 1), is contained by a place so small in comparison with the whole heaven and earth, that the garden, which they imagine to be a corporeal one, is not filled by God, but is so much greater in size than he is that it even contains him as he walks, and the sound of his footsteps is heard. According to their interpretation it is even more absurd that Adam and Eve, fearing God because of their transgression, hid themselves from the presence of God amongst the trees of the garden. For it is not said that they wanted to hide themselves, but that they actually did hide themselves. And how is it, according to their view, that God asks Adam, saying "Where art thou?"[2] (Gen. 3. 9)?

To say that God is in heaven means that he is where Christ, the saints, and the angels are

4. We have discussed these points at greater length in our examination of the contents of the Book of Genesis.[3] But here, that we may not pass over so important a question altogether in silence, it will be sufficient to recall the words spoken by God in Deuteronomy, I will dwell in them and walk in them.[4] For his walking "in the saints" is very like his walking in the garden,[5] since every sinner tries to hide

---

[1] I.e. those who get no further than the literal interpretation.
[2] With this whole passage compare *De Princ.* IV. iii. 1: "And further, when God is said to 'walk in the paradise in the evening' and Adam to hide himself behind a tree, I do not think anyone will doubt that these statements are made by scripture in a figurative manner, in order that through them certain mystical truths may be indicated" (Butterworth's translation).
[3] This is the passage which has some bearing on the date of Περὶ Εὐχῆς. See page 72.
[4] These words are not found in Deuteronomy. They are found in 2 Corinthians 6. 16, where St Paul may be referring to Exodus 29. 45, and Leviticus 26. 12. Deuteronomy 23. 14 bears the closest resemblance in that book to these words.
[5] ὁποῖος γὰρ αὐτοῦ ὁ περίπατος ἐν τοῖς ἁγίοις, τοιοῦτός τις καὶ ὁ ἐν τῷ παραδείσῳ. Delarue omits ὁ after καί.

himself from God and to escape from his sight and shuns speech [1] with him. For thus Cain also went out from the presence of God, and dwelt in the land of Nod over against Eden (Gen. 4. 16). Just as therefore he dwells in the saints, so also he dwells in heaven, whether heaven be every saint who also bears the image of the heavenly (1 Cor. 15. 49) or Christ, in whom all the saved are lights and stars of heaven; or else he dwells there because of the saints who are in heaven, as it has been said,[2] I have lifted up mine eyes unto thee who dost dwell in heaven (Psalm 123. 1). And the verse in Ecclesiastes, Be not hasty to utter a word before God: for God is in heaven above, and thou upon earth below (Eccles. 5. 2), serves to indicate the distance between those who are in the body of our low estate (Phil. 3. 21) and him who is with the angels who are exalted by the help even of the Word and with the holy powers, or with Christ himself.[3] For it is not illogical that he should be the true throne of the Father, called "heaven" by a further piece of allegory, while his Church is called "earth" and is the footstool of his feet (Matt. 5. 34, 35).

The words "Our Father, which art in heaven" assert the distinction of God's essence from all created things

5. Now we have cited these few quotations from the Old Testament which are thought to set God in a place, in order to persuade the reader by every means, according to the ability given to us, to take

---

[1] παρρησίας. Bentley and Delarue read παρουσίας.

[2] ἢ καὶ διὰ τοὺς ἐν οὐρανῷ ἁγίους κατοικεῖ ⟨ἐκεῖ κατὰ⟩ τὸ εἰρημένον. Codex MS., ἢ καὶ διὰ τοὺς ἐν οὐρ. ἁγίους κατοικεῖ τὸ εἰρημένον. Bentley conjectures διὰ τὸ ἐν οὐρανῷ ἁγίους κατοικεῖν. τὸ δ'εἰρημένον . . . Delarue favours this. Koetschau follows Anglus in inserting ἐκεῖ κατά. Anglus considers that the words ἐκεῖ κατά may have been lost by haplography due to their similarity to κατοικεῖ.

[3] It is this "distance" between God and man which the Gnostics sought to bridge with their extravagant systems of semi-divine beings whose work was to free, by fantastically conceived methods, the spiritual seeds or divine sparks which were thought to be hidden in the material bodies of men. It is frequently remarked that Origen has much in common with the Gnostics. There is truth in this, for they addressed themselves to the same problems and were conditioned by much the same intellectual preconceptions. But the differences between Origen's teaching and Gnosticism are great. This section is an indication of Origen's essential orthodoxy. The Mediator is the one Word of God "in whom all the saved are lights and stars of heaven". The angels and other "holy powers" have their part to play, but it is not the part of saviours.

XXIV. 1 ON PRAYER

divine Scripture in a more lofty and spiritual sense whenever it seems to teach that God is in a place.[1] It was appropriate to examine these quotations in connection with the phrase "Our Father, which art in heaven", since this phrase as it were distinguishes [2] the essence of God from all begotten things. For in those things whose nature it does not share,[3] there indwells a certain glory of God and power from him, and, so to speak, an effluence of his divinity.

"Hallowed be thy name" : this seems to suggest that the Father's name is not already hallowed

XXIV.—1. "Hallowed be thy name." The man who uses this petition [4] is sometimes asserting that what he prays for has not yet come to pass; and sometimes, having obtained it, he is asserting that it endures not of itself and asks that it be preserved, since it is clear, so far as the actual words are concerned,[5] that according at least to

---

[1] When a passage of Scripture, taken in its literal sense, involved some impossibility, this, for Origen, was a hint to look deeper for some mystical meaning. See note 1 on p. 85.

[2] οἱονεὶ ἀφιστάντι. Codex MS., ἀφιστάς, and so Delarue. Koetschau follows Anglus, who points out that there is nothing to which ἀφιστάς may be referred. He therefore suggests the dative, agreeing with τῷ „ πάτερ ἡμῶν " etc., thus making Origen suggest that the phrase "Our Father etc." signifies the separation of God's essence from his creatures, since it is a reminder that God is in heaven and we on earth.

[3] οἷς γὰρ οὐ κοινωνεῖ, scil. ἡ οὐσία τοῦ θεοῦ, suggests Koetschau.

[4] Some such personal subjects for παρίστησι must be supplied in English. See next note.

[5] ὅτε μὲν παρίστησι τὸ μὴ γεγονέναι πω, περὶ οὗ εὔχεται, ὁτὲ δὲ τούτου τυχὼν τὸ μὴ παραμένειν αὐτὸ καὶ τηρεῖσθαι ἀξιοῖ, φανερὸν ὅσον ἐπὶ τῇ λέξει ἐνταῦθα. A difficult sentence. Codex MS. has ὅτε μὲν ... ὅτε δὲ τούτου τυχὸν τὸ μὴ παραμένον αὐτό ... Bentley suggests εἴτε μὲν ... εἴτε δὲ ... and is followed by Delarue. This makes translation easier : "whether it asserts ... or whether having obtained this it asks that that which endures not of itself may also be preserved, it is clear ...".

Anglus would rewrite ὁ εὐχόμενος ὅτε μὲν ... ὅτε δὲ, τούτου τυχών, τὸ μὴ παραμένον αὐτῷ ... ἀξιοῖ · φανερὸν δὲ ...

In Koetschau's text παρίστησι must be understood with τὸ μὴ παραμένειν as well as with τὸ μὴ γεγονέναι. His retention of Anglus' τυχών is awkward; for the subject of παρίστησι is the phrase "Hallowed be thy name", regarded as itself praying. So in English we could say "this prayer, or this phrase, asserts ... asks".

The φανερόν clause must be regarded (in Koetschau's text) as a kind of accusative absolute.

Matthew and Luke we are bidden to say "Hallowed be thy name" as though the name of the Father were not yet hallowed. And how, it might be said, does a man ask for God's name to be hallowed as not being already hallowed?[1] Let us consider what is meant by the "name" of the Father, and the words "be hallowed".

What is meant by the "name" of God? "Name" strictly denotes essence. We cannot grasp God's essence completely, and can only say that it is holiness

2. Now a name is a summary designation, indicative of the proper quality of him who is named. For example, there is a proper quality of Paul the Apostle, a quality of the soul in accordance with which his soul is of such and such a kind, a quality of the mind, in accordance with which it contemplates [2] things of such and such a sort, and a quality of his body, in accordance with which it is of such and such a sort. Now what is peculiar in these qualities and not shared by anyone else (for there is no other man in the whole of nature who is exactly like Paul) is expressed by the name "Paul". But in the case of men, when their proper qualities as it were become changed, their names also are rightly changed according to Scripture. For when the quality of Abram was changed he was called "Abraham", and when that of Simon was changed he was named "Peter", and when that of Saul who persecuted Jesus, he was designated "Paul". But in the case of God, who himself is invariable and ever immutable by nature, the name which is as it were given to him is ever one, the "He who is" spoken of in Exodus (Ex. 3. 14), or any other name which conveys the same meaning. Since, therefore, when we think of anything to do with him, we all have some conception of God, but we do not all understand his essence (for there are few and, if I may say so, fewer than few who grasp his holiness [3] which is in all things), we are very properly taught that our conception of God should be that he is holy, that we may see his holiness as one who creates,[4] is provident, judges,

---

[1] Origen offers no answer to this question here, but returns to it in xxv. 2. Koetschau suggests that some connecting word has fallen out after ἡγιασμένον, e.g. καὶ πρῶτον τί . . .

[2] θεωρητικός (scil. νοῦς). So Bentley, Anglus, and Delarue. Codex MS., θεωρητική.

[3] ἁγιότητα. So Codex MS. Bentley and Delarue read ἰδιότητα.

[4] τὴν ἐν ἡμῖν ἔννοιαν περὶ θεοῦ ἁγίαν γενέσθαι, ἵν'ἴδωμεν αὐτοῦ τὴν ἁγιότητα κτίζοντος . . . Bentley, followed by Delarue, reads ὑγιῆ γενέσθαι, ἂν ἴδωμεν αὐτοῦ τὴν ἰδιότητα. Koetschau describes this as too violent and

elects, abandons, welcomes and rejects, deems each man worthy of honour and punishes each according to his deserts.

Certain Old Testament references to God's name are in fact references to God's holiness

3. For in these and in similar ways is expressed, so to speak, the proper quality of God which I consider is called the "name" of God in the Scriptures: in Exodus, Thou shalt not take the name of the Lord thy God in vain (Ex. 20. 7), and in Deuteronomy, Let my utterance be waited for as the rain, my speech descend as the dew, as the shower upon the tender herb, and as snow upon the grass; because I have called upon the name of the Lord (Deut. 32. 2, 3), and in the Psalms, They shall remember thy name in all generations [1] (Psalm 45. 17). For he who fits his conception of God to things which are unsuitable does take the name of the Lord his God in vain; and he who can utter words like rain which works together with those who hear for the fruitfulness of their [2] souls, and offers words of consolation like dew, and by the vehemence [3] of his words of edification provides a shower most beneficial or snow most efficacious to his hearers, is able to do these things because of this name. Considering these things, and his own need of God that maketh perfect, he calls to his aid him who is the true supplier of these aforementioned things. And everyone that clearly understands the things of God remembers them rather than learns them, even though he seems to be taught by someone else or thinks that he himself discovers the mysteries of religion.[4]

---

unnecessary. But the Greek of the codex MS. has to be wrested to give good sense. Τὴν ... γενέσθαι strictly means "that our conception of God is holy", which is not what the sense demands. Origen seems to be suggesting that the best "omnibus" conception of God is that he is holy, and that his holiness is manifest in all his manifold activities.

[1] Having quoted three O.T. references to the name of God, Origen proceeds to give his exegesis of them. These particular quotations do not seem to give much weight to the point Origen is making in this section, namely that the "name" of God denotes his essence, which may be best understood as holiness. Sometimes Origen gives the impression that he kept a stock book of scriptural quotations on various subjects from which, as need arose, he would make a choice to illustrate his points, but without always ensuring that his choice was apt.

[2] αὐτῶν. Codex MS. and Delarue, ἑαυτῶν.

[3] ῥύμῃ. So codex MS. Bentley and Delarue, ῥώμῃ.

[4] This sentence gives Origen's exegesis of Psalm 45. 17 quoted above, "They shall remember etc.". Origen here subscribes to the Platonic doctrine

To exalt God's name is for a man to overcome sin and rise to the knowledge of God's essence

4. And just as he who prays must consider what is said here, and ask that the name of God may be hallowed, so it is said in the Psalms, Let us exalt his name together (Psalm 34. 3), the prophet bidding us [1] with all harmony in the same mind and with the same accord to attain to the true and lofty knowledge of God's essence.[2] For this is to "exalt [3] the name of God together", when a man partakes [4] of an effluence of divinity by being lifted up by God, and by having overcome his enemies, who are thus unable to rejoice at his fall, and exalts the very power of God of which he has obtained a share. This is declared in the twenty-ninth Psalm (A.V. thirtieth) in the words, I will extol thee, O Lord: for thou hast lifted me up, and hast not made my foes to rejoice over me (Psalm 30. 1). And a man extols God by dedicating a dwelling-place for him in himself, for the title of the Psalm says, A Psalm and Song at the dedication of the house of David.

The use of the imperative in "Hallowed be thy name" is equivalent to the optative. (But Tatian is wrong in assuming this is so with other imperatives)

5. Again with regard to the words "Hallowed be [5] thy name", and what is said subsequently in the imperative mood, it must be said that

of Recollection, that all human knowledge is a recalling of what has been already learned in a previous existence. Bigg (*Christian Platonists of Alexandria*, 1913 ed., p. 242, n. 2) remarks that this is the only passage in which Origen hints at the doctrine of Recollection. The doctrine of the pre-existence of the soul was one of Origen's speculations which made him unacceptable to fifth-century champions of orthodoxy.

[1] προστάσσοντος τοῦ προφήτου. Codex MS., πατρός, which Delarue keeps. Anglus, Δαυΐδ.

[2] Here, too, we see the wide difference between Origen's teaching and Gnosticism, in spite of superficial similarities. The knowledge (gnosis) which frees man is knowledge of God's essence, not the knowledge of secretly imparted pass-words. And the gnosis of God's essence, Origen insists, involves a knowledge of God's holiness.

[3] τὸ ὑψοῦν. So Anglus. Codex MS., τὸ ὑψοῦντος. Bentley and Delarue, τὸ ὑψοῦν or τοῦ ὑψοῦντος.

[4] τοῦτο γάρ ἐστι τὸ ὑψοῦν ... ⟨ὅτε⟩ μεταλαβών τις ... ὑψοῖ αὐτὴν τὴν δύναμιν. Bentley and Delarue also add ὅτε. Anglus reads μεταλαβὼν δέ τις, and he alters ὑψοῖ into ὑψώσει, thus making τοῦτο refer to the previous sentence.

[5] In the Greek this is in the imperative mood.

the translators frequently used imperatives instead of optatives; as in the Psalms, Let the lying lips be put to silence;[1] which speak iniquity against the righteous (Psalm 31. 18), instead of, "Would that they might be";[2] and, Let the money-lender search out[3] all that he hath; let there be[4] none to help him, in the one hundred and eighth Psalm, concerning Judas (A.V., Psalm 109. 11, 12). For the whole psalm is a prayer about Judas, that such things as these may happen to him. Tatian,[5] not understanding that the words "Let there be"[6] do not on all occasions signify the optative, but sometimes also the imperative, has taken in a most impious way the passage about God saying "Let there be light"[7] (Gen. 1. 3), as though he prayed rather than commanded that there should be light, "because", as he says with blasphemous intent, "God was in darkness". We must ask him how he will take the following: Let the earth bring forth grass (Gen. 1. 11), and, Let the waters under the heaven[8] be gathered together (Gen. 1. 9), and, Let the waters bring forth the living creatures which creep[9] (Gen. 1. 20), and, Let the earth bring forth[10] the living creature (Gen. 1. 24). Is it, then, in order that he may stand upon a firm place that God prays that the waters under the heaven be gathered together unto one place, or is it in order to have a share in those things which spring forth from the earth that he prays, Let the earth bring forth? And what need, like our need for light, has he for creatures of the sea and of the air and of the dry land, that he should pray for them? But if he will admit that it is absurd that God should pray for these things,

[1] ἄλαλα γενηθήτω, imperative.
[2] γενηθείη, optative. Oxford ed. and Delarue, γενηθεῖεν.
[3] ἐξερευνησάτω, imperative.
[4] ὑπαρξάτω, imperative.
[5] Tatian was the second-century compiler of the Diatessaron, a harmony of the Gospels, and the author of an apology addressed "To the Greeks". He was born in the Roman province of Syria, but was probably of Greek parentage. He was possibly taught by Justin Martyr at Rome. Irenaeus says that he fell into heresy after Justin's death.
[6] γενηθήτω, imperative.
[7] γενηθήτω φῶς, imperative. Tatian (according to Origen), thinking that the imperative γενηθήτω always signified a wish or prayer, interpreted "Let there be light" as a wish or prayer on God's part instead of a command.
[8] τὸ ὕδωρ ⟨τὸ⟩ ὑποκάτω τοῦ οὐρανοῦ. Anglus, followed by Koetschau, inserts the τό, as in LXX.
[9] ἑρπετὰ ψυχῶν ζωσῶν. So LXX. Ψυχῶν ζωσῶν is to be taken as a partitive genitive, "the creeping things of (or among) living souls".
[10] This and the preceding three verbs are all imperatives.

expressed as they are in the imperative, surely the same must be said about "Let there be light" as being spoken not as a prayer but as an imperative. I thought it necessary, since the prayer is expressed in the imperative, to mention Tatian's interpretation for the sake of those who have been misled and accepted his impious teaching, against whom we have tried conclusions before.[1]

"Thy kingdom come" is a prayer that God may rule in the heart

XXV.—1. Thy kingdom come. If the kingdom of God, according to the word of our Lord and Saviour, cometh not with observation; neither shall they say, Lo here! or, lo there! but, the kingdom of God is within us (Luke 17. 20, 21) (for the word is very nigh, in our mouth and in our heart) (Deut. 30. 14), it is clear that he who prays that the kingdom of God may come, is (as is meet) praying for the springing up of the kingdom of God which is in him, and that it may bear fruit and be brought to perfection; for every saint has God to reign over him, and obeys the spiritual laws of God who dwells in him as in a well-governed city: the Father is present with him, and Christ reigns with the Father in the soul which has been perfected, in accordance with the words I was mentioning a little earlier, We will come unto him, and make our abode with him (John 14. 23) (and I think that the kingdom of God means the mind's state of blessedness and the ordering of wise thoughts, while the kingdom of Christ means those words which proceed unto salvation for those who hear them, and the deeds of righteousness [2] and of the other virtues which are brought to perfection; for the Son of God is Word and Righteousness). But on the other hand [3] every sinner has the prince of this world to lord it over him, for every sinner is claimed for its own by the present evil world, since he does not surrender himself

---

[1] Anglus notes that Origen attacks Tatian's interpretation of "Let there be light" in *Contra Celsum* vi. 672: παρακούσας δ'οἶμαι [Κέλσος] μοχθηρᾶς αἱρέσεώς τινος, καὶ κακῶς διηγησαμένης τό, γενηθήτω φῶς, ὡς εὐκτικῶς ὑπὸ τοῦ Δημιουργοῦ εἰρημένον. Tatian's heresy is evidently a *bête noire* to Origen. The reference to him is clearly dragged in in the present passage.

[2] Notice that good works have a prominent place in Origen's conception of the perfection of the soul. A purely intellectual or purely emotional mysticism does not satisfy him.

[3] παντὸς ⟨δὲ⟩ ἁμαρτωλοῦ. Bentley, Anglus, and Delarue all insert the δέ, thus making the clause balance παντὸς μὲν ἁγίου prior to the long parenthesis.

XXV. 2　　　　　　ON PRAYER　　　　　　159

to him who gave himself for us sinners, that he might deliver us from this present evil world, and might deliver us according to the will of God and our Father (Gal. 1. 4), as is said in the Epistle to the Galatians. But he who has the prince of this world lording it over him by reason of voluntary sin, also has sin reigning over him. Therefore we are commanded by Paul no longer to be subject to the sin which wills to reign over us, and it is in these words that we are bidden, Let not sin therefore reign in our mortal body, that we should obey the lusts thereof (Rom. 6. 12).

It is appropriate to go on praying even when God's kingdom has come to a man, for its perfection is not possible until God is all in all

2. But someone will say with regard to both "Hallowed be thy name" and "Thy kingdom come", that if he who prays prays in order to be heard, and if his prayer is sometimes heard, then clearly the name of God will sometimes be hallowed for him, as has been said before, and the kingdom of God will come to him. And if this shall be the case with him, how, then, is it appropriate that he should go on praying for things which are already present, as though they were not, saying, "Hallowed be thy name, thy kingdom come"? And if this is so, it will be appropriate on occasion not to say "Hallowed be thy name, thy kingdom come". To this argument we must say that just as he who prays to attain the word of knowledge and the word of wisdom (1 Cor. 12. 8) will appropriately continue to pray for them, since, when his prayer is heard, he will continue to receive more and more ideas of wisdom and knowledge [1]—although he knows only in part how many such ideas he is able to take in at the moment, while that which is perfect and does away with that which is in part shall be revealed [2] when his mind comes in contact with spiritual things

---

[1] Origen means that the more a man knows of God the more he knows there is to know. When, therefore, it is true to any extent that God's name is hallowed and his kingdom established in a man, that man will be quick to realize that the perfection of having God's name hallowed and God's kingdom established in him still lies in front. He will continue, therefore, to pray "Hallowed be thy name, thy kingdom come".

[2] γινώσκων μὲν ὅσα ποτ' ἂν χωρῆσαι ἐπὶ τοῦ παρόντος δυνηθῇ, τοῦ <δὲ> τελείου καὶ καταργοῦντος τὸ ἐκ μέρους τότε φανερωθησομένου . . . Codex MS., φανερωθησόμενον. Koetschau adds δέ to balance the preceding γινώσκων μέν. Bentley and Delarue read τοῦ τελείου, ὡς καὶ καταργοῦντος τὸ ἐκ μέρους, τότε φανερωθησομένου, "that which is perfect being revealed as also doing away with that which is in part when . . .".

"face to face", without sense experience (1 Cor. 13. 9, 10)—so also that which is perfect in respect of God's name being hallowed in each of us, and in respect of the coming of his kingdom, is impossible unless also that which is perfect is come (1 Cor. 13. 10) in respect of knowledge and wisdom, and perhaps also of the other virtues. And we journey towards perfection if, reaching forth unto those things which are before, we forget those things which are behind (Phil. 3. 13). So, then, consummation will come to the kingdom of God which is in us for those of us who strive forward unceasingly, when that which is spoken by the Apostle is fulfilled, namely that Christ, all his enemies being subdued to him, shall deliver up the kingdom to God, even the Father, that God may be all in all [1] (1 Cor. 15. 24, 28). Wherefore, praying without ceasing with that mental disposition which is inspired by the Word, let us say to our Father which is in heaven, "Hallowed be thy name, thy kingdom come".

God's kingdom means the conquest of sin, which must therefore be accomplished in us

3. Moreover, we must understand this about the kingdom of God, that, just as there is no fellowship between righteousness and unrighteousness, nor communion of light with darkness, nor concord of Christ with Belial (2 Cor. 6. 14, 15), so the kingdom of sin cannot co-exist with the kingdom of God. If, then, we wish God to reign in us, let not sin in any way reign in our mortal body (Rom. 6. 12), neither let us obey its commands when it provokes our soul to the works of the flesh, and to works alien from God; but, mortifying our members which are upon the earth (Col. 3. 5), let us bring forth the fruits of the Spirit, in order that the Lord may walk in us as in a spiritual garden, reigning alone over us with his Christ, who within us sits on the right hand of that spiritual power which we pray to receive (cf. Matt. 25. 64), and is seated until all his enemies within us become a footstool of his feet (Psalm 110. 1), and every principality and authority and power is done away from us. For these things can happen in each one of us, and the last enemy can be destroyed, even death (1 Cor. 15. 26), that in us too Christ may say, O death, where is thy sting? O grave, where is thy victory? (1 Cor. 15. 55). Now, therefore, let that which is corruptible in us put on the holiness and incorruption which consist in chastity and all pureness, and let that

---

[1] Cf. *De Princ.* III. vi for Origen's doctrine of the Consummation.

which is mortal clothe itself with the Father's immortality, death being brought to nought (cf. 1 Cor. 15. 53), so that with God reigning over us we may even now be amid the good things of regeneration and resurrection.

"Thy will be done in earth, as it is in heaven." We must do nothing contrary to God's will, as all who belong to heaven obey his will

XXVI.—1. Thy will be done in earth, as it is in heaven.[1] Luke after "Thy kingdom come" omits this clause and puts "Give us day by day our ἐπιούσιος bread" (Luke 11. 2, 3).[2] These words therefore we have set down as being found in Matthew only. Let us examine them in connection with what precedes them. Let us who pray whilst we are still "in earth", understanding that the will of God is done "in heaven" by all who belong to heaven, pray [3] that the will of God in all things may also be done by us who are "in earth", as it is by them. This will come to pass if we do nothing contrary to his will. And when the will of God is upheld by us who are on earth, as it is in heaven, then being made like unto them which are in heaven, inasmuch as like them we bear the image of the heavenly (1 Cor. 15. 41), we shall inherit the kingdom of heaven, while those who "in earth" come after us pray to be made like unto us who will then be "in heaven".

But "in earth, as it is in heaven" may refer also to the two preceding clauses

2. However, the clause "in earth, as it is in heaven", according to Matthew who alone gives it, can be taken as common to all, so that what we are bidden to say in the prayer is this, Hallowed be thy name in earth, as it is in heaven. Thy kingdom come in earth, as it is in heaven. Thy will be done in earth, as it is in heaven. For the name of God is hallowed by those who are in heaven, and the kingdom of God is present with them, and the will of God is done in them; all of which

---

[1] Γενηθήτω τὸ θέλημά σου ὡς ἐν οὐρανῷ καὶ ἐπὶ γῆς. Codex MS., ἐν οὐρανοῖς, and so Delarue. Koetschau here follows Anglus' suggestion, οὐρανῷ bringing the passage into conformity with Origen's previous quotation of it.
[2] The clause in question is omitted by the best MSS. of Luke. R.V. also omits it.
[3] εὐξώμεθα. So codex MS. Delarue, εὐξόμεθα.

things are wanting to us who are "in earth", but can be true for us if we make ourselves worthy of obtaining God who hears our prayer for all these things.

A difficulty in this petition is solved if " heaven " is interpreted of Christ, and " earth " of the Church

3. But the phrase "Thy will be done in earth, as it is in heaven" might prompt one to ask,[1] How is the will of God done [2] in heaven where there is spiritual wickedness (Eph. 6. 12), on which account the sword of God shall be bathed even in heaven (Isa. 34. 5)? And if we pray thus, that the will of God may be done in earth, as it is done in heaven, shall we not perchance unconsciously be praying that what is contrary to us may also remain in earth, where these things also come from heaven, forasmuch as many who are "in earth" become wicked because of the spiritual wickedness which is in the heavenly places overcoming them (Eph. 6. 12)?[3] But if one takes "heaven" allegorically and says that it is Christ and that "earth" is the Church[4] (for what throne so worthy of the Father as Christ? and what footstool of God's feet so worthy as the Church?), he will easily solve the question by saying that each member of the Church must pray so to receive the Father's will as Christ received it, who came to do the will even of the Father, and perfected it every whit. For a man can, by being joined unto him, become one spirit[5] with him, thereby receiving his will, so that as it is perfected in heaven even so it may be perfected in earth. For he that is joined unto the Lord, according to Paul, is one spirit (1 Cor. 6. 17). And I think that this interpretation will not lightly be rejected by one who considers it carefully.

[1] ζητῆσαι δ' ἄν τις διὰ τὸ γενηθήτω etc. Codex MS., ζήτησας. Bentley and Delarue also read ζητῆσαι.

[2] πῶς γεγένηται. So codex MS. and Delarue. Ox. ed., γένηται. Koetschau in a footnote conjectures πῶς γὰρ γένηται.

[3] The problem is this: Holy Scripture says that there is wickedness in heaven. When, therefore, we pray that God's will may be done in earth *as it is in heaven*, are we not praying for a continuance of wickedness on the earth? Faced by such a difficulty in the literal interpretation, Origen turns to the mystical interpretation.

[4] Cf. XXIII. 4 *ad fin.*

[5] δυνατὸν γὰρ κολληθέντα αὐτῷ ἓν γενέσθαι πνεῦμα. Delarue reads κολλᾶσθαι αὐτῷ καὶ ἓν γενέσθαι πνεῦμα. Codex MS. gives κωλυθτ (sic).

The risen Lord's words "All power is given unto me, as in heaven so in earth", bear out this interpretation [1]

4. But anyone who denies it will compare what is said to the eleven disciples by the Lord, at the end of this Gospel after the resurrection: All power is given unto me, as in heaven so in earth (Matt. 28. 18). For he possesses power over the things which are in heaven, and declares that he has received also power in earth; for the things which are in heaven have, even beforehand, been enlightened by the Word, but at the consummation of the age, the things also which are in earth, by the power given to the Son of God, imitate those things over which the Saviour received power,[2] and are perfected [3] in heaven. It is as if, therefore, he wishes to receive his disciples through their prayers as fellow-workers unto the Father, in order that, when the things which are in earth have been set right because of the power [4] which he has received "as in heaven so in earth", like unto the things which in heaven are subject to truth and to the Word, he may bring them to the blessed fulfilment of those over whom he has power. And he who takes "heaven" to be the Saviour, and the "earth" the Church, and who asserts "heaven" to be the firstborn of every creature (Col. 1. 15) upon whom the Father rests as upon a throne, may find [5] that the Man whom he (i.e. the Saviour) has put on, brought into union with that power [6] in that he has humbled himself, becoming obedient unto death (cf. Phil. 2. 8), says after the resurrection, "All power is given

---

[1] This seems to me to be the intention of this section. But the argument is far from clear. The saying "All power is given unto me, as in heaven so in earth", if taken in its plain sense, would preclude interpreting "heaven" as Christ, in so far as it speaks of Christ having power *in heaven*. One is tempted to suggest that Origen has fallen into the expositor's fault of fastening on a passage similar in phrasing to the one under consideration and forcing its meaning to substantiate some point or other. This invariably increases difficulties, and this seems to be the case in this section.

[2] The Eternal Word, the brightness of God's glory, is thought of as the Light of heaven. Hence, when the effects of redemption are completed at the consummation (see *De Princ.* III. vi), he will be as truly the Light of the redeemed earth.

[3] τά, ὧν ἐξουσίαν ὁ σωτὴρ ἔλαβεν, ἐν οὐρανῷ κατορθουμένων. So codex MS. Bentley and Delarue read κατορθούμενα, agreeing with the τά.

[4] ⟨διὰ⟩ τὴν ἐξουσίαν. Codex MS. has no διά. Delarue reads τῇ ἐξουσίᾳ.

[5] εὕροι ἄν. Codex MS., εὑρεῖν. Anglus, εὗρεν. Bentley and Delarue, ἐρεῖ.

[6] ἐκείνῃ τῇ δυνάμει. Bentley and Delarue, ἐκείνου. Δύναμις here refers to the divine power of the Word, to which the Manhood was united.

unto me, as in heaven so in earth"; for the Man in the Saviour [1] receives power over the things which are in heaven, even the things which belong unto the Only-begotten, that mingled with [2] his divinity, and united with him, he may be a partaker with him.[3]

The spiritual powers of wickedness are not truly in heaven, but by reason of their evil disposition are more properly described as in earth

5. But since the second interpretation [4] does not yet solve the difficulties about how the will of God is done in heaven, when the spiritual powers of wickedness in the heavenly places wrestle against those who are in earth, it will be found possible to solve the question on this interpretation as follows: for, just as he who is still "in earth" and has his citizenship in heaven, and lays up treasure in heaven,

---

[1] τοῦ κατὰ τὸν σωτῆρα ἀνθρώπου, i.e. the Humanity of Christ.

[2] ἀνακιρνάμενος. So codex MS. and Delarue.

[3] Anglus cites other passages in Origen which stress the union of the divine and human natures in Christ. *Contra Celsum* II. 394, "This we say, not separating the Son of God from Jesus; for after the Incarnation (μετὰ τὴν οἰκονομίαν) the soul and body of Jesus are made one (ἓν ... γεγένηται) with the Word of God." Ibid. III. 474, "We are convinced that his mortal body, and the human soul in him, have changed (or passed over, μεταβεβηκέναι) into God, not by fellowship only with that Word, but by union and mingling (ἀνακράσει)." Ibid. V. 608, "We say that the Word ... is closely united and made one (ᾠκειῶσθαι καὶ ἡνῶσθαι) with the soul of Jesus." Ibid. VI. 669, "The soul of Jesus is joined fast (κεκόλληται) with the Lord, the very Word, very Wisdom, very Truth, and very Righteousness ... and if this is so, the soul of Jesus and the firstborn of every creature are not two." *Comm. on John* I. 37, "the manhood of the Son of God mingled with his divinity (ἀνακεκραμμένον)" (Brooke's ed., Vol. I, p. 44). We may mention also the illustration which Origen uses in *De Princ.* II. vi. 6 to describe the union of the Word with the human soul of Jesus. This is the illustration of the fire into which iron is placed. The fire heats and penetrates the iron and it becomes a glowing mass. The fire and the iron are one, yet the fire is still fire, and the iron is still iron.

The extension of the allegorization of heaven as Christ and earth as the Church in section 4 is exceedingly difficult to follow. The thought seems to be that since the Manhood of Christ is united with the Eternal Word the phrase "All power is given unto me, as in heaven so in earth", spoken by the risen Saviour, may be taken as the declaration of Christ's Manhood that henceforth that sacred Manhood shares the power of the Eternal Word.

[4] The second interpretation is the mystical (namely, that heaven means Christ, and earth means the Church), the first being the literal.

having his heart in heaven, and bearing the image of the heavenly, is no longer "of the earth" nor of the world below, but is of heaven and the heavenly world, which is better than this—not indeed so far as his position in space is concerned, but by reason of his will [1]—so also the spiritual powers of wickedness which still dwell in the heavenly places, and have their citizenship in earth, and lay up treasure in earth by plotting and wrestling against men, bearing the image of the earthy, which is the beginning of the Lord's creation made [2] to be mocked at by the angels (Job 40. 14, LXX; cf. A.V., 40. 19), are not heavenly, nor do they dwell in heaven, by reason of their evil disposition. Therefore whenever "Thy will be done in earth, as it is in heaven" is said, it must not be thought that they are "in heaven" who by their presumption have fallen together with him who fell from heaven like lightning (Luke 10. 18).

Another possible interpretation is that " earth " refers to sin and the sinner, " heaven " to the good

6. And perhaps when our Saviour says that we must pray that the will of the Father be done as in heaven so also in earth, he is not entirely bidding that prayers be made for those that are in earth as in a place, that they may be made like those that are in the heavenly place; but he orders this prayer, willing that all things that are "in earth", that is to say, bad things, and things which are closely united with the earthy, be made like unto the things that are good, and that have their citizenship in heaven, and have all become "heaven". For the sinner, wherever he may be, is "earth" [3] and will pass to his

---

[1] Notice that Origen says that it is by their *will* that men may be said to be in heaven whilst in earth. Again there is no concession to emotional or even intellectual mysticism.

[2] ὅστις ἐστὶν ἀρχὴ πλάσματος κυρίου, πεποιημένος . . . Πεποιημένος is to be taken with ὅστις. So Anglus. Codex MS. and Delarue have πεποιημένου, which must be taken with πλάσματος.
Anglus notes that Origen refers this quotation from Job allegorically to the Devil; cf. *Comm. on John* I. 17 (Brooke's ed., Vol. I, p. 20), ibid. xx. 20 (Brooke, Vol. II, p. 66).
Likewise the phrase "image of the earthy", which St Paul in 1 Cor. 15. 49 applies to Adam and his seed, Origen applies to the Devil; cf. *Comm. on John* xx. 20 (the passage mentioned above), and *Comm. on Matt.* xv. 18.

[3] ὅπου ποτ' ἂν ᾖ, ἐστὶ γῆ. So also Bentley and Delarue. Codex MS., ὅπου ποτ' ἄν ἐστιν ἡ γῆ. Anglus, ὅπου ποτ' ἄν, ἐστὶ γῆ. Cf. Gen. 3. 19; Tert., *De. Orat.* IV. This interpretation of "heaven" and "earth" is simpler than that in sections 3 and 4. It also has a more directly homiletic value.

kindred earth in some way or another, unless he repent. But he who does the will of God, and does not disobey the spiritual laws of salvation, is "heaven". So, then, whether we are still "earth" because of our sin, let us pray that the will of God [1] may be extended over us for our amendment, just as it came upon those before us who became "heaven" or who are "heaven"; or whether we are not "earth", but are already counted "heaven" unto God, let us ask that the will of God may be fulfilled in earth, that is to say, in the bad, just as in heaven, so that earth may, so to speak, be made into heaven, that it may no longer be earth, but all things become heaven. For if the will of God be so done in earth, as it is in heaven (interpreted in this way), the earth will not remain earth; so that, to speak more clearly, using another illustration, if the will of God is done in the licentious, as it is in the self-controlled, then the licentious will be self-controlled; or if the will of God is done in the unrighteous as it is done in the righteous,[2] then the unrighteous will be righteous. Therefore, if the will of God is done in earth as it is done in heaven, then we shall all be "heaven". For the flesh which profiteth nothing (John 6. 63), and blood which is akin to it, cannot inherit the kingdom of God (1 Cor. 15. 50), but they could be said to inherit, if they should be changed from flesh and earth and dust and blood into the heavenly substance.

"*Give us this day our ἐπιούσιος bread*": *this is not a petition for material bread*

XXVII.—1. Give us this day our ἐπιούσιος [3] bread (Matt. 6. 11); or as Luke has it, Give us day by day our ἐπιούσιος bread (Luke 11. 3). Since some suppose that we are bidden to pray for corporeal bread, it is fitting to remove the false opinion they create through this interpretation, and to establish the truth concerning "ἐπιούσιος bread". We must therefore say to them, How is it that he who says we must ask for heavenly and great things,[4] bids us bring

[1] τὸ θέλημα τοῦ θεοῦ. Delarue omits τοῦ θεοῦ.
[2] ἢ ὡς γεγένηται τὸ θέλημα τοῦ θεοῦ ἐπὶ τοὺς δικαίους, ⟨ἐὰν οὕτω γένηται⟩ καὶ ἐπὶ τοὺς ἀδίκους. Koetschau adds the bracketed words, which are not in codex MS. or Delarue. Anglus adds οὕτω γένηται.
[3] We leave this word, of which the meaning is much disputed, untranslated. As we shall see, Origen's various suggestions as to its meaning make it difficult to translate the word exactly to convey the meaning he attaches to it. See appended note on p. 220 ff. for a discussion of the meaning.
[4] Origen refers the petition for bread to what he considers to be the governing principle of prayer.

a petition to the Father for something which is earthly and small (for bread which is digested into our flesh is not "heavenly", nor is it a "great" request to ask for it), as though—according to them—he has forgotten what he taught?

Passages in John 6 bear this out: the true bread is Christ himself

2. But we, following the Master himself, who teaches us about bread, will explain these words by others. In the Gospel according to John he says to those who came to Capernaum to seek him, Verily, verily, I say unto you, Ye seek me, not because ye saw the miracles, but because ye did eat of the loaves, and were filled (John 6. 26). For he that has eaten of the loaves blessed by Jesus, and is filled therewith, the more seeks to understand the Son of God more perfectly, and hastens to him. Wherefore well does he bid them, saying, Labour not for the meat which perisheth, but for that meat which endureth unto everlasting life, which the Son of man shall give unto you (John 6. 27). And when his hearers at this inquired and said, What shall we do that we might work the works of God? Jesus answered and said unto them, This is the work of God, that ye believe on him whom he hath sent (John 6. 28, 29). And God sent his word, and healed them (Psalm 107. 20), that is to say, those who were sick, as it is written in the Psalms. Those who believe in this word are they that work the works of God which are the meat that endureth unto everlasting life. Again he says, My father giveth you the true bread from heaven. For the bread of God is he which cometh down from heaven, and giveth life unto the world (John 6. 32, 33). And true bread is that which nourisheth the true man who is made in the image of God: he who is nourished thereby grows in the likeness of the Creator. But what is more nourishing to the soul than the Word, or what is more precious to the mind of him who receives it than the Wisdom of God? And what has a closer correspondence to a rational nature than truth?

3. But if any man suggests an objection to this,[1] saying that he

---

[1] I.e. an objection to Origen's theory that "bread" in the petition means Christ himself. Such an objection might be made on the ground that Christ, if he had meant this, would have made his meaning clearer, instead of teaching us to pray for bread as though it were something other than himself. Origen's reply is that, although there are passages where Christ speaks of bread in the ordinary sense, there are several passages in John 6 where he speaks of himself as bread, which provide justification for Origen's interpretation of this petition.

would not in that case have taught us to ask for ἐπιούσιος bread as for something other (than himself),[1] let him hear that in the Gospel according to John also, while on one occasion he discourses about bread as something other than himself, yet on another he discourses as himself being bread: *as of something other than himself* in these words, Moses gave you bread from heaven, not the true bread; but my Father giveth you the true bread from heaven (John 6. 32); but to those who said to him, Evermore give us this bread, he says, *as of himself*, I am the bread of life: he that cometh to me shall never hunger; and he that believeth on me shall never thirst (John 6. 34, 35). And a little later, I am the living bread which came down from heaven: if any man eat of this bread, he shall live for ever; and the bread that I will give is my flesh, which I will give for the life of the world (John 6. 51).

The bread which is the Word himself is provided for the strong in faith

4. And since all food is called "bread" in Scripture,[2] as is clear from what is written of Moses, He did neither eat bread forty days nor drink water (Deut. 9. 9), while the word which nourishes is manifold and diverse (for all are not able to receive nourishment from the solidity and strength of divine doctrine), for this reason wishing to provide food for training fitted for the more perfect, he says, And the bread that I will give is my flesh, which I will give for the life of the world (John 6. 51); and a little later, Except ye eat the flesh of the Son of man, and drink his blood, ye have no life in you. Whoso eateth my flesh, and drinketh my blood, hath eternal life; and I will raise him up at the last day. For my flesh is meat indeed, and my blood [3] is drink indeed. He that eateth my flesh, and drinketh my blood, dwelleth in me, and I in him. As the living Father hath sent me, and I live by the Father; so he that eateth me, even he shall live by me

---

[1] Anglus suggests the insertion of παρ' αὐτόν here. This is not in codex MS. nor accepted by Delarue or Koetschau. It must, however, be understood.

The protasis in the objector's argument is suppressed. What the objector is presumed to say is, "If you (Origen) are right, and 'bread' means Christ himself, surely he would not have taught us to pray for it as though it were something else."

[2] Cf. *Comm. on John* x. 13 (Brooke, Vol. I, p. 202).

[3] αἷμά μου. Codex MS., πόμα μου, and so Delarue.

(John 6. 53–57). This is the true meat, Christ's flesh, which, being Word, became flesh, as it is said, And the Word was made flesh (John 1. 14). And whenever we eat and drink him, then he dwells among us [1] (John 1. 14); and as often as it is distributed, then are fulfilled the words "We beheld his glory" (John 1. 14). This is that bread which came down from heaven: not as the fathers did eat and are dead: he that eateth of this bread shall live for ever (John 6. 58).[2]

The weak in faith need weaker food, i.e. simpler teaching

5. Paul, moreover, discoursing to the Corinthians as unto "babes", and as unto those who "walk as men", says, I have fed you with milk, and not with meat: for hitherto ye were not able, neither yet now are ye able. For ye are carnal (1 Cor. 3. 1–3). And in the Epistle to the Hebrews, And ye are become such as have need of milk, and not of strong meat. For everyone that useth milk is unskilful in the word of righteousness: for he is a babe. But strong meat belongeth to them that are of full age, even those who by reason of use have their senses exercised to discern both good and evil (Heb. 5. 12–14). And I think that the words, One believeth that he may eat all things: another, who is weak, eateth herbs (Rom. 14. 2), are not spoken in the first place about bodily food, but about God's words which nourish the soul; for the man of great faith and fullest stature whom he indicates by the

---

[1] ὅτε δὲ ⟨φάγοιμεν καὶ⟩ πίοιμεν αὐτόν, καὶ ἐσκήνωσεν ἐν ἡμῖν. Koetschau adds φάγοιμεν καί to bring the sentence into conformity with "Except ye eat the flesh of the Son of man, and drink his blood" above.
Codex MS. has ὅτε δὲ πίωμεν αὐτόν, which Delarue keeps.

[2] It is remarkable that Origen does not in this section appear to mention the Eucharist. But ancient writers by no means always do what modern readers expect of them. He does write elsewhere about the Eucharist (e.g. *Comm. on John* XXXII. 24; *Comm. on Matt.* XI. 14; *Contra Celsum* VIII. 784), and he teaches an allegorization of the action: the eating and drinking is the assimilation of the Word of God. "Now we are said to drink the blood of Christ not only in sacramental rite, but also when we receive his words in which life consists, as he himself says, The words that I spake are spirit and life" (*Hom. in Num.* XVI. 9). In the passage under consideration, then, although specific mention of the Holy Communion is not made, it is probable that it was in Origen's mind, and that he assumed it would be in his readers' minds. The phrase "as often as it is distributed" (ἀναδιδῶται), however, may refer to the Eucharist. It should be added that just as the allegorization of a passage of Scripture implies no disbelief on Origen's part in the literal sense, so his "allegorization" of the sacrament implies no disbelief in its validity as a means of grace.

words "One believeth that he may eat all things" is able to partake of them all, but he that is weaker, and less fully grown, whom he means to signify when he says "another, who is weak, eateth herbs", is sufficed by a simpler teaching which does not produce full strength.

It is better for the simpler to assimilate the simpler teaching than to be overbold

6. And what Solomon says in the Proverbs I think teaches that he who is not able to receive the more vigorous and greater teaching because of his simplicity (provided that there are not errors in his mind) is better than the more skilful and clever man who sets about things in a larger way, but who does not clearly discern the principle of the peace and harmony of all things. His words are as follows, Better is a dinner of herbs where love and grace are than an ox from the stall and hatred therewith (Prov. 15. 17). We have often taken a plain and simple meal with good conscience when dining with those not able to offer us more, in preference to a spate [1] of words rising against the knowledge of God which, with great speciousness, promises a teaching alien from the Father of our Lord Jesus who gave the law and the prophets. So, then,[2] that we be not sick in soul for lack of food, nor die unto God for famine of the word of the Lord (cf. Amos 8. 11), let us ask of the Father the living bread, which is the same as the ἐπιούσιος bread, trusting the Master who is our Saviour, believing and living more rightly.[3]

The meaning of ἐπιούσιος. Only found in the prayer. Probably invented by the Evangelists to represent an Aramaic word. It is probably connected with οὐσία, "substance", and applied to "bread" means "of the divine substance".

7. We must now also grasp the meaning of ἐπιούσιος. And the first thing to be realized is this, that the word ἐπιούσιος is not used by any of the Greeks, or philosophers, nor is it in general use in the

---

[1] ὕψος, literally "height", "sublimity".
[2] Origen comes back to the point after his digression on St Paul's words about the proper spiritual sustenance for the weaker brethren as compared with the stronger. This digression has not been very relevant to Origen's main theme that in this petition of the Lord's Prayer "bread" means the Word of God.
[3] The foregoing section brings out clearly the contrast between Origen and the Gnostics. The Gnostics had nothing but contempt for the intellectually ill-equipped.

XXVII. 7   ON PRAYER   171

customary vocabulary of ordinary people, but it seems to have been invented by the Evangelists. At least, both Matthew and Luke agree about it without any difference at all and use it.¹ The translators of the Hebrew have done a similar thing also in other cases. For what Greek ever used the word ἐνωτίζου ² or ἀκουτίσθητι ³ instead of εἰς τὰ ὦτα δέξαι ⁴ and ἀκοῦσαι ποίει σε? ⁵ Very similar to the word ἐπιούσιος ⁶ is a word written by Moses as spoken by God, Ye shall be unto me a περιούσιος (A.V., peculiar) people (Ex. 19. 5). And both words seem to me to have been derived from οὐσία (substance), the one indicating bread which is united in the Substance ⁷ and the other signifying the people which lives close to (περί) the Substance ⁸ and shares therein.

¹ συνηνέχθησαν γοῦν ὁ Ματθαῖος καὶ ὁ Λουκᾶς περὶ αὐτῆς μηδαμῶς διαφερούσης, αὐτὴν ἐξενηνοχότες. So codex MS. and Delarue.
² ἐνωτίζου is found in LXX of Job 33. 1, 31; 34. 16; 37. 14; Isa. 1. 2.
³ Anglus notes that the passive ἀκουτίσθητι is nowhere found in LXX. He conjectures ἀκούτισον, which is found in, e.g., Song of Songs 2.14; 8.13.
⁴ Literally, "take into your ears".
⁵ Literally, "make yourself hear". ποίει σ⟨ε⟩. Codex MS., ποιεῖς. Anglus, Bentley, and Delarue emend to ποίει. Koetschau's emendation makes the phrase the equivalent of "listen" ("make yourself to hear"). Origen's point is that as the translators in the Septuagint have used words and phrases which would not be used by a Greek, such as the two cited for the imperative of "to listen", so, he suggests, the Evangelists have manufactured a word in the case of ἐπιούσιος.
⁶ ἰσομοία τῇ „ἐπιούσιον" προσηγορίᾳ. Codex MS., ἐπιουσίῳ, and so Delarue. Anglus suggests ἐπιούσιον, the accusative being the case used in the Lord's Prayer. Delarue has προσηγορία, taking it as the subject of ἐστὶ . . . γεγραμμένη—"very similar to ἐπιούσιος is a word written by . . .".
⁷ τὸν εἰς τὴν οὐσίαν συμβαλλόμενον. In the absence of the personal pronoun, the phrase can hardly be translated as Fleury (in Migne) takes it: "*panem qui in substantiam nostram convertatur*". Συμβάλλω seems to be used in its normal sense of "put together with". In view of Origen's belief that "bread" refers to the Word, τὴν οὐσίαν most probably here refers to the divine substance; thus in praying for ἐπιούσιος bread, we are praying that we may be fed by Christ himself who is perfect man united with the divine substance. Ἐπιούσιος, then, meaning literally "into the divine substance", cannot be easily rendered into English. "Bread which is of the divine substance" conveys Origen's suggestion, though it does not clearly reproduce the force of the prefix ἐπι-.
⁸ τὸν περὶ τὴν οὐσίαν καταγινόμενον. It is most probable that τὴν οὐσίαν here also refers to the divine substance, and I have therefore used the capital S. Περί has the same sense of close association as in the frequent phrase οἱ περί τινα. Origen's suggestion, then, is that περιούσιος λαός means the people who are close to God's substance or being.

The two main philosophical meanings of the word οὐσία, *"substance"*

8. Now those who assert that the hypostasis [1] of incorporeal things is primary [2] think of what is properly substance in terms of incorporeal things [3] whose essence is fixed and can neither admit of addition nor suffer subtraction (for this latter is the property of bodies in which there is increase and decline due to their being in a state of flux, and which need some outside agent to come upon them, strengthening and nourishing them; and if more comes upon them at a time than flows away, there is increase, but if less, decrease; and some bodies, perhaps, not admitting any action from outside at all, are, so to speak, in a pure diminution). But others [4] who think that the hypostasis of incorporeal things is secondary, while that of bodies is primary,[5] have the following

[1] The word is used here in its literal sense of "underlying reality". It later came to be used in the orthodox formula of the Trinity for "Person", in which sense also Origen frequently uses it.

[2] I.e. that before material things came into being there existed incorporeal Forms, Ideas, or Patterns.

[3] τοῖς μὲν προηγουμένην τὴν τῶν ἀσωμάτων ὑπόστασιν εἶναι φάσκουσι νενόμισται κατὰ τὰ ἀσώματα, e.g. Plato, *Timaeus*, 34 B.C., where it is said that the "soul of the world" was created before bodily substances, and that God made the soul prior to the body in which it is eventually to be incarnate; cf. also *Timaeus Locrus* IV. Origen in this section describes the two main theories of substance (οὐσία) held by the disciples of Plato or the Academicians, and the Stoics. The distinction is broadly that the Academicians, who regard the world of archetypes (Forms or Ideas) as primary, think of substance as the eternal immutable Form, of which the particular thing partakes, and to whose reality it is but a shadowy approximation. For example the οὐσία of a chair—that which makes it what it is—is the Form of the chair, which is regarded as having a real existence in the immaterial "world" of Forms, and which (in a way not made clear by Plato) enters into the particular chair, and gives it its distinctive being. In this sense οὐσία is "fixed and can neither admit of addition nor suffer subtraction".

The Stoics on the other hand took the more matter-of-fact position that the οὐσία of a thing is the primary matter of which it consists. This primary matter they conceived of as without form or quality.

The whole section impresses the reader as a mere display of erudition on Origen's part. This analysis of the philosophical meanings of οὐσία is not really helpful to his main purpose of elucidating the meaning of ἐπιούσιος.

[4] I.e. the Stoics. Cf. Diogenes Laertius, VII. 134, 150, on Zeno.

[5] I.e. that material things are the first and only true reality and that the Forms or Ideas postulated by Plato are but mental abstractions. Put very briefly the distinction is that Plato said, e.g., Whiteness is primary. Material white things of different kinds come afterwards as shadows of or participations in Whiteness. The Stoics, who in this, broadly speaking, followed Aristotle,

XXVII. 8　ON PRAYER

definitions of it: substance is either primary matter [1] of that which exists, and that which exists consists of it; or it is the matter of bodies,[2] and bodies consist of it; or of things that have a name,[3] and things that have a name consist of it; or the primary subsistence, without qualities; or the underlying pre-existing principle of entities; or that which is susceptible of all kinds of change and alteration, but itself is unalterable in its own principle;[4] or that which endures all alteration and change. According to these, substance is without quality and without form in its own principle,[4] neither has it any determined magnitude, but it underlies [5] every quality as though it were a place made ready for it. The operations and actions, commonly so called, in which its movement and nature may consist, they call distinctively [6] "qualities". They say that in its own principle, substance does not partake of any of these things, yet it is always inseparable from one or other of them as it happens,[7] being none the less susceptible to all the operations of the efficient cause whenever it acts and produces change. For the energy which is present with it and which pervades

said that white things were primary, and denied the existence objectively of Whiteness. The distinction is very similar to that between the Idealists and Materialists of to-day. Stoic doctrine was, however, lifted above crass materialism by its recognition of the principle of reason as active in the universe.

[1] ἡ πρώτη . . . ὕλη. Delarue, ἡ πρώτη. Cf. Diog. Laert. VII. 150: οὐσίαν δέ φασι τῶν ὄντων ἁπάντων τὴν πρώτην ὕλην ὡς καὶ Χρύσιππος . . . καὶ Ζήνων.

[2] ἡ τῶν σωμάτων. Delarue, ἡ τῶν σωμ.

[3] ἡ τῶν ὀνομαζομένων. Delarue, ἡ τῶν ὀνομ. Here and in the preceding two notes the article seems preferable.

[4] κατὰ τὸν ἴδιον λόγον.

[5] ἔγκειται. So Koetschau in his text. In his note he cites Anglus' suggestion of ὑπόκειται as probably right. "Ἔγκειται, "inheres in", is less suitable with καθάπερ ἑτοιμόν τι χωρίον.

[6] διατακτικῶς. Fleury read διατατικῶς, and translated "*extensiori sensu*" (in Migne).

[7] ἀεὶ δέ τινος αὐτῶν ἀχώριστον εἶναι πάθει τήνδε. Here πάθει may mean "by reason of its passive state", οὐσία here being regarded as the "matter" which is passive, and awaits the action of an agent to actualize its potentialities. But I prefer to give it its other sense of "that which befalls", "an incident", and to translate "as it happens", which seems to me to give emphasis to the contrast between οὐσία as it is in its own nature or principle, and as it is in practical experience. But Arnim's conjecture may well be right. He places a comma after εἶναι, and reads παθητὴν δὲ οὐδὲν . . ., "Yet it is always inseparable from one or other of them, and is none the less in a passive and receptive state to all . . .".

the universe is the cause of every quality and of the functions connected with it.[1] They say that it is changeable throughout and divisible throughout, and that any substance can be mingled with any other, but by being united with it.[2]

The bread we ask for is capable of feeding our minds in so far as we assimilate it (i.e. according as we surrender ourselves to the Word) [3]

9. Having said this in the course of our investigation about the word "substance", which was occasioned by the phrase "ἐπιούσιος bread", and "περιούσιος people", in order to distinguish the meanings of "substance", since, according to what was said beforehand, the bread which we ought to ask for was bread for the mind,[4] we must of necessity regard substance and "the bread" as cognate; so that just as material bread imparted to the body of him who feeds on it passes into his substance, so the living bread which came down from heaven (John 6. 51), imparted to the mind and soul, communicates

---

[1] τῶν περὶ αὐτὴν αἴτιος ἂν οἰκονομιῶν. The presence of ἂν is difficult. Bentley and Delarue suggest ἂν ᾖ, Anglus ἂν εἴη, making it a cautious assertion.

[2] Cf. Diog. Laert. VII. 150–1.

[3] This too is a difficult section. The argument seems to be this. The bread we ask for in the Lord's Prayer is the Word of God. This is bread for the nourishment of the mind. Bread is cognate with the substance of the eater: e.g. material bread easily passes into the physical substance of him who eats it. So, then, the "bread of the mind" is cognate with the substance of the mind, or rational soul, and capable of communicating to it its own immortal nature.

This suggests a meaning for ἐπιούσιος rather different from that suggested in XXVII. 7, where according to the most probable interpretation of Origen's meaning ἐπιούσιος is "of the *divine* substance". According to Origen's suggestion in the section under consideration ἐπιούσιος ἄρτος could be paraphrased (for literal translation is impossible) "bread which in substance is cognate with our minds".

The two ideas come together, however, inasmuch as both here and in XXVII. 7 Origen connects ἐπιούσιος with οὐσία. On the Godward side the ἐπιούσιος ἄρτος is bread which is united with the Divine Essence, i.e. the Word of God; on the manward side it is the food of the mind's substance.

[4] νοητός. Origen refers here to his discussion of the word "bread" in XXVII. 1–6, where, although the phrase ἄρτος νοητός is not used, it is in several places clear that he thinks of the bread as the Word of God which nourishes the mind.

its own power to him who surrenders himself to the nourishment derived therefrom. And thus it will be the ἐπιούσιος bread for which we ask.[1] And again, just as he who feeds is of varying strength according to the quality of the food, whether it is solid and suitable for athletes or of milk and herbs, so it follows, since the Word of God is given either as milk fit for babes, or as herbs suitable for the sick, or as flesh appropriate for those engaged in struggle, that each [2] of those who are fed, in proportion as he has surrendered himself to the Word, is able to accomplish this or that and to become such or such. There is, however, what is thought to be food, yet is harmful, and other food produces sickness, and yet other food cannot even be digested; and all these are to be referred by analogy to different doctrines which are thought to give nourishment.[3] Ἐπιούσιος bread, then, is that which corresponds most closely to the rational soul and is cognate with its very substance, producing at the same time health, a good condition, and strength, in the soul, and communicating its own immortality (for the Word of God is immortal) to him who eats thereof.

This bread is also called "Tree of life" and "Wisdom of God". Angels as well as men partake of it

10. This ἐπιούσιος bread appears to me to have been called by another name in Scripture, namely "Tree of life", upon which whoever puts forth his hand and takes of it shall live for ever (Gen. 3. 22). And by a third name this tree is called "Wisdom of God" by Solomon in the following words, She is a tree of life to them that lay hold upon her, and unto those that lean upon her as upon the Lord, safe (Prov. 3. 18). And since the angels also feed upon the wisdom of God, being given power to perform their proper works from their contemplation in truth with wisdom, it is said in the Psalms that the angels also take food, the men of God who are called Hebrews partaking with the angels, and, as it were, even becoming table-companions with them. The words are as follows, Man did eat angels' bread (Psalm 78. 25).

---

[1] καὶ οὕτως ἔσται ὃν αἰτοῦμεν ἄρτον ἐπιούσιον. So codex MS. Delarue suggests καὶ οὗτος ἔσται ὃν αἰτοῦμεν, ἄρτος ἐπιούσιος.

[2] ἢ ὡς σαρκὸς ἀγωνιζομένοις προς⟨καίρως⟩, ἕκαστον . . . Codex MS. has πρὸς ἕκαστον. Bentley and Delarue, προσφόρως, ἕκαστον . . . Anglus deletes πρός.

[3] I.e. heretical teachings of more or less gravity, and teaching on subjects which are "too high for man".

For let not our mind be so poor as to think that the angels for ever partake of and feed upon a sort of corporeal bread which, as is narrated, came down from heaven upon those who came out of Egypt,[1] and that it was this selfsame bread which the Hebrews shared with the angels who are the ministering spirits of God.

There is a sense in which men may give angels food

11. We shall not find it irrelevant, as we are inquiring into the meaning of ἐπιούσιος bread, and the tree of life, and the wisdom of God, and the food common to holy men and angels, to give attention also to the three men recorded in Genesis as having turned in to Abraham's house and partaken of three measures of fine meal kneaded to make cakes (Gen. 18. 2–6), in case these things, when stripped bare, have been spoken in a figurative sense;[2] for the saints are able sometimes to give a share of intellectual and rational food not only to men, but also to more divine powers, either to help them or to prove what most nourishing food they have been able to procure for themselves; and the angels rejoice at and feed upon this proof and are the more ready to co-operate in every way, and henceforth to conspire for a comprehension of more and greater truths on the part of him who, provided only with the nourishing doctrines formerly enjoyed, has made them rejoice,[3] and, if I may use the expression, nourished them. Nor is it to be wondered at if a man gives food to angels, when even Christ confesses that he stands at the door and knocks, that he may come in to him that opens to him and may sup with him of the

---

[1] I.e. the literal interpretation of Ps. 78. 25.

[2] μή ποτε γυμνῶς τροπικῶς ταῦτα εἴρηται. So codex MS. Delarue, μήποτε οὐ γυμνῶς ἀλλὰ τροπικῶς ταῦτα εἴρηται, taking γυμνῶς in the sense "literally" = κυρίως. But, as Anglus points out, Origen regards the literal sense as a garment concealing the spiritual sense of Scripture. When this is stripped off the spiritual meaning lies bare, and we have τὰ γυμνὰ πνευματικά. Hence the phrase under consideration means literally "in a nakedly figurative sense", i.e. with the garment of the literal sense stripped off; cf. De Princ. IV. ii. 8: τὸ ἔνδυμα τῶν πνευματικῶν, λέγω δὲ τὸ σωματικὸν τῶν γραφῶν, "the outer covering of the spiritual truths, I mean the bodily part of the Scriptures" (Butterworth's trans.).

[3] τοῦ ἐπὶ προτέροις παρεσκευασμένου τροφίμοις μαθήμασιν, εὐφράναντος. Codex MS., παθήμασιν. Delarue reads παρεσκευασμένοις, "of him who has made them rejoice at the nourishing doctrines provided". But τοῦ παρεσκευασμένου is the subject of εὐφράναντος.

things he possesses (Rev. 3. 20), after which he himself will impart his own good things to him who has first entertained the Son of God according to his ability.

A warning: it is also possible to feed on the Devil. There is a sense in which all spiritual powers and men may be food for one another

12. He, then, who partakes of the ἐπιούσιος bread, being strengthened in his heart, becomes a son of God; but he who has part in the dragon is nothing but a spiritual Ethiopian,[1] by the snares of the dragon changing himself into a serpent, so that even if he says he desires to be baptized he is reproached by the Word, and hears the words, Serpents, generation of vipers, who hath warned you to flee from the wrath to come? (Matt. 3. 7). And David says of the body of the dragon upon which the Ethiopians feast, Thou didst crush the heads of the dragons in the water (thou brakest the head of the dragon in pieces),[2] thou gavest him to be meat to the people of the Ethiopians (Psalm 73. 13, 14). But if it is not incongruous, since the Son of God subsists substantially, and the adversary also subsists, that each of them should become the food of this or that man, why do we hesitate to admit, at least in respect of all the powers,[3] good and bad, and in respect of men, that each one of us can feed upon all these?[4] Peter certainly, when he is about to hold communion with the centurion Cornelius, and those who were gathered together with him in Caesarea, and afterwards to make the Gentiles also partakers of the words of God, sees the vessel let down from heaven by the four corners, wherein were all manner of four-footed beasts and creeping

---

[1] See the quotation from Psalm 73 below. Two thoughts are combined in this section: (*a*) Those who feed on the Devil, or dragon (i.e. obey the Devil's teaching), may be called Ethiopians in accordance with Psalm 73, which says that dragons are the food of the Ethiopians. (*b*) By feeding on the Devil, or serpent, they themselves become serpents, and the words of John the Baptist may be applied to them, "Ye generation of vipers . . .".

[2] ⟨σὺ συνέθλασας τὴν κεφαλὴν τοῦ δράκοντος,⟩. With Anglus, Koetschau inserts these words, which Origen has in quoting the Psalm in *Comm. on Matt.* XVI. 26. Delarue has σὺ συνέτριψας τὰς κεφαλὰς τοῦ δράκοντος.

[3] ἐπί γε πασῶν τῶν δυνάμεων. Delarue ἐπί τε.

[4] Anglus cites the same idea in *Hom. in Levit.* VII.: "*Post Christi carnem, mundus cibus est Petrus et Paulus, et omnes apostoli: tertio loco discipuli eorum: et sic unusquisque pro quantitate meritorum, vel sensuum puritate, proximo suo efficitur cibus.*" We are influenced for good or bad (our souls are fed or poisoned) by the company we keep.

things and wild beasts of the earth (Acts 10. 11, 12); at which time also he is bidden to rise, kill and eat, being commanded also, after he had refused and said, Thou knowest that nothing common or unclean hath at any time entered into my mouth (Acts 11. 8), to call no man common or unclean (Acts 10. 28), because things which are cleansed by God ought not to be called common by Peter; for the text says, What God hath cleansed, that call not thou common (Acts 10. 15). So, then, the clean and unclean meat which is distinguished in the Law of Moses by the names of many animals, refers to the different characters of rational men,[1] and teaches us that some are useful for our nourishment, and of others the opposite is true, until God cleanses them all, or some of every kind,[2] and makes them such.

The derivation of ἐπιούσιος from the verb ἐπιέναι ("of the age to come") is less likely. The meaning of "this day". In the Scriptures "day" frequently signifies an age

13. Since this indeed is so, and since there is this difference in meats, our ἐπιούσιος bread is the one above all those mentioned concerning which we ought to pray, that we may be worthy of it, and, being fed by God the Word who was in the beginning with God, may be transformed into God.[3] But someone may say that ἐπιούσιος [4] is formed from the verb ἐπιέναι (to come upon), so that we are bidden to ask for the bread which belongs to the age to come, that God by anticipation may grant it to us now, so that what should be given as it were to-morrow, is given us to-day ("to-day" being taken as the present age, and "to-morrow" as the age to come). But as the former interpretation is better, at least in my judgement, let us examine the

---

[1] Note this mystical interpretation. Origen, prompted by Peter's vision in which the various unclean animals stood for men regarded by the Jews as unclean, applies the same interpretation to the unclean animals listed in the Law of Moses (e.g. Lev. 11).

[2] ἢ τοὺς ἀπὸ παντὸς γένους. So codex MS. Delarue conjectures ἢ τινας.

[3] θεοποιηθῶμεν. A favourite idea in Alexandrine theology. Cf. Athanasius, *Oratio contra Arianos* 1. 39: "He was God and then was made man that we might be made God." The idea follows naturally here from Origen's exegesis of "bread" and ἐπιούσιος. The bread on which man feeds is the Word of God who is of the substance of God; and the substance of this bread passes over into the substance of him who partakes of it.

[4] ἐρεῖ δέ τις τὸ ἐπιούσιον. So Anglus. Codex MS. and Delarue, τὸν ἐπιούσιον.

XXVII. 14   ON PRAYER   179

word "to-day" which is joined [1] to the phrase in Matthew, or the "day by day" which is written in Luke. Now it is usual [2] in many places in the Scriptures for every age to be called "to-day", as in the following: He is the father of the Moabites unto this day (Gen. 19. 37), and, He is the father of the children of Ammon unto this day (Gen. 19. 38), and, This saying is commonly reported among the Jews until this day (Matt. 28. 15), and in the Psalms, To-day if ye will hear his voice, harden not your hearts (Psalm 95. 7, 8). And in Joshua this is made very clear, as follows: Turn not away from the Lord in these days (Josh. 22. 16, 18, 19, LXX). But if "to-day" is all this age, perhaps "yesterday" is the age that is past.[3] I suspect that this is meant both in the Psalms and by Paul in the Epistle to the Hebrews; the words in the Psalms being as follows: A thousand years in thy sight are but as yesterday which is past (Psalm 90. 4)—that is the much talked-of millennium [4] which is likened to "yesterday", as distinct from "to-day"; and the Apostle writes, Jesus Christ the same yesterday, and to-day, and for ever (Heb. 13. 8). Nor is it to be wondered at that for God the whole age is measured by the space of one of our days [5]—and I should think even of less.

Possibly the biblical references to the days of the festivals are to be interpreted of ages to come

14. We must also inquire whether the words used of festivals and solemn assemblies, described in terms of days, or months, or seasons, or years (Gal. 4. 10), are analogous to "ages". For if the law has a shadow of things to come (Heb. 10. 1), it must be that the many sabbaths are the "shadow" of many days, and that the new moons begin after intervals of time, being brought to pass by I know not what

---

[1] προσκείμενον. So Anglus. Codex MS. and Delarue, προκείμενον.
[2] ἔθος δή. Delarue, ἔθος δέ.
[3] μή ποτε ἐχθὲς ὁ παρεληλυθώς ἐστιν αἰών. Codex MS., ὁ χθὲς ὁ παρεληλυθώς ἐστιν αἰών. So Delarue.
[4] χιλιονταετηρίς. Bentley and Delarue, χιλιετηρίς. The adjective διαβόητος indicates Origen's dislike of Chiliasm, which he attacks elsewhere, e.g. *De Princ.* II.
[5] τῷ θεῷ τὸν ὅλον αἰῶνα τῆς παρ'ἡμῖν μιᾶς ἡμέρας διαστήματος λόγον ἔχειν. So Anglus. Codex MS., διαστήματι λόγον λέγειν. Bentley, τῷ θεῷ τῶν ὅλων τὸν ὅλον αἰῶνα τοῦ παρ'ἡμῖν μιᾶς ἡμέρας διαστήματος λόγον ἔχειν. Delarue gives the text of codex MS. but approves Bentley's emendation.

moon in conjunction with some sun. And if the first month and the tenth day until the fourteenth (Ex. 12. 2, 3, 6) and the feast of unleavened bread from the fourteenth until the one and twentieth (Ex. 12. 18) contain a shadow of things to come, who is wise [1] and so close a friend of God as to discern the first of many more months, and the tenth day thereof, and so on? And what need is there for me to speak of the feast of the seven weeks (Deut. 16. 9) and of the seventh month (Lev. 16. 29), the new moon of which is a day of trumpets and on the tenth of which is a day of atonement (Lev. 23. 24, 27, 28), which are known to God alone who ordained them? And who has grasped the mind of Christ [2] sufficiently to understand the seventh years of the freeing of Hebrew servants and the release of debts and the resting of the holy land from tillage (Ex. 21. 2; Lev. 25. 4–7; Deut. 15. 1 ff.)? There is also a feast greater than the feast of the seven years, called Jubilee (Lev. 25. 8 ff.); and to imagine what this represents at all clearly, or the laws therein which are to be fulfilled in reality, is beyond anyone except him who [3] has beheld the Father's will concerning the arrangement of all the ages in accordance with his unsearchable judgements and his ways which are past finding out (Rom. 11. 33).[4]

[1] Delarue here quotes a note from the Oxford edition, which points out that in the same way that in Jewish thought the Temple and its apparatus were held to be constructed upon the model of the universe (cf. ἅγιον κοσμικόν, Heb. 11. 1), so here Origen suggests that the successive Jewish festivals represent successive "ages" in the history of the people. In a similar way the Epistle to the Hebrews (4. 9) makes the sabbath the analogy of the sabbath rest for the people of God. It is suggested that Origen interprets the ages (aeons) as of future periods of time in opposition to the Valentinians, who identified them with the pre-existing aeons of Gnostic cosmology. The writer praises Origen's intention, but regrets the overlarding of "the simplicity of the gospel with the dreamings of Gentile philosophy about infinite worlds succeeding one another in turn, and with the tenets of the Academy about the revolutions of heavens round to the same points, and with the restoration of all things in the 'great year' of Plato".

[2] Χριστοῦ. So codex MS. Delarue suggests θεοῦ.

[3] οὐδενός ἐστι ⟨πλήν⟩ τοῦ ... Bentley and Anglus also add the clearly necessary πλήν. Delarue notes that Fleury had ἐστιν εἰ μὴ τοῦ.

[4] Origen's conception is that "the end is always like the beginning" (*De Princ.* I. vi. 2): "So far as I am able to judge ... the order of our human race was constituted in the hope of restoring it in the age to come, or in the ages beyond that, when there shall be the 'new heaven and new earth' of which Isaiah speaks, to that unity which the Lord Jesus promises ... 'that they all may be one'" (*De Princ.* I. vi. 2, Butterworth's trans.). But because of free

ON PRAYER

The "consummation of the ages" by Jesus does not necessarily preclude other ages to come

15. But there has often arisen a doubt in my mind when I compare two texts of the Apostle, how there is a consummation of ages [1] at which Jesus hath appeared once to put away sin, if there are to be ages coming after this one. His words are as follows, first in the Epistle to the Hebrews: But now once in the consummation of the ages [1] hath he appeared to put away sin by the sacrifice of himself (Heb. 9. 26); and in the Epistle to the Ephesians, That in the ages to come he might show the exceeding riches [2] of his grace in his kindness towards us (Eph. 2. 7).[3] Venturing a conjecture [4] about these great matters, I think that just as the consummation of a year is the last month, after which comes the beginning of another month, so perhaps as many ages fulfil as it were a year of ages,[5] the present age is a consummation after which certain future ages will come, of which the beginning is the age to come, and in those ages to come God will show the riches of his grace in kindness, the great sinner and blasphemer against the Holy Spirit being held by his sin throughout the whole of this present age, and in that which is to come hereafter, from its beginning to the end, faring [6] I know not how.

---

will and the fact of sin and failure, ages may pass before the final consummation when God shall be all in all. Thus Origen seems to hold that there is a succession of ages, of which the present world and its order is but one. But all this is presented very tentatively in *De Princ.* I. vi. Cf. also III. v. 3 and III. vi.

[1] συντέλεια αἰώνων. A.V. translates "end of the world".
[2] τὸ ὑπερβάλλον πλοῦτος. So Bentley. Codex MS., τὸ ὑπερβάλλον πλῆθος. Anglus reads here τὸν ὑπερβάλλοντα πλοῦτον on the strength of τὸν πλοῦτον τῆς χάριτος below. Codex Alex. has τὸ ὑπερβάλλον πλοῦτος in Eph. 2. 7.
[3] The problem is that Heb. 9. 26 implies that "the consummation of the ages" took place at the Incarnation. In what sense, then, can Eph. 2. 7, which speaks of "ages to come", be understood?
[4] στοχαζόμενος. Note that Origen does not dogmatize on this subject.
[5] Cf. *Comm. on Matt.* xv. 31.
[6] οἰκονομησομένου. Almost the equivalent of the English colloquial "managing". So codex MS. Delarue suggests οἰκονομηθησομένου, "being treated". The whole phrase, Delarue notes, is a hint at Origen's speculation that the Devil will eventually be saved. See *De Princ.* III. vi. 5–6.

Meditation on the meaning of "the ages" brings realization of our need for the true bread both "this day" (in this age) and "day by day" (in the ages to come)

16. When a man sees these things, and with his understanding reflects upon the week of ages, and so beholds a certain holy sabbath, and upon the month of ages, and so sees the holy new moon of God, and upon the year of ages, and so also sees the festivals of the year [1] when every male must appear before the Lord God (Deut. 16. 16), and upon the years that are analogous to these great ages, and so gains an understanding of the holy seventh year, and diligently ponders the seven times seven years of ages in order to praise him who ordained such great principles, how can he disparage the smallest part of an hour of the day of so great an age, and will he not do everything possible in order that, being made worthy by preparation here to obtain the ἐπιούσιος bread to-day,[2] he may receive it also day by day (for it has now become clear from the aforesaid what "day by day" means)?[3] For he who "to-day" prays to God who is from infinity unto infinity, not only concerning "to-day",[4] but also in some sense concerning what is needful "day by day", will be enabled to receive, from him who is able to give exceeding abundantly above all that we ask or think (Eph. 3. 20)—if I may use something of an exaggeration—things beyond those which eye hath not seen, and things beyond those which ear hath not heard, and things beyond those which have not entered into the heart of man (1 Cor. 2. 9).

---

[1] ἵνα συνίδῃ τὰς τοῦ ἐνιαυτοῦ γε ἑορτάς. Oxford ed. and Delarue have τε for γε. The force of the γε, if it is the right reading, is hard to convey in English. The thought seems to be that if a man meditates on the "year of ages" (and what Origen means by that phrase is not made clear, though possibly he intends to suggest a succession of 365 ages), he will come to see the significance *at any rate* of the yearly festivals.

The whole passage is difficult. It is possible that Origen means that just as a week, with the sabbath day's rest at the end of it, mystically represents the sabbath rest of God, so the month and the year must represent still greater delights in the economy of God.

[2] From his speculative flights Origen comes back to the practical Christian duties.

[3] I.e. "to-day" represents this present age, and "day by day" represents the ages to come.

[4] περὶ τῆς σήμερον. Bentley, Anglus, and Delarue read τοῦ σήμερον, "that which concerns to-day".

The true bread is ours, for according to Paul all things are ours (1 Cor. 3. 22)

17. These considerations seem to me to have been a very necessary study in order that the words "this day" and "day by day" may be understood when we pray that ἐπιούσιος bread may be given us of his Father.[1] And if in the last book,[2] in which is written not "Give us this day our ἐπιούσιος bread", but "Give us day by day our ἐπιούσιος bread", we first of all examine[3] the word "our", we must none the less[4] consider how this bread is ours. The Apostle indeed teaches that "whether life or death or things present or things to come, all" belong to the saints[5] (1 Cor. 3. 22). But it is not necessary to speak of this word[6] at the moment.

"Forgive us our debts, as we also forgive our debtors." Our debts are our duties towards all[7]

XXVIII.—1. And forgive us our debts, as we also forgive our debtors (Matt. 6. 12), or as Luke has it, And forgive us our sins; for we also forgive everyone that is indebted to us (Luke 11. 4). Concerning debts the Apostle too says, Render to all their dues; tribute to whom tribute is due; fear to whom fear; custom to whom custom;

---

[1] ἀπὸ τοῦ πατρὸς αὐτοῦ. Delarue omits τοῦ. Anglus suggests ἡμῶν for αὐτοῦ. Koetschau takes αὐτοῦ as referring to Christ, the living bread.
[2] εἰ κατὰ τελευταῖον δὲ βιβλίον. So Delarue. Codex MS. has εἰ καί. St Luke's Gospel seems to be meant, but it is a curious phrase to use for it.
[3] πρότερον ἐξετάζομεν. Delarue reads ἐξετάσομεν in his text, following Oxford ed. In his footnote he suggests ἐξητάσαμεν. But Origen has nowhere given particular attention to the word ἡμῶν. He is clearly putting a hypothetical case, and either present or future tense is demanded. Anglus gives the whole passage up as too corrupt to recover Origen's meaning. The meaning, indeed, is far from clear.
[4] ὅμως γε. Codex MS. and Delarue, ὅμως τε.
[5] Origen's meaning seems to be that therefore, *a fortiori*, the ἐπιούσιος bread belongs to the saints.
[6] ⟨περὶ οὗ⟩ οὐκ ἀναγκαῖον ἐπὶ τοῦ παρόντος λέγειν. Περὶ οὗ is not in codex MS. Delarue suggests περὶ οὗ or περὶ ὧν. The former is preferable as the sentence clearly refers to a discussion of the word ἡμῶν.
[7] In this chapter Origen deals in masterly fashion with some of the common duties of the Christian life, a welcome relief to the reader after the excursus into philosophy, the etymological discussion and the obscure speculations about "the ages" of Chapter XXVII.

honour to whom honour. Owe no man anything, but to love one another (Rom. 13. 7, 8). So, then, we are debtors and have certain duties not only in giving, but also in the word of gentleness and such deeds as these, and moreover we ought [1] to have a disposition of this kind towards them. Now since we owe this debt, we either repay it by fulfilling what is enjoined by the divine law, or else in contempt of sound teaching we do not repay it, but remain in our debts.

We have debts to our brethren, fellow citizens, strangers, elders, and to our own bodies and souls

2. And we must be of the same mind in the case of our debts towards the brethren, both those who are regenerated together with us in Christ according to the word of our religion, and those who are born of the same mother or father as ourselves. There is also a debt towards our fellow citizens, and another debt common to us all towards all men, particularly strangers and particularly those who are old enough to be our fathers,[2] and yet another towards certain whom it is right for us to honour as sons or brothers. He, therefore, who does not perform the things that ought to be fulfilled for the brethren remains a debtor in respect of the things he has not done. In the same way if, when things are due to men from us out of the kindly spirit of wisdom, we should be found wanting,[3] the debt is the greater. Moreover, in what concerns ourselves we owe a debt to use the body in a certain way, and not to waste the flesh of the body through love of pleasure; and we owe a debt too to apply the same care to the soul, and to make provision for the sharpening of the mind and of our speech, that it may be without barb, and profitable, and in no wise idle. Indeed, whenever we fail to perform towards ourselves those debts which we owe ourselves, our debt becomes the heavier.

[1] ὀφείλομεν. "We are debtors" and "we ought" are the same word in Greek; cf. the English "we owe" and "we ought", which are cognate.

[2] πρὸς πάντας ἀνθρώπους, ἰδίᾳ μὲν ξένους ἰδίᾳ δὲ καὶ ἡλικίαν πατέρων ἔχοντας. Koetschau follows E. Klostermann's emendation. Codex MS., ἰδίᾳ μὲν ξένους ἰδίᾳ δὲ καὶ ἡλικίαν πατέρων ἔχοντας. Delarue has ἰδίᾳ πρὸς ξένους, ἰδίᾳ δὲ καὶ πρὸς τοὺς ἡλικίαν πατέρων ἔχοντας. In Koetschau's reading ξένους and ἔχοντας explain ἀνθρώπους.

[3] ἐλλείποιμεν. Delarue prefers ἐλλείπομεν.

We have debts to God, to Christ, to the Holy Spirit, and to the angels

3. And in addition to all these debts, since we are God's handiwork and fashioning above all else, we owe a debt to preserve a certain disposition towards him, even love with all our heart and with all our strength and with all our mind (Luke 10. 27; Mark 12. 30); unless we succeed in this, we remain God's debtors, sinning against the Lord. And who shall pray on our behalf for this? For if a man sin against a man, then they shall pray [1] for him: but if [2] he sin against the Lord, who shall pray for him? as Eli says in the First Book of Kings (LXX, 2. 25; A.V., 1 Sam. 2. 25). But we are also debtors of Christ, who purchased us with his own blood, even as every slave is a debtor of his purchaser since so much money has been given for him.[3] There is also a debt towards the Holy Spirit which we pay when we do not grieve him whereby we are sealed unto the day of redemption (Eph. 4. 30); and if we grieve him not, we bear the fruits which are required of us, since he himself is with us and quickens our soul. Again, even if we do not know exactly who the angel of each one of us is that beholds the face of the Father which is in heaven (Matt. 18. 10), yet it is clear to each of us, if we consider it, that we are debtors in certain respects to him also.[4] And if we are in the theatre of the world and of angels and of men (1 Cor. 4. 9), we must know that just as he who is in a theatre owes a debt to say or do certain things in the sight of the spectators, and if he does not do them he is punished since he has affronted the whole theatre, so also we are debtors to the whole world and to all the angels and to the race of men in respect of those things which, if we will, wisdom will teach us.

---

[1] προσεύξονται. So Anglus. Codex MS., προσεύξηται. Delarue has προσεύξεται.

[2] ἐὰν ⟨δὲ⟩. Δέ is not in codex MS., which Delarue follows.

[3] Note the reference to the Atonement in terms of ransoming. The Church has throughout the centuries stated the doctrine of the Atonement in language taken from social or political ideas of the time. In the early centuries of Christianity the widespread institution of slavery and the practice of manumission provided a readily understood illustration of the saving work of Christ. But, as always, the pressing of the details of the illustration brought many of the Fathers into absurdity.

Origen frequently represents the death of Christ as a ransom price paid to Satan to free men from slavery. Cf. *Comm. on Matt.* xvi. 8.

[4] For Origen's belief in guardian angels see vi. 4 *ad fin.* and xi. 1.

There are special debts owed by particular persons, e.g. widows, deacons, presbyters, bishops, husbands, wives

4. And apart from these more general debts there is also a debt of a widow who is provided for by the Church, and another of a deacon [1] and another of a presbyter, while the debt of a bishop is the heaviest of all, required by the Saviour of the whole Church, and recompense is taken if he should not repay it.[2] And the Apostle speaks of a common debt of husband and wife when he says, Let the husband render unto the wife the debt; and likewise also the wife unto the husband (1 Cor. 7. 3), and he adds, Defraud ye not one the other (1 Cor. 7. 5), and since it is possible for those who read this work to gather, from what has been said, what their own debts are, what need is there for me to say how many debts we owe, debts for which we shall either be held if we repay them not, or released if we pay them? But it is not possible for one who is in this life not to be a debtor every hour of night and day.

These debts, if unpaid, will speak against us at the judgement

5. But when he is a debtor a man either repays the debt or else defrauds somebody of it. Now in this life it is possible to repay, and it is possible to defraud. And there are some who owe no man anything; and some, paying back much, owe little; and others, repaying a little, owe more; and perhaps there is one who repays nothing but owes everything. But he at least who repays everything so as to owe nothing, achieves this in time, although he needs remission for his former debts;[3] and this remission can well be gained by one who for some time has been zealous to become the sort of man who owes none of those things for which, as being unpaid, he was liable.[4] These lawless actions, engraved in the mind, become the handwriting that is against us (Col. 2. 14), by which we shall be judged as though from documents

---

[1] Note the clear reference to the three orders of the ministry, and the implication that their responsibilities and therefore their functions differ. Cf. *Hom. in Jerem.* xi: "More is required of me (as a presbyter) compared with a deacon, and more is required of a deacon than a layman; but of him who is appointed (ἐγκεχειρισμένος) head of us all still more is required." Cf. also *Hom. in Ezech.* v.

[2] ἀποδιδοῖτο. So Anglus. Codex MS., ἀποδιδῶτο; so Delarue.

[3] I.e. he is still blameworthy in that he was in the past a debtor.

[4] ὥστε μηδὲν ὀφείλειν τῶν ἐπιβαλλόντων ὡς οὐκ ἀποδιδομένων. So Anglus and Delarue. Codex MS., ἀποδιδομένοις.

written by us all, so to speak, with our own hand, to be produced as evidence [1] when we shall all stand before the judgement seat of Christ that every one may receive the things done in his body, according to that he hath done, whether it be good or bad (Rom. 14. 10; 2 Cor. 5. 10). The following passage in Proverbs also refers to these debts: Give not thyself for a surety, thou who dost respect thy person; for if he has nothing with which to pay, they shall take away thy bed from under thy side (LXX, Prov. 22. 26, 27).

The knowledge of our own failure to pay debts should make us more gentle to those who are in debt to us

6. But if we are debtors to so many, there are certainly some also who are debtors to us. For some are debtors to us because we are men, some because we are citizens, others because we are fathers, some because we are sons, and besides these, wives are debtors to husbands and friends to friends. Therefore whenever any of our many debtors behave somewhat negligently in the matter of the repayment of what is due to us, we shall act the more kindly, bearing ourselves without malice towards them, mindful of how many of our own debts we have often failed to pay, not only to men, but also to God himself. For mindful of the things which, being debtors, we have not paid, but kept back when the time elapsed in which we ought to have performed certain deeds towards our neighbour, we shall be more gentle towards those who are in debt to us and have not paid their debt; and particularly so if we do not forget our transgressions against the Godhead and the wickedness against the Highest which we have uttered either in ignorance of the truth or in displeasure at circumstances which have befallen us.

This is illustrated by the Parable of the Wicked Servant, and other sayings of our Lord

7. But if we will not be more gentle towards those who are in debt to us, we shall suffer the same as the man who did not forgive his fellow servant the hundred pence, from whom, although he had been

---

[1] προαχθησομένων. So codex MS. Bentley and Anglus, προαχθησόμενον; Delarue, προαχθησομένου to agree with the οὗ preceding: "the handwriting ... by which we shall be judged ... and which will be produced ...". With the idea, expressed in this sentence, that sins remain engraved in the mind, cf. *De Princ.* II. x. 4, where it is said that "signs and forms" are impressed on the mind at the moment of sinning.

previously forgiven, according to the parable in the Gospel, his master, having imprisoned him, exacts what had been forgiven before, saying, O thou wicked and slothful servant; shouldest not thou also have had compassion on thy fellow servant, even as I had pity on thee? Cast him into prison until he pays all that is due. And to this the Lord adds, So likewise shall the heavenly Father do also unto you, if ye from your hearts forgive not every one his brother (Matt. 18. 30–35).[1] Yet we must forgive those who have sinned against us when they say that they repent, even if our debtor does this many times; for, If thy brother trespass against thee seven times in a day, and seven times turn again to thee, saying, I repent; thou shalt forgive him (Luke 17. 4). But towards those who do not repent we are not harsh, but they that are such do themselves harm; for, He that refuseth instruction hateth himself (Prov. 15. 32). But even in the case of such we must by every means seek to bring healing to one who is so completely perverted as not even to perceive what harms himself and to be drunk with a drunkenness more deadly than that of wine, the drunkenness that is caused by the darkness of wickedness.

Both Luke and Matthew imply we should forgive all who are in debt to us. We ourselves are able to forgive sins against our own persons. The Apostles and those like them have power to forgive or retain sins in God's name

8. When Luke says, Forgive us our sins (for sins are constituted when we are debtors and do not pay), he means the same as Matthew, who does not seem to give a place [2] to the man who is willing *only* to forgive those debtors who repent, for he says that it was laid down by the Saviour that we must add in our prayer, For we also ourselves forgive *every one* that is indebted to us (Luke 11. 4). We all, however, have power to forgive sins committed against us, as is clear from the words, As we also forgive our debtors (Matt. 6. 12), and, For we also ourselves forgive every one that is indebted to us (Luke 11. 4). But he who is breathed upon by Jesus, as were the Apostles, and can be known by his fruits, as having received the Holy Spirit and been made spiritual

---

[1] This seems to be an instance of Origen quoting from memory. "Wicked and slothful" is from another parable (Matt. 25. 26); "Cast him . . . all that is due" is in narrative form in Matt. 18. 30, 34.

[2] χώραν. So Delarue (see his comment on Anglus' note), although χῶρον appears in his text.

XXVIII. 9   ON PRAYER   189

by being led by the Spirit like the Son of God to all those things which are to be done in accordance with reason,[1] forgives whatsoever God forgives and retains those sins which cannot be cured, and in this, just as the prophets when they spoke not their own, but the things of the divine will, he also ministers to God who alone has power to forgive.[2]

The Apostles, however, may not grant forgiveness to all, for the Spirit teaches them that, as under the Old Covenant, certain sins may not be forgiven

9. The passage in the Gospel according to John concerning the forgiveness which is of the Apostles is as follows: Receive ye the Holy Ghost; whose soever sins ye remit, they are remitted unto them: whose soever ye retain, they are retained (John 20. 22, 23). If a man takes this without examination, he might blame the Apostles for not granting remission to all, in order that all might be forgiven; whereas they retain the sins of some, so that because of them those sins are retained with God also. It will be useful to take an example from the law in order to understand that remission of sins which comes from God to men through men. Those who are priests according to the law are prevented from offering sacrifice for certain sins that their trespasses may be forgiven for whom the sacrifices are offered. And the priest, who has power over certain involuntary sins and an offering for misdemeanours, does not, it is to be supposed, even to this day, offer a burnt-offering and a sin-offering for adultery or wilful bloodshed or any other more grievous offence [3] (cf. Num. 15. 27, 31). So, then, the Apostles, and those who are made as the Apostles, being priests after the order of the Great High Priest in that

[1] This phrase appears to refer to the work of the priesthood.
[2] Origen in several places refers to confession of sins in the presence of the Church's ministers: *Hom. in Luc.* XVII; *Hom.* ii *in Psalm.* XXXVII. 6; *Hom. in Lev.* II. 4.
[3] καὶ οὐ δή που τὴν περί τινων ἐξουσίαν ὁ ἱερεὺς ἀκουσίων ἢ πλημμελημάτων ἀναφορὰν ἔχων ἤδη καὶ περὶ μοιχείας ἢ ἑκουσίου φόνου ἢ τινος ἄλλου χαλεπωτέρου πταίσματος προσφέρει ὁλοκαύτωμα καὶ περὶ ἁμαρτίας.
Delarue follows Ox. ed. in reading οὐδέπου.
Koetschau in a footnote prefers ἐξουσίαν ὁ ἱερεὺς ἀκουσίων ἢ <ἑκουσίων> πλημμελημάτων ἀναφορᾶς ἔχων.
καὶ περὶ ἁμαρτίας. Codex MS., ἢ περὶ ἁμαρτ., and so Delarue. Koetschau reads καί to conform with Psalm 39. 6, LXX (A.V., Psalm 40. 6).

they possess knowledge of God's service, know, being taught by the Spirit, for what sins sacrifices may be offered, and when, and how; and they know, too, for what sins this may not be done. Even so the priest Eli, knowing that his sons Hophni and Phinees were sinners, when he was unable to help them in any way to repentance of their sins, confesses even that he despairs of this happening in the words, If a man sin against a man, then they shall pray for him: but if he sin against the Lord, who shall pray for him? (1 Sam. 2. 25).

These are the sins "unto death" of which St John speaks

10. There are some who, I know not how, have taken to themselves powers beyond the priestly dignity, perhaps because they are unversed in the craft of the priesthood, and boast that they can forgive idolatries, and remit fornications and adulteries, as though through their prayer for those who have dared to do these things, the sin which is unto death is loosed. For they do not read the text, There is a sin unto death: I do not say that a man shall pray for it (1 John 5. 16).[1] Neither must we pass over in silence the most valiant Job, who offers sacrifice for his sons, saying, It may be that my sons have devised evil in their hearts against God (Job 1. 5). For he is offering sacrifice for sins of which there is a doubt whether they have been committed, and moreover which have not proceeded even as far as the lips.

"And lead us not into temptation." In view of the fact that the whole of life is a temptation, what does this petition mean?

XXIX.—1. And lead us not into temptation, but deliver us from evil (Matt. 6. 13). The phrase "but deliver us from evil" is omitted by Luke [2] (11. 4). Unless the Saviour is bidding us pray for impossible things, it seems to me worth inquiring how we are bidden to pray that we do not enter into temptation, when the whole life of men

---

[1] Origen shows himself a rigorist here, and his rather tart words are aimed at those who supported a less rigorous church discipline. In his later works Origen himself expressed less rigorous views. See Bigg, *Christian Platonists of Alexandria*, 1913 ed., pp. 262 f. *The Shepherd* of Hermas (early second century) is our first written evidence of a movement away from the rigorism of Hebrews 6. 4–6. Hermas was prepared to allow *one* opportunity of repentance and restoration to grievous sinners after Baptism. Origen discusses 1 John 5. 16 also in *Hom. in Lev.* XI. 2.

[2] So the best MSS. The clause is not in R.V., but appears in A.V.

upon earth is a time of temptation. For inasmuch as we are on the earth, invested with the flesh that warreth against the spirit (1 Pet. 2. 11; Gal. 5. 17), whose mind is enmity against God, since it cannot in any way be subject to the law of God, we are in temptation.

Scripture supports the contention that man's whole life is a temptation [1]

2. Now that the whole of human life upon earth is a time of temptation we learn from Job in the following words: Is not the life of men upon earth a time of temptation? (Job 7. 1, LXX); and from the seventeenth Psalm the same is shown in the words, In thee I shall be delivered from temptation (Psalm 17. 29, LXX). But Paul too, writing to the Corinthians, says that God grants us not to escape temptation, but not to be tempted beyond our power; he says, There hath no temptation taken you but such as is common to man: but God is faithful, who will not suffer you to be tempted above that ye are able; but will with the temptation also make a way to escape, that ye may be able to bear it (1 Cor. 10. 13). For whether the wrestling is against the flesh that lusteth and warreth against the spirit (Eph. 6. 12; Gal. 5. 17) or against the life of all flesh [2] (Lev. 17. 11) (which is synonymous with the body which the intelligence, otherwise called the heart, inhabits) [3]—and such is the wrestling of those who are tempted with temptations which are "common to man"; or whether,

---

[1] In characteristic fashion Origen quotes copiously from Scripture to support his contention that the whole life of men upon earth is a time of temptation.

[2] πρὸς τὴν ψυχὴν πάσης σαρκός, i.e. blood. Lev. 17. 11 (LXX) has ἡ γὰρ ψυχὴ πάσης σαρκὸς αἷμα αὐτοῦ ἐστιν, "For the life of all flesh is the blood thereof"; cf. also A.V. The early Hebrew belief, of which there are several vestiges in their sacrificial ceremonies, was that the blood was the "nephesh" or life principle (Gk. ψυχή). Anglus remarks that there is here a μετάληψις, or substitution of the word ψυχή for αἷμα, the blood in which the ψυχή has its seat. Thus the phrase is the equivalent of "whether the wrestling is against flesh . . . or against blood". Origen's parenthesis explains that what he means is simply the body which the intelligence (τὸ ἡγεμονικόν), or "heart" as it was sometimes called, inhabits—i.e. he is referring to the struggle against temptations arising from the lower part of man's nature.

[3] (ἥτις ἐστὶν ὁμωνύμως ᾧ ἐγκατοικεῖ σώματι τὸ ἡγεμονικόν, ὃ καλεῖται καρδία). The ἥτις must be taken to refer to both σάρκα and τὴν ψυχὴν πάσης σαρκός.

In ancient thought parts of the body were the seats of various faculties and emotions: cf. the frequent biblical word "bowels" representing compassion.

as with athletes who have made progress and are more perfect, no longer wrestling against flesh and blood or tested by temptations that are common to man, which they have now trodden under foot, our struggling is against principalities, and against powers, and against the rulers of the darkness of this world, and against spiritual wickedness (Eph. 6. 12), in either case we are not released from temptation.

This is true even of the righteous

3. How, then, is it that the Saviour bids us pray that we enter not into temptation, when God tempts all men in some way? For remember, says the Jewess—not [1] only to the elders of those days but also to all those who read her book—what things he did with Abraham, and how he tried Isaac, and what happened to Jacob in Mesopotamia of Syria, when he kept the sheep of Laban, his mother's brother. For not as he tried them in the fire for the examination of their hearts doth the Lord that scourgeth them that come near unto him for their admonishing take vengeance on us [2] (Judith 8. 26, 27). And that it is universally true of all the righteous, David shows when he says, Many are the afflictions of the righteous (Psalm 34. 19), and the Apostle in the Acts, That we must through much tribulation enter into the kingdom of God (Acts 14. 22).

Were, then, the Apostles not heard in their prayers, since they suffered so many temptations?

4. And unless we understand what escapes the majority concerning the prayer that we enter not into temptation, we shall have to say that the Apostles were not heard when they prayed, since they experienced so great and innumerable sufferings throughout their whole life, in labours more abundant, in stripes more abundant, in prisons above measure, in deaths oft [3] (2 Cor. 11. 23), and Paul alone five times

---

[1] ἡ 'Ιουδαία [εἰ] οὐ. So codex MS. The reference is to Judith. Koetschau brackets the εἰ. Oxf. ed. and Anglus, 'Ιουδὶθ οὐ. Delarue, 'Ιουδαῖθ οὐ.

[2] καὶ ἡμᾶς ἐκδικεῖ ὁ εἰς νουθέτησιν μαστιγῶν κύριος τοὺς ἐγγίζοντας αὐτῷ. LXX of Judith 8. 27 has καὶ ἡμᾶς οὐκ ἐξεδίκησεν, ἀλλ' εἰς νουθέτησιν μαστιγοῖ κύριος τοὺς ἐγγίζοντας αὐτῷ. (A.V., "Neither hath he taken vengeance on us: but the Lord doth scourge them that come near unto him, to admonish them.")

[3] Anglus suspects that carelessness on the part of a scribe accounts for the variation here from the Greek text of 2 Cor. 11. 23.

received of the Jews forty stripes save one, thrice was he beaten with rods, once was he stoned, thrice he suffered shipwreck, a night and a day he spent in the deep (2 Cor. 11. 23–25), a man troubled on every side, and perplexed and persecuted and cast down (2 Cor. 4. 8, 9), who confesses that, Even unto this present hour we hunger and thirst, and are naked, and are buffeted, and have no certain dwelling-place; and labour, working with our own hands; being reviled, we bless; being persecuted, we suffer it: being defamed, we intreat (1 Cor. 4. 11–13). And if the Apostles did not achieve success in their prayer, what hope is there that any man who is inferior to them when he prays will find God answering him?

Further indications from Scripture that no circumstance of life is exempt from temptation

5. The words in the twenty-fifth Psalm (A.V., Psalm 26), Examine me, O Lord, and prove me; try my reins and my heart (Psalm 26. 2), will very easily be taken, by anybody who does not carefully examine what the meaning of the Saviour's command is, to be the opposite of what our Lord taught about prayer.[1] Has anyone ever thought that men were outside the scope of temptations whose tale he knows, having himself completed it?[2] And what occasion is there upon which a man is confident as not having to struggle that he may not commit sin? Is a man poor? Let him take heed lest he steal and swear by the name of God (Prov. 30. 9). But is he rich? Let him not be confident; for he that is full can be a liar, and be lifted up and say, Who sees me?[3] Not even Paul, who was enriched in all utterance and in all knowledge (1 Cor. 1. 5), was delivered from the danger of sinning by exalting himself above measure on this account, but needs Satan's goad to buffet him, lest he should be exalted above measure (2 Cor. 12. 7). And even if a man be of good conscience in himself and flies away from evil,[4] let him read what is said in the

---

[1] I.e. Psalm 26. 2 seems to be a prayer that we *may* be led unto temptation. But Origen delays his explanation of what the meaning of this clause is until section 9.
[2] πειρασμῶν ... ὧν ᾔδει τὸν λόγον συμπεπληρωκώς; Characteristically again Origen appeals to experience as well as to a wide range of biblical texts.
[3] LXX of Proverbs 30. 9 has ἵνα μὴ πλησθεὶς ψευδὴς γένωμαι, καὶ εἴπω, τίς με ὁρᾷ; ἢ πενηθεὶς κλέψω, καὶ ὀμόσω τὸ ὄνομα τοῦ θεοῦ.
[4] ἀναπτερωθῇ ἀπὸ τῶν κακῶν. Codex MS., ὑπὸ τῶν κακῶν, and so Delarue. Anglus, taking ἀναπτερῶ in its common meaning of "to furnish

Second Book of Chronicles concerning Hezekiah, who is said to have failed from the pride of his heart (2 Chron. 32. 25, 26).[1]

Poverty, riches, and moderate means all bring temptation

6. And since we have not said much about the poor man, let anyone who is confident, as though there were no temptation with regard to poverty, know that the Snarer lays snares to cast down the poor and needy (Psalm 37. 14), and especially when, according to Solomon, The poor man withstandeth not threatening (Prov. 13. 8, LXX). And what need is there to relate how many have received their allotted place in punishment together with the rich man in the Gospel (Luke 16. 22–24) because of their corporeal riches which they have not rightly administered, and how many who bear their poverty ignobly, living in a more servile and base manner than befits saints, have fallen away from the heavenly hope? Nor are those who are between these, between riches and poverty, entirely free from sinning in their moderate possessions.

The same is true both of health and sickness

7. But the man who is healthy in body and strong thinks he is beyond the reach of all temptation because of his very health and strength.[2] And to what others except those who are strong and healthy belongs the sin of defiling the temple of God (1 Cor. 3. 17) no man will venture to say, because the meaning of the passage is clear to all.[3] And what man that is sick escapes from the incitements to

with new wings", "to make light and active again" (see Liddell and Scott), emends to ὑπὸ τῶν καλῶν. With Koetschau's reading, ἀναπτερῶ must have the sense of raising the feathers to fly away.

[1] The actual words of LXX are καὶ ἐταπεινώθη Ἐζεκίας ἀπὸ τοῦ ὕψους τῆς καρδίας αὐτοῦ.

[2] Delarue punctuates with a question-mark: "But does the man . . .?"

[3] Delarue punctuates, καὶ τίνων ἄλλων ἢ . . . ἐστὶν ἁμάρτημα τὸ φθείρειν τὸν ναὸν τοῦ θεοῦ; οὐ τολμήσει τις, διὰ τὸ ἐκκεῖσθαι πᾶσι, σαφῶς τὰ κατὰ τὸν τόπον εἰπεῖν. This must be translated: "And to what others except . . . belongs the sin of defiling the temple of God? No man will venture to say clearly what the passage means (Fleury, "*quae ad hunc locum pertinent*") since it is obvious to all." This seems to lack all point. Koetschau's punctuation provides excellent sense. The position of σαφῶς causes the ambiguity.

XXIX. 8   ON PRAYER   195

defile the temple of God,¹ since he has the opportunity at that time and very easily admits thoughts of impurity? But what need is there to tell how many things besides such thoughts disturb him unless he keep his heart with all diligence (Prov. 4. 23)? For many, being overcome by trouble, and knowing not how to bear sickness bravely, are proved then to be sick in soul rather than in their bodies; and many because they shun dishonour, being ashamed to bear the name of Christ nobly, have fallen into everlasting shame.

And of worldly honour and servility

8. But a man thinks he enjoys rest as not suffering temptation when he receives glory in the eyes of men. And is it not a hard thing that is announced to those who are exalted by their glory in the eyes of the many as though it were for good—"They have their reward from men" (Matt. 6. 2)? And is not this an astonishing saying, How can ye believe, which receive honour one of another, and seek not the honour that cometh from God only? (John 5. 44)? And why should I make a list of the sins of pride of those who are considered noble, and the cringing submission of those who are called ignoble towards those who are thought their betters—cringing submission which is due to their ignorance ² and which turns away from God those who have no true friendship in them but only simulate what is the fairest thing among men, even love? ³

---

¹ Codex MS. has τίς after θεοῦ. Koetschau brackets it as a copyist's slip. Delarue omits it without mention.

² καὶ τῶν λεγομένων δυσγενῶν διὰ τὸ ἀνεπίστημον τὴν πρὸς τοὺς ὑπερέχειν νομιζομένους ὑπόπτωσιν θωπευτικὴν ... It is possible, however, that διὰ τὸ ἀνεπ. is to be taken with τῶν λεγ. δυσγ.—"of those who are called, through ignorance, 'ignoble'".

³ ... θωπευτικὴν, ἀφιστᾶσαν θεοῦ τοὺς γνησίαν μὲν φιλίαν οὐκ ἔχοντας τὸ δὲ κάλλιστον τῶν ἐν ἀνθρώποις, τὴν ἀγάπην, ὑποκρινομένους; Delarue, placing a comma after ἀφιστᾶσαν θεοῦ, conforms to Fleury's translation, "*submissionem adulatoriam ortam ex imperitia avertentemque a Deo, qua ante illos procidunt qui superiores esse videntur, qui sinceram quidem amicitiam non habent et ... charitatem simulant*". But this is to take τοὺς γνησίαν ... ὑποκρινομένους as explanatory of τοὺς ὑπερέχειν νομιζομένους, which is unlikely Greek.

This petition, then, is not a prayer that we may escape temptation, but that we may not be overcome by it.[1]

9. So, then, as has been said above, all the life of man upon the earth is a temptation (Job 7. 1, LXX). Let us therefore pray to be delivered from temptation, not by not being tempted (for this is impossible, especially for those who are on earth), but by not being overcome when we are tempted. Him who is overcome when he is tempted I take to enter *into* temptation, being entangled in its nets.[2] And the Saviour, having entered into those nets for the sake of those who had been previously caught in them, bending and looking forth through the nets, as is said in the Song of Songs [3] (2. 9, LXX), gives answer to those who have been previously caught by them and have entered into temptation, and says to those who are his bride, Rise up, come, my neighbour, my fair one, my dove (Song of Songs 2. 10). I will add also this, in order to prove that there is no time free of temptation for men: not even he who meditates upon the law of God day and night (Psalm 1. 2), and practises to effect the saying, The mouth of the just shall meditate wisdom (Prov. 10. 31), is released from temptation.

There is temptation even in studying the Scriptures

10. Why need I tell how many have misinterpreted what is proclaimed in the Law and the Prophets when they have devoted themselves to the study of the sacred Scriptures, and have devoted themselves either to ungodly and impious doctrines or to those that are foolish

---

[1] Origen now comes to his explanation of this petition.

[2] This clause in the Lord's Prayer has puzzled many simple Christians. If successful resistance to temptation is a means of strengthening character, why is it that our Lord bids us pray that we be not led into temptation? Tertullian, in commenting on this clause (*De Oratione* 8), attributes temptation to the Devil, and interprets the petition as a prayer for the entire removal of sin, and the succeeding petition, "deliver us from the evil one", as explanatory of it. Origen sees in temptation an instrument of God for the perfecting of men (see *De Princ.* III. ii. 3). Origen's interpretation of the clause under consideration gives a certain emphasis to the word "into". We do not pray that we may not be tempted, but that we may not be led into temptation so that it engulfs and overcomes us.

[3] Origen sees in this verse of Solomon's Song an allegory of the Incarnation, by which the Saviour entered into the nets of temptation in order to free men, who were entangled there.

and ridiculous, since so many who do not seem to be guilty of the charge of careless reading fail in this way? And many also have failed in the same way [1] in their reading of the Apostles' and Evangelists' writings, through their own foolishness fashioning anew another Son or Father different from him who is spoken of and known to the saints according to the truth.[2] For he who does not understand the truth about God or his Christ has fallen away from the true God and his Only-begotten. And he does not in reality worship [3] the being whom his foolishness, thinking it to be Father and Son, has fashioned; and this happens to him because he has not understood the temptation that there is in reading the Holy Scriptures and does not stand armed as for a struggle which is even at that time close upon him.

But does not the word "lead" imply that God does sometimes cause a man to be overcome by temptation?

11. We must pray, then, not that we may not be tempted (for this is impossible), but that we may not be engulfed[4] by temptation, which happens to those who are held within it and overcome. Since, then, elsewhere than in the prayer, it is written [5] "that ye enter not into temptation" (Luke 22. 40) (and how this can be is clear from what we have already said), while in the prayer we must say to God the Father, "Lead us not into temptation", it is worth while to see how we must understand that God leads one who has not prayed, or one whose prayer is not answered, into temptation. For it is incongruous to think, when a man who is overcome enters into temptation, that *God* leads him into temptation as though delivering him over to be overcome. And the same incongruity also is encountered in whatever way one tries to explain the words, "Pray that ye enter not into temptation". For if it is an evil thing to fall into temptation (which we pray may not happen to us), is it not absurd to think that the good God who cannot bring forth evil fruits engulfs anyone in evil?

[1] Lit. "have suffered (or experienced) the same".
[2] Anglus detects here a reference to the Marcionites. See note on p. 198.
[3] I.e. the devotions of the Gnostics cannot be dignified by the name of worship.
[4] περιβληθῶμεν, lit. "surrounded". This word again emphasizes Origen's interpretation of the phrase as a petition not to be led *into* temptation so as to be completely surrounded and overwhelmed by it.
[5] After γέγραπται Anglus reads εὔχεσθε; Lommatzsch, προσεύχεσθε. The editor in Migne, *P.G.*, adds εὔχεσθε, although Delarue does not have it.

Romans 1 *does speak of God delivering men up to sin*

12. It will be useful, therefore, to compare with these texts what is said by Paul in the Epistle to the Romans in the following terms: Professing themselves to be wise, they became fools, and changed the glory of the uncorruptible God into an image made like to corruptible man, and to birds, and fourfooted beasts, and creeping things. Wherefore God gave them up to uncleanness through the lusts of their own hearts, to dishonour their own bodies between themselves (Rom. 1. 22–24); and a little later, For this cause God gave them up unto vile affections: for even their women did change the natural use into that which is against nature: and likewise also the men, leaving the natural use of the woman, burned (Rom. 1. 26, 27) and so on; and again a little later, And even as they did not like to retain God in their knowledge, God gave them over to a reprobate mind, to do those things which are not convenient (Rom. 1. 28). However, in all this, we must give some attention to those who cleave the Godhead into two, and ask those who think that the good Father of our Lord is different from the God of the law,[1] whether it is the good God who leads one who has not attained his prayer "into temptation", and whether it is the Father of the Lord who gives those who have sinned in any way "up to uncleanness through the lusts of their hearts, to dishonour their own bodies between themselves", and whether, relieved of judging and punishing as they say he is, he gives them up "unto vile affections", and "to a reprobate mind to do those things which are not convenient", since they would not be in "the lusts of their hearts" unless they were given over to them by God, nor would they have succumbed to "vile affections" unless they were given over to them by God, nor would they fall into a "reprobate mind" except God gave over thereto those who were thus condemned.[2]

---

[1] The Marcionites. Marcion, finding much that is recorded in the Old Testament and the sin and suffering that occurs in the world to be inconsistent with God's love, invented another "god", a god of justice, to account for these facts. This dualism enabled the Marcionites to identify the God spoken of in such passages as that under consideration with the god of law and justice, rather than the good Father of our Lord.

[2] The point lying behind this rather involved rhetorical question put by Origen to the Marcionites is that the God who can lead into temptation, whom they think to be an inferior god, is nevertheless the God whom our Lord addresses as Father in the Lord's Prayer. It is a *reductio ad absurdum* of the Marcionite position.

The Marcionites evade the difficulty by explaining these passages as referring to another god. The true explanation is that God in his concern for man's eternal welfare allows some to continue in evil, that they may become satiated, and finally repent

13. I know well that these things will greatly disturb them, and for this reason they have fashioned [1] another god, other than the maker of heaven and earth; for discovering many such things in the Law and the Prophets they have taken offence at him who utters such words, as being not good. But because of the difficulties connected with the phrase "Lead us not into temptation", on account of which we were led to compare also the words of the Apostle,[2] we must now consider whether we can find any worthy explanations of the incongruities.[3] My opinion is indeed that God deals with each rational soul with a view to its eternal life, while each soul always possesses its own free will and of its own volition either it is in a better state according as it ascends to the height of goodness, or else it descends [4] in different ways because of negligence to such or such a great depth [5] of evil.[6] Since, then, a speedy and short recovery gives rise in some to contempt for those diseases into which they have fallen as being easily curable, so that after regaining their health they fall into the same a second time, in the case of such it is reasonable that he will allow the evil which to a certain extent increases, permitting it to be diffused so widely in them as to be incurable,[7] in order that by lingering long in the evil and

---

[1] ἀναπλάσαντας, to be taken with the ἐκείνους above. So Anglus. Codex MS. and Delarue have ἀναπλάσαντες.

[2] I.e. Romans 1. 22 ff.

[3] The difficulties in the petition have now been faced and Origen proceeds to the explanation of them.

[4] ⟨ἢ⟩ καταβαίνουσαν. Bentley and Anglus also add ἤ.

[5] χύσιν, literally "heap", "abundance".

[6] In Origen's thought the possession of free will leads to the fall and rise of souls according as free will is used rightly or misused. These movements might go on through ages subsequent to this until the final consummation. It was a matter of accusation against Origen by his later enemies that this doctrine involved the transmigration of souls (e.g. Justinian, *Ep. ad Mennam*). The rise and fall of souls is discussed by Origen at length in *De Princ.* I. iv, vi, viii; III. i. 23; IV. iii. 10, and touched on in several other places.

[7] περιόψεται τὴν ἐπί τι κακίαν αὔξουσαν, καὶ ἐπὶ πλεῖστον χεομένην ἐν αὐτοῖς ἀνίατον ὑπερορῶν. Fleury: "*si malitiam in istis neglexerit et contempserit crescere et ita diffundi ut insanabilis fiat.*" The use of the word ἀνίατον is inappropriate, in that Origen a line or two later speaks of their eventual cure.

having their fill of the sin they lust after, they may become satiated and perceive the harm they have taken, hate what they formerly welcomed, and being cured may find themselves able more surely to derive benefit from the health of their souls which consists in their being healed; as, for example, the mixed multitude once among the children of Israel fell a lusting: and they sat and wept, and the children of Israel also, and said, Who shall give us flesh to eat? We remember the fish, which we did eat in Egypt freely, and the cucumbers, and the melons, and the leeks, and the onions, and the garlick: but now our soul is dried away; there is nothing at all, beside this manna, before our eyes (Num. 11. 4–6). Then a little later it is said, And Moses heard them weep throughout their families, every man at his door (Num. 11. 10). And again a little later the Lord says to Moses, And say thou unto the people, Sanctify yourselves against to-morrow, and ye shall eat flesh: for ye have wept before the Lord, saying, Who shall give us flesh to eat? for it was well with us in Egypt: and the Lord will give you flesh to eat, and ye shall eat flesh. Ye shall not eat one day, nor two days, nor five days, neither ten days,[1] nor twenty days; for a whole month shall ye eat, until it come out at your nostrils, and it be loathsome unto you: because that ye have despised the Lord which is among you, and have wept before him saying, Why came we forth out of Egypt? (Num. 11. 18–20).

God's satiating the people in the wilderness illustrates this. Its purpose was to free them from lust

14. Let us consider, then, the story, and see whether it has been of use to you that we have adduced it to explain the incongruity in the clause, "Lead us not into temptation", and in the words of the Apostle.[2] The mixed multitude among the children of Israel fell a lusting and wept, and the children of Israel with them. And it is clear that as long as they did not possess what they lusted after they could not be satiated nor be rid of their evil condition.[3] But the merciful and good God, when he gave them what they lusted after, wanted to give it in such a way as not to leave in them any lust. Therefore he says that they shall eat flesh not for one day only (for the evil condition would have remained in the soul, which would have been on fire and aflame with it, if they had participated in the flesh only for a short while); and neither does he give them what they lust after for

---

[1] οὐ⟨δὲ⟩ δέκα ἡμέρας. Codex MS., οὐ δέκα; so Delarue.
[2] Rom. 1. 22 ff.   [3] τοῦ πάθους.

two days; but wishing to satiate them with it, it is not as if he *promises* it, but rather (to him who is able to understand) he threatens them through those things which he seemed to bestow on them, when he says, Nor shall ye spend five days only in eating flesh, nor twice this number, nor yet twice that, but for so long shall ye eat, devouring flesh for a whole month, until that which ye thought good and your lusting for it, so blameworthy and base, comes out at your nostrils [1] like a choleric disease,[2] in order that I may release you from mortal life no longer with lust in your hearts, and that thus coming forth, as men who are pure from lust and remembering by how many pains ye were released from it, ye may be unable in any wise to fall into it again; or if this does ever happen, after long intervals of time, if, forgetful of the sufferings you endured through your lust, ye take not heed to yourselves and do not assimilate the Word which perfectly frees you from every disease, that ye may fall [3] into evil, and that later when the lust of earthly things [4] has come upon you ye may again pray to obtain a second time the things ye now lust after, after a period of hating them,[5] and thus to hasten back then to the good things,

---

[1] I.e. both the flesh is expelled from the body and the lust from the soul.

[2] μετὰ χολερικοῦ πάθους: cf. ἔσται ὑμῖν εἰς χολέραν of Numbers 11. 20, translated in A.V. "and it be loathsome unto you". Χολέρα, a disease in which the humours of the body (χολαί) are violently discharged by vomiting and stool (Liddell and Scott).

[3] περιπέσητε. So Delarue. Codex MS., περιπεσεῖτε. The subjunctive is to be taken after ἵνα, and as parallel with ἀπαλλάξω ... δυνηθῆτε: "in order that I may release you ... and that ... ye may be unable ... or if ... that ye may fall".

[4] τῆς γενέσεως ἐπιθυμήσαντες, a puzzling phrase. Fleury translates "*cum vos nascendi cupido incesserit*". Anglus urges that Origen is using γένεσις in the philosophical sense as denoting "things of the world". He instances this usage in Ocellus, Suidas, Philo, Celsus (ap. Origen, *Contra Celsum* VII. 727), and Origen himself (*Contra Celsum* VII. 728, VIII. 786–8). This seems likely. It is not probable that Origen here introduces the idea of re-birth. If γένεσις is to be translated "birth", the passage must be taken as a clear indication that Origen held a doctrine of transmigration of souls. He was certainly accused of this by his later enemies. Jerome (*Ep. ad Avitum* 7) attributes to Origen the words "At the end of this world each man that must pass into another world will receive the beginnings of a fresh birth". See Butterworth, *Origen on First Principles*, p. 145, note 5.

[5] τυχεῖν ὧν ἐπιθυμεῖτε, μισήσαντες τὸ ἐπιθυμούμενον. So codex MS. Anglus suggests ἐπεθυμεῖτε, μισήσαντες δὲ τό ... But this does not ease a difficult passage. "The things ye now lust after" (present tense) are the heavenly delights.

even the heavenly food which men despise when they yearn after[1] the worse.

In a similar way God deals with the reprobates mentioned in Romans 1, *that they may be finally purified and cleansed*[2]

15. A fate like unto theirs they too then will suffer who have changed the glory of the uncorruptible God into an image made like to corruptible man, and to birds, and fourfooted beasts, and creeping things (Rom. 1. 23), being abandoned and given up to uncleanness through the lusts of their own hearts, to dishonour their own bodies (Rom. 1. 24), who have attributed to a body without soul or feeling the name of him who has given to all sentient and rational creatures the power not only of perception but also of rational perception, and to some even the power of perfect and moral perception and understanding. And justly are such men forsaken in their turn by the God whom they have forsaken, and given up by him unto vile affections, receiving the recompense of the error (Rom. 1. 27) by which they loved filthy[3] pleasure. For the recompense of their error comes when they are given up unto vile affections, rather than when they are purged in the fire of wisdom[4] and when in prison they have each of their debts exacted from them unto the uttermost farthing (Matt. 5. 25, 26). For when they are given up unto vile affections (not only those which are in accordance with nature, but also many which are unnatural), they are contaminated and coarsened by the flesh, as though no longer then possessing soul or mind, but becoming nothing but flesh. But in the fire and the prison it is not the recompense of their error that they receive, but (together with salutary pains)

---

[1] ὠρέχθησαν. So codex MS. Anglus, ὠρέχθητε. Delarue and Lommatzsch, ὠρεχθήσατε.

[2] This section shows clearly Origen's belief that punishment is not eternal, but is remedial, a preparation of the soul for a further advance towards its final destiny. Cf. *De Princ.* II. v. 3; II. x. 4–8.

[3] ψωρώδους, literally "scabby".

[4] τῷ φρονίμῳ πυρί. The reference is to the fire of purgatory. Cf. Clement of Alexandria, *Strom.* VII. 6 *ad fin*: "We say that the fire sanctifies not flesh, but sinful souls; meaning not the all-devouring vulgar fire, but that of wisdom (πῦρ οὐ βάναυσον, ἀλλὰ τὸ φρόνιμον), which pervades the soul which passes through fire" (trans. Wilson, Ante-Nicene Christian Library). Cf. also Clem. Alex., *Paedagogus* III. 8 and *Eclog. Prophet.* XXV. Origen, *Hom. in Ezech.* 1, has "*ignis sapiens*", as also Minucius Felix, *Octavius* XXXV. 3. Cf. Isa. 4. 4 and Mal. 3. 2.

God's beneficence [1] for the purifying of the evils of their error which come upon the lovers of pleasure, and they are delivered from all the filth and blood in the which, when they were soiled and wallowed, they were not even able to think of their salvation by reason of the destruction in which they were involved.[2] God therefore shall wash away the filth of the sons and daughters of Zion, and shall purge the blood from the midst of them by the spirit of judgement and by the spirit of burning (Isa. 4. 4). For he cometh like a furnace fire and like fullers' soap [3] (Mal. 3. 2), washing and cleansing those who are in need of such medicines because they did not like, when tested,[4] to retain God in their knowledge (Rom. 1. 28). If they are given over [5] willingly to these medicines they will come to hate the reprobate mind (Rom. 1. 28); for God wills not [6] that good should come to anybody as by compulsion, but by free will [7] (since there may be some who from their long association with evil scarcely realize the shame of it, and turn away from it because they falsely conceive it to be good).

God's hardening of Pharaoh's heart was likewise for Pharaoh's eventual benefit. "Lead us not into temptation" is a prayer that we may do nothing to merit such drastic treatment

16. And consider whether it is for this reason also that God hardens Pharaoh's heart, that he might be able to say what he actually did say

---

[1] Origen similarly describes the fires of purgatory in *Contra Celsum* v. 588: οὐχ ὡς μάγειρόν φαμεν τὸ πῦρ ἐπιφέρειν τὸν θεόν, ἀλλ'ὡς εὐεργέτην τῶν χρῃζόντων πόνου καὶ πυρός.

[2] τῇ σφῶν ἀπωλείᾳ. Anglus suggests ἐν τῇ σφῶν ἀπωλ. to conform to LXX of Esther 8. 6, to which Origen possibly alludes.

[3] πόα πλυνόντων. So codex MS. Oxf. ed. ποία. Literally "grass", the word by which LXX translates Heb. בֹּרִית ("borith"). Some detergent prepared from grass is meant.

[4] δεδοκιμασμένως. Delarue, δεδοκιμασμένους.

[5] παραδοθέντες. So Koetschau corrects παραδιδόντες of codex MS. Anglus inserts ἑαυτούς. Delarue does not correct the text, but the editor of Migne, *P.G.*, adds ἑαυτούς.

[6] οὐ γὰρ βούλεται. Delarue omits γάρ.

[7] That the soul possesses free will is a cardinal doctrine of Origen's. The doctrine lies behind his cosmological theory. The possession of free will is the cause of the rise and fall of souls (see note 6, page 199), and ages may elapse before all are restored. The present passage shows Origen's belief that the soul's free will is always respected by God. Cf. *De Princ.* III. iii. 5, "The soul always possesses free will, both when in the body and when out of the body; and the will's freedom always moves in the direction either of good or of evil" (Butterworth, op. cit., p. 228).

when his heart was softened, The Lord is righteous, and I and my people are wicked (Ex. 9. 27). But he needs to be hardened further, and to endure further sufferings, lest, because he ceases to be hardened too quickly, he belittles the hardening as an evil, and comes to deserve a hardening even many times greater.[1] If, then, it is not unfitting that nets are spread for birds (Prov. 1. 17, LXX), as is said in Proverbs, while God with good reason leads us into the net, according to him who said, Thou broughtest us into the net (Psalm 66. 11), and without the will of the Father not even the meanest sparrow among the birds of the air falls into the net (cf. Matt. 10. 29) (for what falls into the net falls because it has not rightly used the power of the wings which were given it to raise itself aloft), let us pray that we may do nothing which will merit our being led into temptation by the righteous judgement of God, since everyone who is given up to uncleanness through the lusts of his own heart [2] is led (sc. into temptation), and so is everyone who is given up to vile affections, and everyone who, inasmuch as he did not like to retain God in himself, is given over to a reprobate mind, to do those things which are not convenient.[3]

The usefulness of temptation is to make clear what we are

17. The usefulness of temptation is this:[4] through temptations those things which our soul has admitted, and which are unknown to all except God, unknown even to ourselves, become manifest, that we may no longer be unaware what manner of men we are, but, recognizing them, may perceive, if we will, our own evils, and give thanks for the good that has been shown to us through the temptations. And that the temptations which come upon us come that we may appear what we are, or that what is hidden in our heart may be made known, is shown by what is said by the Lord in Job, and what is written in Deuteronomy; the passages are as follows: Dost thou think

---

[1] Pharaoh was, therefore, led into temptation (in the sense which Origen gives to this phrase), but it was for his eventual repentance.

[2] τῆς καρδίας ἑαυτοῦ. So Oxford ed. and Anglus. Codex MS. and Delarue, τῶν καρδιῶν ἑαυτοῦ.

[3] The sum of Origen's argument, then, is that to be led into temptation is to be overwhelmed by it (section 9). God may thus deal with souls, but it is for their eventual restoration.

[4] After the theoretical discussion of the significance of temptation, Origen now deals with the practical usefulness of it. And he ends the chapter (section 19) with a spirited exhortation to steadfastness and a word of encouragement.

XXIX. 19   ON PRAYER   205

that I have answered thee otherwise than that thou shouldest appear righteous? (Job 40. 3, LXX), and in Deuteronomy as follows: *And he humbled thee, and suffered thee to hunger, and fed thee with manna, and led thee in the wilderness, where there was the serpent that biteth,' and the scorpion and drought, that what was in thine heart might be made known* (Deut. 8. 3, 15, 2).

Instances from the Scriptures of temptation making manifest the true characters of those tempted

18. And if we will recall the story, we must know that Eve's proneness to be deceived and the corruption of her imagination [1] did not arise at the time that she disobeyed God and listened to the serpent; but existed before, and were then made manifest, since it was on this account that the serpent came to her, knowing her weakness by his own craftiness (Gen. 3. 1 ff.). Again neither did wickedness begin to exist in Cain when he killed his brother (for even before, *Unto Cain and to his offering God* who knoweth the heart *had not respect* (Gen. 4. 5)), but his wickedness came out into the open when he slew Abel. And again if Noah, having drunk the wine which he had husbanded, had not become drunk and made himself naked, neither the rashness and impiety of Ham towards his father nor the respect and reverence of his brothers towards him who begat them would have been shown (Gen. 9. 20–24). And Esau's plot against Jacob seemed to have the theft of his blessing as an excuse (Gen. 27), but even before this his soul had the roots of one who was a fornicator and profane (Heb. 12. 16). And we should not have known the shining example of Joseph's continence, fortified as he was against being taken by any lust, if his master's wife had not loved him (Gen. 39. 7 ff.).

An exhortation to prepare against future temptation, knowing that God will supply what may still be needful when we have done our utmost

19. Therefore in the intervals between the succession of temptations let us make a stand against those that are to come, and let us make preparations for all that can happen, in order that, whatever may come, we may not be convicted of unreadiness, but may be

---

[1] ἰστέον ὅτι τὸ ⟨τῆς Εὔας⟩ εὐεξαπάτητον καὶ τὸ σαθρὸν τοῦ λογισμοῦ αὐτῆς. So Anglus. Delarue suggests ἰστέον ἐν τῇ Εὔᾳ, ὅτι τὸ ... Bentley has τοῦ λογισμοῦ τῆς Εὔα.

known to have composed ourselves [1] with the utmost care. For when we bring to perfection all that is in our power, God, who works together for good in all things for those who love him (cf. Rom. 8. 28), will supply what is lacking because of human weakness, for by his unfailing foreknowledge he foresees what, of themselves, they will one day be.[2]

"*But deliver us from evil*": *this God does, not by taking away the evil, but by enabling us to withstand it*

XXX.—1. In the words, Lead us not into temptation, Luke seems to me to have included also the force [3] of the words, Deliver us from evil.[4] And surely it is natural [5] that the Lord should have spoken more briefly to the disciple,[6] inasmuch as he had been helped,[7] but to the majority, who needed clearer teaching, more plainly. Now God delivers us from evil, not when the enemy that wrestles against us does not attack us at all with his own devices, whatsoever they may be, or through the ministers of his will, but rather when we conquer, manfully making a stand against the things that happen to us.[8] In this

---

[1] ἑαυτοὺς συγκροτήσαντες, lit. "welded ourselves together".

[2] τοῖς κατὰ τὴν ἀψευδῆ πρόγνωσιν αὐτοῦ, ὅ τι ποτὲ ἔσονται παρ' αὐτοὺς, προεωραμένοις. So Anglus, taking παρ' αὐτοὺς as meaning "*per se*", "*sua sponte*", or "*ex proprio arbitrio*". Codex MS. and Delarue, παρ' αὐτοῖς.

[3] δυνάμει δεδιδαχέναι, lit. "to have taught really". Fleury, "*re ipsa docuisse*".

[4] Note that the best MSS. of Luke 11. 4 omit ἀλλὰ ῥῦσαι ἡμᾶς ἀπὸ τοῦ πονηροῦ. Cf. R.V. with A.V.

[5] καὶ εἰκός γε. So Anglus and Lommatzsch. Codex MS., καὶ εἰκός τε. So Delarue.

[6] Note that according to Luke it is "one of his disciples" who asked, "Lord, teach us to pray" (11. 1).

[7] ἅτε δὴ ὠφελημένον, i.e. by previous instruction from our Lord. Possibly ἤδη, already, is to be read instead of δή.

[8] A paraphrase may help the reader to follow Origen's argument here. God delivers us from evil, not by causing our evil enemy to cease his attacks, but by helping us to withstand evil. So, according to Paul, he delivers us from afflictions, not by causing them to cease, but by giving us his aid so that we are not distressed. Paul says "We are afflicted on every side, yet not distressed". The afflictions are still present. The distinction between "affliction" and "distress", as the underlying Hebrew words show, is that the former is experienced involuntarily, but "distress" is due to a succumbing of the will. Paul's words mean, then, that evils may still attack us, but God gives us aid to endure them; and this is precisely what we pray for when we say "deliver us from evil".

way also we interpret the words, Many are the afflictions of the righteous: and he delivereth them out of them all (Psalm 34. 19). For God delivereth from afflictions, not when afflictions no longer come upon us (at least if Paul intends the words "afflicted on every side" (2 Cor. 4. 8) to mean "not yet free from affliction"), but when, being afflicted, by the help of God we are by no means distressed,[1] the word "afflicted" traditionally among the Hebrews signifying a calamity which happens against one's will, while the word "distressed" is used of one who with full power of choice is overcome by tribulation and has surrendered to it.[2] Wherefore Paul rightly says, We are afflicted on every side, yet not distressed. I consider that the following verse in the Psalms is also similar to it:[3] Thou hast enlarged me when I was in affliction [4] (Psalm 4. 1). For by the help and presence of the Word of God who comforts and saves us, our cheerfulness and stoutness of mind which comes from God in the time of calamity is called "enlargement".

The story of Job illustrates this

2. In the same way, therefore, we are to think of a man being delivered from evil. God delivered Job not by the fact that the Devil [5] had not received power to surround him with these or those temptations (for he had received it), but by the fact that [6] in all that happened to him he sinned not at all before the Lord, but was proved righteous; for he who said, Doth Job fear God for nought? Hast not thou made an hedge about him, and about his house, and about all that he hath

---

[1] ⟨οὐ⟩ μὴ στενοχωρούμεθα. Delarue, μὴ στεν. Koetschau suggests the οὐ has fallen out after θεοῦ by haplography.

[2] Delarue takes the Hebrew word which Origen here makes θλίβεσθαι represent to be צרה, which is found in Psalm 34. He suggests that the Hebrew equivalent of στενοχωρία intended by Origen is מצהק. Anglus suggests a different interpretation of the passage—that Origen's meaning is that Paul in 2 Cor. 4. 8 is introducing a distinction between the meaning of two similar words κατά τι πάτριον παρ' Ἑβραίοις, after the manner of the Hebrew tradition.

[3] ὅμοιον δὲ τούτῳ. Codex MS. and Delarue, ὅμοιον δὲ τοῦτο.

[4] ἐν θλίψει. A.V. has "in distress". But we must translate "in affliction" here, since the word has the same root as that used by Paul in the phrase "We are afflicted on every side".

[5] ⟨τὸν διάβολον⟩. Not in codex MS. Added by Anglus and Lommatzsch. Delarue omits, but the editor of Migne, *P.G.*, inserts.

[6] ἀλλὰ ⟨τῷ⟩. So Anglus and Lommatzsch.

on every side, and blessed his works,[1] and increased his cattle in the land? But put forth thine hand, and touch all that he hath, and surely he will curse [2] thee to thy face (Job 1. 9–11), was put to shame as having then falsely accused Job, who suffered these great calamities does not, as the adversary said, curse [3] God to his face, but even when delivered over to the tempter perseveres in blessing the Lord, rebuking his wife when she said, Curse the Lord and die, and reproving her in the words, Thou speakest as one of the foolish women. If we have received good things at the hand of the Lord, shall we not endure the evil?[4] (Job 2. 9, 10). And a second time also the Devil spoke to the Lord about Job, Skin for skin, all that a man hath will he pay for his life. But put forth thine hand and touch his bone and his flesh, and he will surely curse thee to thy face (Job 2. 4, 5). But overcome by the champion of virtue, he is proved false. For although he suffered the greatest hardships, he persevered, in nothing sinning with his lips before God. But Job, having had two struggles and conquered, does not have to undergo a third such contest. For the wrestling with three temptations had to be reserved for the Saviour, as is recorded in the three Gospels, when our Saviour, known in his manhood, overcame the enemy in all three.

The necessity of beseeching God that in temptation we be not consumed

3. Therefore, having examined these things with some care, and scrutinized them among ourselves, that we may know what we are doing when we ask God that we enter not into temptation and that we may be delivered from evil, being made worthy to be heard of God because we ourselves hear him, let us beseech him that when we are tempted we be not killed, and when we are cast beneath the fiery darts of the Evil One (Eph. 6. 16), we be not set on fire by them. Now those who are "set on fire by them" are all they whose hearts, in the words of one of the twelve prophets, have become like an oven (Hos. 7. 6); but they are not set on fire who, with the shield of faith, quench all the fiery darts which are launched at them by the Evil One

---

[1] ⟨τὰ δὲ⟩ ἔργα αὐτοῦ εὐλόγησας. Koetschau adds τὰ δέ as in LXX of Job 1. 10.

[2] εὐλογήσει, representing a Hebraic euphemism.

[3] εὐλογεῖ. Codex MS. and Delarue, εὐλόγει. Koetschau takes it as present in view of the following ἐπιμένει.

[4] τὰ κακά. Delarue omits τά.

(Eph. 6. 16); for they have within them rivers of water springing up into everlasting life (John 4. 14), which do not suffer the attack of the Evil One to increase,[1] but easily bring it to nought [2] by the flood of divine and saving thoughts which are formed in the soul of him who studies to become spiritual, by his contemplation of truth.

Advice about disposition and posture in prayer, and other practical matters

XXXI.—1. After this it seems to me in place, in order to deal completely with the question of prayer, to say something by way of introduction about the disposition and posture which he who prays ought to have, and about the place in which prayer should be made, and the region towards which one should look, if circumstances permit,[3] and about the time which is suitable and desirable for prayer, and any other similar points. The word "disposition" is to be referred to the soul, and "posture" to the body. Now Paul, as we said above,[4] is describing disposition when he talks of the necessity of praying without wrath and doubting, but he is describing posture in the words, Lifting up holy hands (1 Tim. 2. 8). This seems to me to have been taken from the Psalms, where we read, The lifting up of my hands as the evening sacrifice (Psalm 141. 2). And concerning place, I will therefore that men pray everywhere (1 Tim. 2. 8); while concerning region, in the Wisdom of Solomon, That it might be known that we must prevent the sun to give thee thanks, and at the dayspring pray unto thee (Wisd. 16. 28).

Disposition: there must be due preparation of mind, quieting of disturbing thoughts, a fastening of attention on God, and a spirit of forgiveness. The most desirable posture is that of outstretched hands and uplifted eyes whenever circumstances permit

2. It seems to me, then, that he who intends to come to his prayer, if he lays something of a foundation and prepares himself, becomes more attentive and alert throughout the whole of his prayer—if he

---

[1] ἰσχῦσαι τὸ τοῦ πονηροῦ. Delarue, τὰ τοῦ πονηροῦ (sc. βέλη). Anglus reads τὸ τοῦ πονηροῦ πῦρ. Koetschau's comment on this is that πῦρ does not suit the verb λύω. Codex MS. has τὰ τοῦ πονηροῦ.
[2] αὐτὸ λύοντας. Delarue reads αὐτά.
[3] χωρὶς πάσης περιστάσεως.
[4] See IX. 1.

puts aside every temptation [1] and perturbation of mind, and reminds himself, so far as he can, of the majesty to which he draws near, and that it is impious to draw nigh thereto yawning, and careless, and, as it were, contemptuous, putting away all intruding thoughts, and in this way comes to his prayer; if he stretches forth his soul, so to speak, before his hands and stretches his mind to God before his eyes, and, before he takes his standing position, raises his intelligence from the ground and makes it stand before [2] the Lord of the universe, putting away all remembrance of wrongs against any who may seem to have injured him, just as a man wishes God not to remember wrongs against him, if he has injured and sinned against many of his neighbours or if he is conscious in himself of things done in defiance of right reason.

For neither can a man who bears as it were the image of those characteristics which become the soul in prayer, doubt in the case of the body also that although there are innumerable dispositions of the body, that which involves the stretching out of the hands and the uplifting of the eyes is to be preferred before all.[3] And these things I assert must be particularly observed, apart from any adverse circumstance; for when there is an adverse circumstance [4] it is fitting that permission be given sometimes to pray sitting because of some disease of the feet which cannot be regarded lightly, or even lying down because of fevers or such sicknesses; and in some circumstances,[5] for example if we are on a voyage, or business does not allow us to return [6] and fulfil our obligation of prayer, it is possible to pray without any pretence of doing this.[7]

Genuflection is appropriate when sins are confessed

3. And we must know that genuflection is necessary when a man is going to accuse himself of his sins before God, beseeching healing for them and remission of them, for it is a type of Paul who fell down and

[1] πάντα πειρασμόν. Bentley, followed by Delarue, reads καὶ πάντα περισπασμόν ("distraction").
[2] στήσαντα. So Anglus. Codex MS., στῆσαι.
[3] πάντων προκριτέον. So codex MS. Anglus, πασῶν (scil. καταστάσεων). If a change is to be made Koetschau prefers πάντως.
[4] μετὰ γὰρ περιστάσεως.
[5] διὰ περιεστῶτα. So Anglus. Codex MS., διὰ περιεστῶτος; so Delarue.
[6] μὴ ἐπιτρέπῃ ἀναχωροῦντας ἡμᾶς ... So Anglus. For ἡμᾶς codex MS. has μή, which Delarue deletes.
[7] I.e. standing and raising the hands.

humbled himself saying, For this cause I bow my knees unto the Father of whom the whole family in heaven and on earth is named (Eph. 3. 14, 15). When he says, That at the name of Jesus every knee should bow, of things in heaven, and things in earth, and things under the earth (Phil. 2. 10), the Apostle seems to me to be indicating spiritual genuflection, called genuflection in that each thing that has being falls down before God at the name of Jesus and humbles itself before him.[1] For we must not in any way understand the heavenly bodies to be so formed as to possess physical knees, since their bodies have been proved to be spherical [2] by those who accurately treat of these things. But he who will not admit this, will yet admit, unless he shamelessly refuses to see reason, that each member has a function, lest anything should have been created by God for the heavenly bodies to no purpose; and he is in error in either case, whether he says that bodily members were made for them by God to no purpose and not for their own particular work, or whether he says that the bowels and rectum [3] perform their own particular function even in the heavenly places.[4] And a man will be very foolish if he thinks that, as is the case with statues, the outward appearance only is that of a man, and not also the inward parts. I make these remarks as I examine the question of genuflection and observe that, At the name of Jesus every knee

[1] οὕτως ὀνομαζομένην παρὰ τὸ ὑποπεπτωκέναι τῷ θεῷ ἐν τῷ ὀνόματι Ἰησοῦ [καὶ] ἕκαστον τῶν ὄντων ⟨καὶ⟩ αὐτῷ ἑαυτὸν τεταπεινωκέναι. Koetschau omits the first καί with Anglus. Delarue keeps it. Codex MS. has καὶ ἑκάστου. Delarue, καὶ ἕκαστον. Koetschau follows Anglus in inserting the second καί.

[2] Cf. Plato, *Tim*. VII. 33B; *Tim. Loc.* II. 94D; Aristotle, *De Anim.* I. 2 (and elsewhere). Anglus points out that there is nothing in the passage under consideration to justify the later belief that Origen taught that the resurrection body would be spherical. So Justinian (*Ep. ad Mennan*): "He (Origen) says that in the resurrection the bodies of men rise spherical." Cf. H. Chadwick, "Origen, Celsus and the Stoa", *J.T.S.*, Vol. XLVIII, No. 189-90, pp. 42-3.

This passage has strong points of similarity with Plato, *Tim*. VII. 33B, where Plato is discussing the shape of the cosmos. To interpret τὰ ἐπουράνια here of the risen bodies of men, without strong reason, is impossible.

[3] τὸ ἀπευθυσμένον ἔντερον. So codex MS. Bentley and Delarue read ἀπευθυμμένον.

[4] Origen, who accepts the theory that the heavenly bodies are spherical, argues that those who will not do so, but believe that the heavenly bodies have bodily members, are forced to hold one of two errors: (*a*) that God creates bodily members which do not perform any function; (*b*) or if they do perform their proper function, then the heavenly bodies digest and evacuate food!

shall bow, of things in heaven, and things in earth, and things under the earth (Phil. 2. 10). The same also is written in the prophet: Unto me every knee shall bow (Isa. 45. 23).

Any place may be appropriate, provided no sin has been committed there, though it is doubtful whether the bedroom of the married is suitable

4. And concerning place, we must know that every place is made suitable for prayer by him who prays well; for, In every place offer incense unto me, saith the Lord (Mal. 1. 11), and, I will therefore that men pray everywhere (1 Tim. 2. 8). And so that every man may perform his prayers in quiet and without distraction, it is in order to choose in his own house, if there is room, the place of greatest honour, so to speak, and thus to pray,[1] duly considering, however, apart from his general examination of it, whether sin has ever been committed, or anything contrary to right reason been done, in this place in which he prays. For (otherwise)[2] it is as though he has made not only himself but also his place of prayer such that God turns his attention away from it.[3] And when I consider this topic still further, I must give voice to an opinion which, if it be grievous, yet perhaps is not lightly to be disregarded by one who examines the matter carefully. For it must be considered whether it is a holy and pure thing to intercede with God in the place of intercourse—not unlawful intercourse, but[4] that which is allowed by the Apostle's word by

---

[1] ἔχει δὲ καὶ τεταγμένον ὑπὲρ τοῦ ἐφ' ἡσυχίας μὴ περισπώμενον τὰς εὐχὰς ἐπιτελεῖν ἕκαστον, ἐπιλεξάμενον τοῦ ἰδίου οἴκου, ἐὰν ἐγχωρῇ, τὸ σεμνότερον, ἵν' οὕτως εἴπω, χωρίον, οὕτως εὔχεσθαι. Fleury takes τεταγμένον with χωρίον: "*Potest etiam ... certum ac definitum in privatis aedibus ... eligere locum, ut ita dicam, sanctiorem.*" The wide separation of the two words seems to be against this. I take ἔχει τεταγμένον together—lit. "it has been settled", "it is in order". Liddell and Scott comment on the use of ἔχω with the participle: "This seems the first step towards the modern use of the auxiliary verb 'to have'."

[2] The insertion of some such word is needed.

[3] ὡς φυγεῖν ἐκεῖθεν τὴν ἐπισκοπὴν τοῦ θεοῦ.

[4] ἐν γὰρ τῷ τόπῳ τῆς ⟨οὐ⟩ παρανόμου μίξεως ἀλλὰ ὑπὸ τοῦ ... MSS. Holmiensis and Colbertinus have τῆς παρανόμου μίξεως ὑπὸ τοῦ ... Anglus, οὐ μόνον τῆς παρανόμου μίξεως, ἀλλὰ καὶ τῆς ὑπὸ τοῦ ... Bentley and Delarue, τῆς ἀπαρανόμου μίξεως ὑπὸ τοῦ ...

Origen's distrust of the flesh is apparent here in the suggestion that a bedroom lawfully shared by husband and wife is not a suitable place for prayer.

permission and not of commandment (1 Cor. 7. 6). For if it is not possible to find time for prayer as one ought, "except it be with consent for a time" (1 Cor. 7. 5) that a man applies himself thereto, perhaps we ought to consider also whether (such a) place is suitable.

The place of common prayer is also the meeting-place of angels, the power of our Lord, and departed saints

5. But a place of prayer possesses something of joy in addition to the benefit it bestows, being the place of the coming together of the faithful, and, as one may reasonably believe, of angelic powers who are present at the gatherings of the faithful,[1] and of the power of our Lord and Saviour himself, and moreover of holy spirits also (I believe both those who have fallen asleep, and also, as is clear, those who remain alive), even if it is not easy to say how.[2] And with regard to angels one must consider the following: if the angel of the Lord encampeth round about them that fear him, and delivereth them (Psalm 34. 7), and if Jacob speaks truth, not only of himself but of all those that are devoted to God, when he says to him that understands, The Angel which redeems me from all evil (Gen. 48. 16), it is reasonable to suppose that, when many are gathered together in sincerity for the glory of Christ, each one's angel that is round about each of those that fear God, encamps with the man whose guardianship and guidance have been entrusted to him.[3] So there is a twofold Church when the saints are gathered together, one of men, and the other of angels. And if Raphael says that he has carried up the prayer of Tobit alone for a remembrance, and after him, that of Sarah (Tobit 12. 12), who later became his daughter-in-law [4] in that she married Tobias, what are we to say when many more come together in the same mind and

---

[1] Yet another illustration of Origen's strong belief in the ministrations of angels.

[2] οἶμαι δὲ ὅτι καὶ προκεκοιμένων, σαφὲς δὲ ὅτι καὶ ἐν τῷ βίῳ περιόντων, εἰ καὶ τὸ πῶς οὐκ εὐχερὲς εἰπεῖν. This is difficult. It seems to me that the two participles προκεκ. and περιόντων are to be taken with πνευμάτων ἁγίων. Origen means that of the "holy spirits" some have fallen asleep, some remain alive. The latter are obviously present at the place of prayer. He believes the former are also present, though it is not easy to say how this happens. But the δέ after οἶμαι is awkward. Yet the whole sentence is but loosely bound together in a conversational style.

[3] Cf. XI. 1.

[4] τῆς ὑστέρως νύμφης γενομένης. Codex MS., τῆς ὑστέρας. But, as Anglus points out, Tobias had no previous wife. He therefore reads ὕστερον.

heart and are made one body in Christ?[1] And with regard to the power of the Lord being present with the Church, Paul says, When ye are gathered together, and my spirit, with the power of the Lord Jesus (1 Cor. 5. 4), the power of the Lord Jesus being united not only with the Ephesians,[2] but also with the Corinthians. And if Paul when still clothed in the body considered himself to be united in his spirit [3] at Corinth,[4] we must not give up hope that thus also the blessed who have departed are present in spirit at the gatherings of the Church, perhaps more so than one who is in the body. Wherefore we must not belittle prayers therein, for they bestow a singular grace on anyone who in sincerity comes to the assembly.

But the place where wicked men gather is probably the meeting-place also of wicked angels

6. And as the power of Jesus, and the spirit of Paul and of those like him, and the angels of the Lord who encamp around every saint, meet and come together with those who gather together in sincerity, so one must wonder whether perchance, if a man be not worthy of a holy angel, he does not also deliver himself over to an angel that is a devil [5] because of his sins and transgressions in despite of God.[6] For such a man, if there are but few like him, will not long escape the notice of the providence of the angels in their attendance upon the divine will which guards [7] the Church, and then providence will bring

---

[1] Origen's argument seems to be that as Sarah shared the benefits of the angel's ministry by virtue of her kinship with Tobit, it may be expected that those who are made one family in Christ will enjoy an even greater ministry of angels. There is no hint in the LXX of Tobit of Sarah's prayers being brought by Raphael before God in virtue of her kinship with Tobit.

[2] Paul wrote 1 Corinthians from Ephesus.

[3] A reference to the words καὶ τοῦ ἐμοῦ πνεύματος in 1 Cor. 5. 4.

[4] ἐν τῇ Κορίνθῳ. Anglus, τοῖς ἐν τῇ K., which reads more easily.

[5] ἐὰν ἁγίου ἀγγέλου ἀνάξιός τις ᾖ καὶ ἐπιδῷ ἑαυτὸν ἀγγέλῳ διαβόλῳ. So Anglus, except that he reads ἀγγέλῳ διαβόλου. Codex Holmiensis has καὶ ἐπὶ τῷ ἑαυτὸν ἀγγέλλων διαβόλῳ. Colbertinus has ἑαυτὸν ἀγγέλῳ διαβόλῳ παραδῷ, which Delarue follows.

[6] δι' ὧν ἁμαρτάνει καὶ θεοῦ καταφρονῶν παρανομεῖ. So Codex Holm. and Oxford ed. Colbertinus, followed by Delarue, has δι' ὧν ἁμαρτάνων παρανομεῖ.

[7] ὑπηρεσίᾳ τοῦ θείου βουλήματος, ἐπισκοποῦντος. Koetschau remarks that Anglus' emendation ἐπισκοπούντων is probably right, in which case translate "of the angels who in their attendance upon the divine will guard the Church".

the trespasses of such an one to the notice of many. But if men of this sort become numerous as human societies do, and meet together to transact mundane business, they shall not have the guardianship of the angels. This is made clear in Isaiah when the Lord says, Not even if ye come to appear before me (Isa. 1. 12); for he says, I will turn away mine eyes from you: and if ye make many prayers, I will not hear you (Isa. 1. 15). For it may be that instead of the twofold rank of holy men and blessed angels mentioned above, there comes together again a twofold gathering of impious men and wicked angels; and in the case of an assembly of this sort, it may be said both by the holy angels and by pious men, I have not sat with the council of vanity, neither will I go in with transgressors. I have hated the congregation of evil doers; and will not sit with the wicked (Psalm 26. 4, 5).

For the present condition of the Jews witnesses to the fact that whole congregations can be forsaken by God. The common gathering-place of the saints, then, is the best place in which to pray

7. For this reason, too, I think that those in Jerusalem and all Judaea, having fallen into many sins, have become subject to their enemies, because the peoples who have forsaken the law have been forsaken by God and the guardian angels and the protection of holy men. For in this way sometimes even whole congregations are forsaken to fall into temptations, so that even that which they seem to have is taken from them (Luke 8. 18); like the fig tree, accursed and plucked up [1] by the roots because it gave no fruit to Jesus, when he hungered, they are withered (Mark 11. 13 ff.), and if by faith they had a vestige of life-giving power, they lose it. These things I think it has been necessary to say in considering the place of prayer, and suggesting that it is preferable in the place where the saints also come together, who with due piety gather together with the Church.

To pray facing the east is natural and has symbolic value

XXXII. Now also we must say a few things about the region [2] towards which we must look when praying. There being four regions, towards north and south, towards sunsetting and sunrising,

---

[1] ἀρθείσῃ. Anglus notices the discrepancy here from Mark's account of the incident, and suggests ξηρανθείσῃ.
[2] περὶ τοῦ κλίματος.

who would not at once agree that the region towards the sunrising [1] clearly indicates that we ought to make our prayers facing in that direction in symbolic fashion as though the soul beheld the rising of the true light? But, since the door of the house may face in any direction, if a man desires to make his intercessions rather in the direction that the house opens, on the plea that the sight of the heaven has something more inviting about it than looking at the wall, if the doors of the house happen not to look towards the sunrising, we must say to him that since it is by arrangement that the buildings of men open [2] towards this or that region, while it is by nature that the east is preferred before the other regions, we must put that which is by nature before that which is by arrangement. Moreover, according to this argument, why should a man who wishes to pray in an open space pray towards the east rather than towards the west? But if the east is reasonably to be preferred there,[3] why is this not to be done everywhere? And so much for this subject.[4]

The sections of prayer: praise, thanksgiving, confession, petition, and praise again at the end

XXXIII.—1. Now I think that when I have dealt with the sections [5] of prayer, I shall have thus brought my argument to a conclusion. It appears, then, to me that there are four sections to be described, which I have found scattered in the Scriptures, and we must each organize our prayer in accordance with them. These sections are as follows: according to our ability at the beginning and exordium of our prayer we must address praises [6] to God through Christ, who is praised together with him in the Holy Spirit, who is likewise hymned; and after this each must place thanksgiving, both general—enumerating with thanksgiving God's benefits to the many—and for those things

---

[1] τὸ πρὸς ἀνατολήν. Oxf. ed. and Delarue, τὰ πρὸς ἀνατολήν.
[2] θέσει τῶν οἰκοδομημάτων ἀνθρώπων ... διανοιγομένων. So cod. MS. and Delarue. Anglus, θέσει ⟨μὲν⟩ ἀνθρώπων τῶν οἰκ., "by arrangement of men, buildings open ...".
[3] I.e. in an open space.
[4] On praying towards the east, cf. Clement of Alexandria, *Strom.* VII. 1. See p. 42 above.
It must be remarked that in this chapter Origen's spiritual acuteness seems to fail him.
[5] περὶ τῶν τόπων.
[6] δοξολογίας.

ON PRAYER

which each has received privately from God;[1] and after thanksgiving it seems to me that one ought to be a bitter accuser of one's own sins before God, and to ask first for healing so as to be delivered from the state that leads to sin, and secondly[2] for remission of what is past; and after confession, in the fourth place it seems to me we must add petition for the great and heavenly gifts for ourselves, and for people in general, and also for our families and friends; and in addition to all this, our prayer ought to end in praise to God through Christ in the Holy Spirit.

Psalm 104 is an example of praise

2. These sections of prayer, as I said before, I have found scattered in the Scriptures: praise in the hundred and third Psalm (104, A.V.) in these words, O Lord my God, how exceeding great art thou; thou art clothed with honour[3] and majesty, who coverest thyself with light as with a garment: who stretchest out the heavens like a curtain: who covereth his upper chambers with waters: who maketh the clouds his chariot: who walketh upon the wings of the wind: who maketh his angels spirits, and his ministers a flame of fire: who layeth the foundation of the earth that it may be safe; it shall not fall for ever. The deep as a garment is his clothing: the waters shall stand above the mountains. At thy rebuke they shall flee; at the voice of thy thunder they shall be afraid (Psalm 104. 1–7). And the greater part of this Psalm contains praise of the Father. And one can collect many more (such passages) for oneself and see how this section of praise is scattered everywhere (in the Scriptures).

---

[1] καὶ μετὰ τοῦτο τακτέον ἑκάστῳ εὐχαριστίας τε κοινὰς, ⟨τὰς⟩ πρὸς πολλοὺς εὐεργεσίας προσάγοντα ἐπὶ τῆς εὐχαριστίας, καὶ ὧν ἰδίᾳ τέτευχεν ἀπὸ θεοῦ.
Cod. Col. has εὐχαριστίας τε κοινὰς ὑπὲρ τῶν εἰς πάντας εὐεργεσιῶν καὶ ὧν ἰδίᾳ τέτευχεν. So Delarue.
Cod. Holm., εὐχαριστίας τε κοινὰς πρὸς πολλοὺς εὐεργεσίας προσάγοντας ἐπὶ τῆς εὐχαριστίας καὶ ὧν ἰδίᾳ τέτευχεν. So Oxf. ed. Προσάγω seems to be used in the sense of "bringing on", "introducing", one by one.
[2] δεύτερον ⟨δέ⟩. The δέ is inserted by Koetschau, following Anglus.
[3] So A.V. The Gk. word in the text is ἐξομολόγησιν. The verb ἐξομολογοῦμαι has both the meaning of "to confess" and "to give thanks" in N.T. (in LXX its meaning is usually, if not always, "to give thanks"). So the noun ἐξομολόγησις bears both the meaning of "confession" and "thanksgiving".

David provides us with an example of thanksgiving

3. And of thanksgiving let this example, found in the Second Book of Kings (A.V., 2 Samuel), be cited, uttered [1] by David after Nathan's promises to him, being astonished at the gifts of God, and giving thanks for them in these words, Who am I, O Lord, my Lord? And what is my house, that thou hast loved me to this extent? And I am become very small in thy sight, O my Lord; and thou hast spoken of thy servant's house for a great while to come. And this is the law of man, O Lord, my Lord. And what can David say more unto thee? And now, O Lord, thou knowest thy servant. For thy servant's sake thou hast done it, and according to thine own heart hast thou performed all this thy greatness to make it known unto thy servant, that thou mightest magnify thyself, O Lord, my Lord (2 Sam. 7. 18–22).

Examples of confession in the Psalms

4. And as an example of confession, Deliver me from all my transgressions (Psalm 39. 8), and elsewhere, My wounds stink and are corrupt because of my foolishness. I am troubled and bowed down to the uttermost; I go mourning all the day long (Psalm 38. 5, 6).

An example of petition from the Psalms

5. There is an example of petition in the twenty-seventh Psalm (A.V., Psalm 28): Draw me not away with the sinners, and with the workers of iniquity, lest thou destroy me with them (Psalm 28. 3), and other similar passages.

Our prayers should end with praise

6. And it is a good thing to bring one's prayer to an end, having begun with praise, to close also in praise, hymning and glorifying the Father of all, through Jesus Christ, in the Holy Spirit, to whom be glory for ever.

Origen asks for the prayers of his readers and for their indulgence in reading his work

XXXIV. All this I have struggled through as I have been able, my most studious and true kinsmen in piety, Ambrosius and Tatiana,

---

[1] ἀπαγγελλόμενον. Delarue, ἐπαγγελλόμενον.

upon the subject of prayer, and upon the prayer in the Gospels and the prolegomena to it in Matthew. And I do not doubt that if you reach forth unto those things which are before, and forget those things which are behind (Phil. 3. 13), and meanwhile pray for me, I shall be able to receive from God the giver greater things and more divine in addition to all these, and when I have received them, to discourse again on the same subject with greater excellence, depth, and clarity; but for the present please read this with indulgence.

APPENDIX F

ΕΠΙΟΥΣΙΟΣ

DISCUSSIONS of this ἅπαξ λεγόμενον may be found in Moulton's *Grammar of New Testament Greek*, Vol. II, pp. 313-4; F. H. Chase's "The Lord's Prayer in the Early Church" in *Texts and Studies* (Cambridge), I, pp. 45 ff.; Matthew Black's *An Aramaic Approach to the Gospels and Acts* (Clarendon Press, 1946), Part IV, Chapter 7, pp. 149 ff., as well as in the usual commentaries on St Matthew's and St Luke's Gospels.

There are two main questions to be decided: (1) Is the word derived from ἐπί and the participle of εἶναι, or a noun derived from that participle; or is it derived from ἐπί and the participle, or some noun derived therefrom, of ἰέναι? (2) As Origen saw, the Greek word was invented to represent an Aramaic original. What is this Aramaic?

If we knew with certainty the answer to (1) we could pronounce with more confidence on (2). Conversely, if we knew exactly what the Aramaic original was, we should be in a position to give a certain answer to (1). Unfortunately, different answers are given to both questions, and all are supported by strong lines of reasoning.

(1) *The Derivation of ἐπιούσιος from ἐπί and εἶναι (fem. part. οὖσα, or noun οὐσία)*

Moulton holds that the non-elision of ι in ἐπί is not a conclusive argument against derivation from ἐπί and οὐσία.

This is the derivation suggested first by Origen, *De Oratione* XXVII. 7 (see pp. 170 ff.). So also Jerome translates "*supersubstantialis*", by which, he tells us, he means "*super omnes substantias*", i.e. "*praecipuus*", "*egregius*", or "*peculiaris*".

Origen relates the -ούσιος to the divine essence (XXVII. 7), but XXVII. 9 suggests that he takes the word to mean "(bread) which can pass over into (ἐπί) the substance of him who assimilates it".

The Derivation of ἐπιούσιος from ἐπί and ἰέναι (fem. part. ἰοῦσα)

Most modern scholars consider the derivation to be from ἐπί and ἰέναι.

Ἔπειμι means "to come close after", and the fem. participle *ἐπιοῦσα* was used to express the immediately following day. Thus ἡ *ἐπιοῦσα*, if used in the evening, would mean "to-morrow"; if used in the morning, it would mean "the day which is just beginning". So Grotius, Scaliger, Wetstein, Winer, Fritzsche, Schmiedel, Meyer, Lightfoot, Chase, Plummer. Moulton too inclines to the derivation of *ἐπιούσιος* from ἡ *ἐπιοῦσα* used in this sense.

(Debrunner suggests that *ἐπιούσιος* is a substantivizing of *ἐπὶ τὴν οὖσαν (ἡμέραν)*, "for the current day". This view was accepted by Albert Thumb, but by few other scholars.)

(2) *The Aramaic Words behind ἐπιούσιος*

(*a*) Chase (op. cit.) conjectures an original Aramaic phrase behind this clause in the Lord's Prayer, meaning "Our-bread of-the-day give to-us".

For Hebrew and Syrian Christians this phrase would be appropriate when used in the morning. In the evening some adaptation would be necessary. Jerome, commenting on Matt. 6. 11, gives a hint of this. He says "In the Gospel which is called 'according to the Hebrews' I have found, instead of '*supersubstantialis*' bread, *mahar*, which is to say 'of to-morrow', so that the sense is 'Give us to-day our bread for to-morrow', that is, for the future ".

Ἐπιούσιος was an adjective coined from the expression ἡ *ἐπιοῦσα* for the use of Hellenistic Christians. This adjective was especially appropriate in that it would have been equally fitting for use in the morning or in the evening. *Ἡ ἐπιοῦσα (ἡμέρα)* was used both of the day already begun, and also as an equivalent of ἡ *αὔριον* (see Acts 7. 26; 16. 11; 20. 15), and the adjective *ἐπιούσιος* derived from it could equally well be used in the morning or evening.

This adjective, then, Chase argues, was very early used in the assemblies of the Church, and became firmly attached to the noun *ἄρτος* before the first and third Gospels were written. In Matthew, in addition to the adjective, there appears the natural Greek adverbial form of the original Aramaic "of-the-day" in the word *σήμερον*; and in Luke, again in addition to the adjective, there appears a free translation, *τὸ καθ'ἡμέραν*. Thus, in both versions there is strictly a tautology, occasioned by the "devotional conservatism" which retained the adjective *ἐπιούσιος* which had long been used in this prayer in Hellenistic Christian circles.

Chase finds confirmation of his view in James 2. 15 ff., where he claims that the phrase τῆς ἐφημέρου τροφῆς is reminiscent of an original petition in Aramaic for "the bread of the day"; and also in an indirect reference to this clause of the Lord's Prayer in Ephrem,[1] which provides evidence that among Syrian Christians of the fourth century there was a popular version of the Lord's Prayer which contained the phrase "bread of the day". The Arabic version of Tatian's Diatessaron (published by Ciasca in 1888) has "Give us the bread of our day" (i.e., says Chase, the day in which we now are). The Diatessaron was widely used in public worship, and its version of the Lord's Prayer may well have been that which had been used by Christians in worship from the beginning.

Chase admits that the evidence is "no doubt scanty", but he claims that, as far as it goes, it does favour his conjecture that behind the Gospel versions of this clause was an Aramaic phrase meaning "Give us the (or our) bread of the day". The petition is for bodily needs; the adjective is temporal, not qualitative, and is not part of the original form of the petition as taught by our Lord, but is due to liturgical use.

(b) Matthew Black (op. cit.) first gives some attention to Arnold Meyer's theory that the original Aramaic of the petition meant "Bread which is sufficient for us (lahma d^emissathna) give us day by day". Ἐπιούσιος he derives from ἐπὶ τὴν οὐσίαν, meaning "for our necessity", "necessary". (So the Peshitta, "the bread of our necessity".) Black rejects this theory on the grounds that (i) the "bread which is sufficient for us" of the conjectured Aramaic is not the equivalent of "bread of our necessity", the meaning which Meyer assigns to ἐπιούσιος; and (ii) it is very doubtful whether so rare a word as ἐπιούσιος would have been used to express the meaning "necessary", when common Greek words for it were available.

Black himself connects ἐπιούσιος with ἐπιέναι, and especially with ἡ ἐπιοῦσα (ἡμέρα).

The Aramaic original of the clause he considers to be:

> Give us our bread (habh lana lahma)
> Day by day (yoma den w^eyomahra)

"Yoma den w^eyomahra" is a common Semitic expression. Black believes it to be behind the Greek of Luke 13. 32, which should thus be translated, "Behold I cast out demons, and I do cures *day by day*,

---

[1] "The bread of the day shall suffice thee, as thou hast learned in the Prayer."

but one day soon I am perfected"; and Luke 13. 33, which should be translated, "But *day by day* I must needs work; then one day soon pass on". Compare also Gen. 39. 10, where the Jerusalem Targum has "yoma den wᵉyomaḥra"; and Esther 3. 4, where the Targum has "yoma wᵉyomaḥra".

Black's contention, then, is that the petition as taught by our Lord was, very simply, "Give us our bread day by day" ("yoma den wᵉyomaḥra"). "A translator of the Aramaic who failed to recognize the idiom and felt constrained to give a Greek equivalent of the words he found before him would get into difficulties with his rendering of 'yomaḥra'." Matthew's text shows such a misunderstanding. His σήμερον translates "yoma (den)", and ἐπιούσιον is an attempt to provide an equivalent of "(den) wᵉyomaḥra". "Luke retains τὸν ἐπιούσιον, which he no doubt found in Q, but he has combined it with the true tradition, a correct rendering of the Aramaic, τὸ καθ' ἡμέραν."

One weak spot in this argument is that it rests first of all on the fact that "yoma wᵉyomaḥra" was "a common Semitic idiom, and examples in Aramaic are frequent", and secondly on the assumption that the "common" idiom was completely misunderstood.

The discussion of this crux will go on as long as Hellenistic Greek and Hebrew scholarship flourish.

INDEX OF SCRIPTURAL QUOTATIONS AND REFERENCES IN Περὶ Εὐχῆς

The Old Testament

Genesis
1. 3....157
9....157
11....157
20....157
24....157
3. 1 ff....205
8....150 f.
9....151
22....175
4. 5....205
16....152
9. 20–24....205
18. 2–6....176
11....81
19. 37....179
38....179
25. 23....95
27. general....205
28....132
28. 20–22....88
39. 7 ff....205
48. 16....213

Exodus
3. 14....154
8. 8....89
9....89
28–29....89
30....89
9. 27....204
27–28....89
33....89 f.
10. 17–18....90
12. 2, 3, 6....180
18....180
19. 5....171
20. 7....155
21. 2....180
32. 11....123

Leviticus
16. 29....180
17. 11....191
23. 24, 27, 28....180
25. 4–7....180
8 ff....180
27. 1–3....90

Numbers
6. 1–3....90
5....90
13....90
20–21....90
11. 4–6....200
10....200
11. 18–20....200
15. 27, 31....189
30. 1–4....90 f.

Deuteronomy
4. 20....119
8. 2....205
3....205
15....205
9. 9....168
18....123
15. 1....180
9....109
16. 9....180
16....141, 182
23. 1....141
3....141
7–8....141
30. 14....158
32. 2–3....155
6....145
18....145
20....145
43 (LXX)....129

Joshua
10. 12....124 f.
22. 16, 18–19 (LXX)....179

Judges
11. 30–31....92
16. 30....125

1 Samuel
1. 9–11....91 f.
10 ff....116, 123 f.
12–13....87
2. 25....185, 190
12. 16–18....120

2 Samuel
7. 18–20....218

SCRIPTURAL QUOTATIONS AND REFERENCES

1 Kings
17–18. general.................121

2 Kings
20. 1 ff.....................116 f.
23. 15........................102

2 Chronicles
32. 25–26....................194

Esther
3. 6..........................117
4. 16.........................117
9. 26.........................117
13. 8–9......................123
14. 3........................123

Job
1. 5..........................190
   9–11.....................207 f.
   22.........................109
2. 4–5.......................208
   9–10......................208
   10.........................109
3. 8 (LXX)...................120
7. 1 (LXX)..............191, 196
40. 3 (LXX).................204 f.
   14 (LXX)...................165

Psalms
1. 2..........................196
4. 1..........................207
   6..........................108
5. 3..........................115
7. 9..........................105
17. title......................87
   29 (LXX)..................191
20. 7.........................117
22. 22........................130
25. 1.........................107
26. 2.........................193
   4–5........................215
28. 3.........................218
30. title.....................156
   1..........................156
31. 18........................157
33. 17........................117
34. 3.........................156
   7..........................213
   19....................192, 207
37. 14........................194
38. 5–6......................218
39. 8.........................218
44. 25.........................84
45. 17........................155
58. 3..........................95
   4..........................144
   6–7.......................118

Psalms—*continued*
66. 11........................204
73. 13–14....................177
74. 19........................119
78. 25........................175
82. 7.........................140
90. title.....................87
   2...........................96
   4..........................179
91. 13........................120
95. 7–8......................179
102. title....................87
104. 1–7....................217
   24..........................79
107. 20.......................167
109. 1........................102
   8.........................96 f.
   11–12.....................157
110. 1........................160
   4..........................128
119. 62.......................115
123. 1...................107, 152
141. 2...................115, 209
148. 3........................103

Proverbs
1. 17 (LXX)...................204
3. 18.........................175
4. 23.........................195
10. 19........................144
   31........................196
13. 8 (LXX)..................194
15. 17........................170
   32........................188
20. 25.........................91
22. 26–27 (LXX).............187
30. 9.........................193

Ecclesiastes
5. 2..........................152
   5...........................91

Song of Solomon
2. 9–10 (LXX)................196

Isaiah
1. 2..........................145
   12........................215
   15........................215
4. 4..........................203
25. 8.........................118
27. 12........................112
34. 5.........................162
40. 6–8......................135
45. 23........................212
49. 22–23....................129
58. 9.........................109
61. 1.........................151

SCRIPTURAL QUOTATIONS AND REFERENCES

Jeremiah
7. 22–23 108
11. 4 119
15. 1 116
23. 24 110

Daniel
3. 25 (LXX) 123
  50 (LXX) 117, 132
6. 10 115
  22 117

Hosea
7. 6 208
14. 9 .... 87 f.

Amos
8. 11 170

Jonah
2. general 117
  1–3 124

Habbakuk
3. 1–2 (LXX) 124

Zechariah
7. 10 108

Malachi
1. 6 145
  11 212
3. 2 203

The Apocrypha

Tobit
3. 1–2 123
  16–17 111
12. 8 111
  12 .... 111, 213
  15 111

Judith
8. 26–27 192
13. 4–9 117

Wisdom of Solomon
1. 7 110
9. 13–16 79
11. 24 94
16. 28 209

2 Maccabees
15. 13–15 111

The New Testament

Matthew
1. 9–10 .... 116 f.
3. 5 87
  7 177
4. 11 112
5. 1–2 137
  23–24 83
  25–26 202
  34–35 .... 151, 152
  44 82
  45 147
6. 2 .... 139, 195
  5 139
  5–9 138
  7 .... 83, 105, 143, 144
  8 .... 94, 136
  9 127
  9–13 136
  11 166
  12 .... 183, 188
  13 190
8. 10 141
9. 38 82
10. 29 204
  30 113
11. 9 87

Matthew—continued
18. 10 .... 114, 185
  30–35 .... 187 f.
22. 32 131
24. 20 82
25. 35–36 112
  64 160
28. 15 179
  18 163

Mark
1. 35 116
10. 18 130
11. 13 ff. 215
  25 .... 83, 108
12. 30 185

Luke
1. 13 123
4. 19 141
6. 12 116
8. 18 215
9. 38 126
10. 18 165
  19 120
  21 125
  27 185

Luke—continued
- 11. 1 .... 86, 116, 127, 137
- 2 146
- 2–3 161
- 2–4 136
- 3 166
- 4 .... 183, 188, 190
- 5–6 110
- 8 110
- 9–10 110
- 13 110
- 15. 7 111
- 16. 22–24 194
- 17. 4 188
- 20–21 158
- 18. 1–2 110
- 22. 27 112
- 40 .... 82, 197

John
- 1. 12 145
- 14 169
- 51 113
- 4. 14 209
- 35–36 121
- 5. 44 .... 139, 195
- 6. 26 167
- 27 167
- 28–29 167
- 32 168
- 32–33 167
- 34–35 168
- 51 .... 168, 174
- 53–57 .... 168 f.
- 58 169
- 63 166
- 11. 42 116
- 52 112
- 13. 1 149
- 3 149
- 14. 23 .... 143, 149, 158
- 28 149
- 16. 5 149
- 23–24 129
- 17. 1 116
- 20. 17 149
- 22–23 189
- 23 126

Acts
- 1. 20 .... 96 f.
- 2. 21 112
- 7. 60 126
- 10. 9–11 115
- 11–12 .... 177 f.
- 15 178
- 28 178
- 11. 8 178
- 14. 22 192

Acts—continued
- 16. 25 115
- 21. 23 91

Romans
- 1. 22–24 198
- 23–24 202
- 26–27 198
- 27 202
- 28 .... 198, 203
- 6. 12 .... 159, 160
- 8. 9 108
- 13 119
- 14 130
- 15 .... 110, 130, 145
- 16–17 147
- 26 .... 82, 84
- 26–27 .... 84, 124
- 28 206
- 29–30 96
- 37 85
- 9. 11–12 95
- 12–13 95
- 10. 10 147
- 13 112
- 11. 33 180
- 12. 2 147
- 6 132
- 13. 7–8 .... 183 f.
- 14. 2 169
- 10 187

1 Corinthians
- 1. 5 .... 134, 193
- 30 79
- 2. 6 144
- 9 182
- 10 86
- 11 80
- 12–13 80
- 16 80
- 3. 1–3 169
- 17 194
- 22 183
- 4. 9 185
- 11–13 193
- 5. 4 214
- 6. 17 162
- 7. 3 186
- 5 .... 83, 105, 186, 213
- 6 .... 212 f.
- 10. 13 191
- 11. 4–5 .... 83 f.
- 12. 3 146
- 7 132
- 8 159
- 26 112
- 13. 9–10 160
- 10 160
- 12 112

SCRIPTURAL QUOTATIONS AND REFERENCES

1 Corinthians—*continued*
- 14. 15 .... 86, 114
- 15. 9 103
- 10 103
- 24 160
- 26 160
- 28 160
- 41 161
- 49 .... 147, 152
- 50 166
- 53 161
- 55 160

2 Corinthians
- 2. 14–15 108
- 3. 18 .... 107 f.
- 4. 8 207
- 8–9 193
- 5. 10 187
- 6. 14–15 160
- 10. 3 119
- 11. 23 192
- 23–25 .... 192 f.
- 28–29 112
- 12. 4 .... 79 f., 84
- 6–7 82
- 7 .... 103, 193

Galatians
- 1. 4 159
- 15 95
- 4. 1–2 145
- 4 145
- 6 84
- 10 179
- 5. 17 191
- 6. 8 139

Ephesians
- 1. 4–5 96
- 2. 7 181
- 3. 14–15 211
- 20 .... 101, 182
- 4. 30 185
- 5. 27 141
- 6. 12 .... 162, 191, 192
- 16 .... 208, 208 f.

Philippians
- 2. 8 .... 149, 163
- 10 .... 211, 212

Philippians—*continued*
- 3. 13 .... 160, 219
- 20 148
- 21 .... 84, 147, 152
- 4. 13 95

Colossians
- 1. 15 163
- 16 135
- 19 149
- 2. 3 142
- 14 186
- 3. 5 160
- 10 147

1 Thessalonians
- 5. 17 114

1 Timothy
- 2. 1 122
- 8 .... 106, 203, 212
- 8–10 83
- 9–10 107

2 Timothy
- 3. 4 140

Hebrews
- 1. 6 129
- 4. 15 130
- 5. 12–14 169
- 9. 26 181
- 10. 1 179
- 12. 16 205
- 13. 8 179

James
- 5. 17–18 121

1 Peter
- 2. 11 191

1 John
- 2. 1 110
- 3. 8 .... 147, 148
- 9 .... 145, 147
- 5. 16 190

Revelation
- 1. 20 .... 112 f.
- 3. 20 .... 176 f.

INDEX OF PATRISTIC QUOTATIONS AND REFERENCES

Athanasius
Oratio c. Arianos I. 39.............178

Athenagoras
Legatio pro Christianis XI............13

Augustine
Confessiones X. 27.................65

Barnabas
Epistle
XII.........................14
XVI..........................9

Clement of Alexandria
Stromateis
I. 24.....................31, 82
II. 20........................97
 |23........................38
III. 12.......................83
V. 3.........................30
  10.........................30
VI. 9................29, 31, 34 f.
  12.........................29
  14..................28, 33, 144
VII. 1......................216
  6........................202
  7........26, 27, 28, 29, 30, 31,
           32, 33, 34, 35, 37, 38,
           42, 44, 93, 115, 148
  10....................26, 27
  11–14....................27
  12......28, 29, 30, 32, 34, 38, 44
  13...................30, 32
Exhortation to the Heathen (Λόγος προτρεπτικός)
X. 28........................27
  29.........................30
XII. 34....................27 f.
The Tutor (Παιδαγωγός)
II. 4....................30, 37
  9....................30, 38
III. 8......................202
  12.........................34
Extracts from the Prophetical Writings
XXV.......................202

Clement of Rome
Epistle to the Corinthians
29...........................6
38........................6, 12
41...........................6

Clement of Rome—continued
Epistle to the Corinthians—continued
48...........................6
53...........................6
55...........................6
56........................6, 43

The Didache
II............................7
IV..........................7 f.
VIII......................8, 36
XV............................8

Epiphanius
Haereseis
42.........................130

Eusebius of Caesarea
Historia Ecclesiastica
II. 23........................15
IV. 3........................13
V. 5.........................15
VI. 1–39....................47
  46.........................49

Hegesippus
Fragment in Eusebius, H.E. II. 23.....7

Hermas
The Shepherd
Visions
I. 1.........................10
II. 1........................10
Mandates
IX..........................10
X........................10 f.
Parables
II..........................12
IV..........................11
V. 3........................11
  4.........................11

Hippolytus
Apostolic Tradition
XVIII. 1....................21
XXX. 1.....................36
XXXV. 1....................36
XXXVI. 2–8.................36
  12.....................36, 41
  13–14....................36
  15.........................21

230

PATRISTIC QUOTATIONS AND REFERENCES

Ignatius of Antioch
  Eph. xxi.........................6
  Mag. xiv.........................6
  Trall.
    xii...............................6
    xiii..............................6
  Rom.
    iii...............................6
    ix...............................6
  Phil. x...........................6
  Smyrn. xi........................6
  Polycarp
    i..............................6 f.
    vii..............................6

Irenaeus
  Contra Haereses
    iv. 14..........................16
    17..........................16, 17
    18.............................17

Jerome
  Ad Avitum 7....................201

Justin Martyr
  Apology
    i. 13.......................13, 15
    61.........................15, 20
  Dialogue with Trypho
    lxxiv. 3........................15
    xc. 5...........................14
    xciii. 3........................15
    xcvi............................38
      2-3..........................13
    cv. 3-5.........................15
    cviii...........................13
    cxvii...........................16
    cxxxiii. 6......................13

Minucius Felix
  Octavius xxxv. 3...............202

Origen
  Commentaries :
    Song of Songs
      78...........................65
      91...........................64
    Matthew
      xi. 14......................169
      xii..........................96
      xiii.........................96
      xv. 18......................165
        31.......................181
      xvi. 8......................185
        26.......................177
      xxvii. 30...................111
    John
      i. 17.......................165
        30...................65, 128
        37......................164

Origen—continued
  Commentaries—continued
    John—continued
      40..........................130
      ii. 6........................128
      7...........................130
      18..........................128
      x. 13.......................168
      x. 21....................127 f.
      xiii. 57....................111
      xix. 1......................144
      xx. 20......................165
      xxviii. 4....................42
      xxxii. 24...................169
  Homilies
    In Gen.
      i. 13........................64
      15..........................64
    In Levit.
      ii. 4.......................189
      vii.........................177
      xi. 2.......................190
      xiv. 3.......................44
    In Num.
      xvi. 9......................169
      xxvi. 6.....................111
      xxvii.......................64
        12........................65
    In Psalm. II. xxxvii. 6.........189
    In Jerem.
      viii. 2.....................128
      x...........................146
      xi..........................186
    In Ezech.
      i...........................202
      v...........................186
    In Luc.
      xvii........................189
      xxiii........................44
  Epistle to Gregory iv............70
  Epistle to Africanus.............81
  Exhortation to Martyrdom
    xxx. 38......................111
  De Principiis
    Preface......................60
    I. i. 7-9.....................65
      ii.........................128
      ii. 6.......................72
      iv.........................199
      vi.........................199
      vi. 2......................180
      vii........................103
      vii. 4......................104
      vii. 5......................104
      viii.......................199
    ii..........................179
      iii. 6.......................72
      iii. 7.......................60
      v. 3.......................202

Origen—*continued*
  De Principiis—*continued*
     vi. 6...................164
     vi. 7...................60
     x. 4....................187
     x. 4–8..................202
     xi. 6–7.................79
     xi. 7...................61
  III. i. 2..................97
     i. 23...................199
     ii. 3...................196
     ii. 4...................111
     iii. 2–6................114
     iii. 5..................203
     iv. 2...................108
     v. 3....................181
     vi.............160, 163, 181
     vi. 5–6.................181
  IV. ii–iii.................85
     ii. 6...................85
     ii. 8...................176
     ii. 9...................85
     iii. 1..................151
     iii. 10.................199
     iv. 10..................61
  Contra Celsum
     II. 394.................164
     IV. 474.................164
     V. 580..................126
     585.....................103
     586................127, 130
     588.....................203
     608.....................164
     VI. 669.................164
     670.....................72
     672.....................158
     VII. 726................82
     727.....................201
     728.....................201
     VIII. 750...............127
     751.....................126
     761.....................126
     784.....................169
     786–788.................201
     791.....................103

Polycarp
  Epistle to the Philippians XII..........7

Letter of the Smyrnaeans
  (*Martyrdom of Polycarp*)
     VII–VIII................7
     XVII....................43

Tertullian
  Apology
     V.......................15
     XXXII...................23
     XXXIX...................24
  De Baptismo XX............22
  De Corona Militis III.....42
  De Idolatria VII..........42
  De Jejunio
     X.......................38
     XV......................23
  De Oratione
     II–III..................22
     IV..................22, 165
     V.......................24
     VI......................22
     VII.....................22
     VIII....................196
     X.......................23
     XIV.....................41 f.
     XVII....................41
     XXIII...................42
     XXV.............38, 39, 40
     XXIX................23, 24
  De Patientia I............21
  De Poenitentia
     VII–XII.................22
     IX......................24
  Ad Uxorem II..............38

Theophilus of Antioch
  Apologia ad Autolycum
     I.......................14
     II. v...................14

GENERAL INDEX

Abandonment by God, 202 ff.
Absolution, power of, 125 f., 188 ff.
Academy (*see also* Plato), 54, 172, 180
Accidie, 11
Adversary. *See* Devil.
Ages, 57, 59, 178 ff.
Alexander, Bishop of Jerusalem, 49, 50
Alexandria, 47
Allegorical interpretation of Scripture, 53, 84, 118 ff., 132 ff., 140, 149, 150, 152, 162, 178
Allegorization of the Eucharist, 169
Ambrosius, 49, 50, 51, 72, 81, 93, 218
'Ανάμνησις, doctrine of, 155 f.
Angels, 56, 102, 111, 135, 152, 175 ff., 185, 213 ff.
Anglus, 74
Answer of God to prayer, 100 ff., 120 ff.
Apologists, 13 ff.
Apostolic Fathers, 6 ff., 43
Apostolic Tradition. *See* Hippolytus.
Aristides, 13
Aristotle, 48, 54, 128 f., 150, 211
Ascension of Christ, 149 f.
Ascent of the soul, 57, 66
Athanasius, St, 130, 178
Atheists, 93 f.
Athenagoras, 13
Attentiveness in prayer, 142 f., 209 f.
Atonement, 185
Augustine, St, 65

Barnabas, Epistle of, 8 f.
Basilides, 146
Beauty, 135
Bentley, Richard, 74
Bernard, St, 65
Beryllus, Bishop of Bostra, 50
Bigg, Charles, 47 f., 52, 62, 127, 156, 190
Bishops, 186
Black, Matthew, 220, 222 f.
Bodies, nature of, 143 f., 150, 172
Bonaventure, St, 65
Bread,
    of angels, 175 ff.
    interpreted as food for the mind, 174
    interpreted as the Wisdom of God, 175 f.
    interpreted as the Word of God, 167 ff.
Butterworth, G. W., 52, 54, 67, 108, 151, 176, 180, 201, 203

Cadiou, R., 52

Catechetical School, 26, 48
Catechumens, prayers of, 21
Catherine of Genoa, 65, 67
Causality, 97 ff.
Celsus, 13, 201
Chadwick, H., 211
Chase, F. H., 220 ff.
Cheerfulness in prayer, 10
Christ,
    Ascension of, 149 f.
    assistance of, in prayer, 5 f., 110
    example of, in prayer, 116
    humility of, in the Incarnation, 149
    as Light, 163
    love for the soul, 135
    manhood of, 163 f.
    Origen's doctrine of, 55
    personal relation with the Father, 127 f.
    prayer to, 125 ff.
    temptations of, 208
    as True Bread, 167 ff.
    Union of Divine and human in, 57, 163 f.
Church,
    allegorically described as "earth", 152, 162 ff.
    the twofold, 213 f.
Cicero, 79, 103
Clement of Alexandria, 26 ff., 37 f., 42, 44, 52, 61, 66, 83, 93, 97, 108, 115, 144, 148, 202, 216
Clement of Rome, 6, 12, 43
Cockcrow, prayers at, 36, 41
Common Prayer, 213 ff.
Communion of Saints, 111, 213 f.
Companionship with God, 27 ff.
Confession, 15, 22, 30 f., 210 f., 217, 218
Connolly, R. H., 20
Consummation, 56, 59, 67, 160, 163, 180 f.
Contemplation, 66, 69
Creation, Origen's doctrine of, 55, 56, 66 f.
Cross, sign of the, 42
Cyprian, St, 3

Daemons, 56, 58, 102, 114, 118, 146, 164 f., 214 f.
Daniélou, J., 52, 62, 64 ff., 69
Darkness, spiritual, 66
Date of Περὶ Εὐχῆς, 72, 151
Day, interpreted as "age", 178 ff.
Deacons, 186
Debts, 183 ff.
de Faye, E., 52

233

GENERAL INDEX

Delarue, Charles, 73 ff.
Demetrius, Bishop of Alexandria, 48, 49
Departed, prayer for the, 19, 23
Devil, 58, 83, 93, 110, 133, 147 f., 158 f., 165, 177 f., 181, 185, 194, 196, 207 ff.
Dibelius, M., 9
Didache, 7 f., 36
Diogenes Laertius, 172, 173, 174
Dionysius, Bishop of Alexandria, 49
Direction of the body in prayer, 42 f., 215 f.
Disposition of the soul in prayer, 104 f., 209 f.
Dix, Gregory, 20 f., 36
Döllinger, 20
Doubtful-mindedness in prayer, 10
Dualism, Marcionite, 198 f.
Dugmore, C. W., 8, 38 ff., 115

Earth,
 interpreted as the Church, 152, 162 ff.
 interpreted as "sin", 165 f.
Eastward position in prayer, 42 f., 215 f.
Ecstasy, 65, 66
Effective Prayer, scriptural examples of, 116 f.
Efficacy of Prayer, 3, 10 f., 14 f., 24, 70 f., 106
Emperor, prayers for the, 23
Ephrem Syrus, 222
Ἐπιούσιος, meaning of, 170 ff., 220 ff.
Epiphanius, 130
Epistles, prayer in the, 4 ff.
Essence of the Godhead, 127 f., 152 f., 154 ff.
Eternal life as God's purpose for soul, 199
Eucharist, 17, 93, 169
Εὐχή, meaning of, 88 ff.
Eusebius of Caesarea, 13, 15, 47, 50, 72
Evening Prayers, 39, 115 f.

Farges, Albert, 63
Fasting, 23
Fatherhood of God, 144 ff.
Felicitas, St, 19
Festivals, Jewish, 179 f.
Fleury, Claude, 74, 171, 173, 194, 195, 199, 201, 206, 212
Food,
 of Angels, 175 ff.
 of the Devil, 177 f.
 harmful, 175
 for strong and weak in faith, 168 ff., 175
 interpreted as "teaching", 169 f.
Foreknowledge of God, 94 ff., 206
Forgiveness, 106, 108 f., 126, 187 ff., 210
Forms, doctrine of, 172 f.
Freedom of will, 57, 58 f., 67, 69, 71, 97 ff., 165, 199, 203

Fuller, J. M., 21
Future Ages, 57, 59, 67

Genuflection, 210 f.
Glossolalia, 5
Gnosis, Christian, 26 ff., 156
Gnostics, 69 f., 93, 152, 156, 170, 180, 197
God,
 answer of, to prayer, 100 ff., 120 ff.
 essence of, 152 ff.
 Fatherhood of, 144 ff.
 Foreknowledge of, 94 ff., 206
 Giver of life and reason, 202
 Grace of, 79 ff.
 Holiness of, 154 f.
 Immanence of, 67 f.
 Immutability of, 97, 154
 Marcionite doctrine of, 198 f.
 Name of, 154 ff.
 not a body, 150
 not locally circumscribed, 148 ff.
 predestination of, 94 ff.
 providence of, 100 ff.
Gregory of Nyssa, 64, 65, 66
Gregory Thaumaturgus, 50, 51, 70

Harnack, 7
Health, temptations in, 194 f.
Heaven,
 interpreted as Christ, 152, 162 f.
 interpreted as "the good", 165 f.
 not a place, 148 ff.
Heavenly bodies,
 as living beings, 103 f.
 freedom of, 103 f.
 shape of, 211 f.
 souls of, 56, 104
Heavens, ancient view of, 79
Hegesippus, 15
Heiler, F., 3, 31, 71
Heraclas, Bishop of Alexandria, 49
Hermas, 100 ff., 190
Hexapla, 48 f.
Hippolytus, 20 f., 36 ff., 116
Holiness of God, 154 f.
Holy Spirit,
 of adoption, 146
 co-operation of, in prayer, 4 f., 84 ff., 88, 108, 117, 124
 Origen's doctrine of, 55, 188 f.
Homoousion, 128
Hours of prayer, 29, 36 ff., 114 f.
Humility in prayer, 138 f.
Hypostasis, meaning of, 127, 172

Idealism, 173
Ignatius of Antioch, 6

GENERAL INDEX

Image,
  of the earthy, 165
  of God, 64, 69, 108, 147, 167
  of the heavenly, 165
Immanence of God, 66 f.
Imperative Mood, significance of, in Lord's Prayer, 156 ff.
Incarnation, 57, 149, 163 f., 196
Intercession
  in prayer, 15, 22 ff., 31, 124 ff., 217
  of Christ, 5 f.
Irenaeus, St, 9, 16 ff., 157

James, M. R., 73
Jerome, St, 50, 72, 201, 220, 221
Journey of the soul, 64, 70
Judgement, 58, 187
Julius Africanus, 51
Justinian, 199, 211
Justin Martyr, 13, 14, 16, 20 f., 38, 157

Keble, John, 62
Kenosis, 149
Kidd, B. J., 18, 23, 24, 42
Kingdom of God, 158 ff.
Knowledge of God, 68 f.
Koetschau, Paul, 54, 73 ff.

Last Things, 58
Lebreton, Jules, 70
Lewis, C. S., 101
Lietzmann, 9
Light, Christ as, 163
Lightfoot, J. B., 6, 20, 221
Lilley, A. L., 26, 31
Literal interpretation of Scripture, 53, 85, 86, 109, 133, 150 f., 153, 162, 169, 176
Lommatzsch, 75
Lord's Prayer, Matthew's and Luke's versions compared, 136 ff., 161, 166, 171, 179, 183, 188, 190, 206, 221 ff.

Ma'amad, 39
Manhood of Christ, 163 f.
Marcion, 130, 146
Marcionites, 197 ff.
Marcus Aurelius, 14, 15
Marriage, 83, 186
Martyrdom of Polycarp, 43
Martyrs, Acts of, 18 ff.
Materialism, 173
Mattins, 36
Meyer, A., 222
Midnight, prayer at, 36, 41, 115 f.
Millennium, 179
Minucius Felix, 202
Moral interpretation of Scripture, 53, 85
Morning prayers, 36, 39, 115 f.
Moulton, J. H., 220 f.

Movement, 97 ff.
Muratorian Fragment, 9
Mystical interpretation of Scripture. *See* Allegorical.
Mysticism,
  in Clement of Alexandria, 28, 61
  definitions of, 62 f.
  in Origen, 61 ff., 158, 165

Name of God, 154 ff.
Names, significance of, 154
New Testament, prayer in, 3 ff.
Night prayers, 36
Nobility, 135, 139
None, 36 ff., 115 f.

Ocellus, 201
Offices, Daily, 8, 37
Old Testament, examples of prayer in, 116 ff., 132 ff.
One and the Many, 143 f.
Optative significance of imperatives, 156 ff.
Orders of Ministry, 186
Origen,
  as apologist, 53 f.
  doctrine of, 52 ff.
  humility of, 59, 181
  interpretation of the Bible, 53, 85
  life of, 47 ff.
  teaching on prayer, 61 ff.
  Treatise on Prayer,
    date, 72, 151
    editions, 74 f.
    manuscripts, 73
  as theologian, 52 f.
  universalism in, 58, 181
  works of, 50 f.
Ostentation, 138 f.
Owen, E. C. E., 18

Pantaenus, 52
Pantheism, 66 f.
Passivity of the soul, 67
Pelagianism, 59
Perpetua, St, 18 f.
Persecution, 18 f., 47, 49, 50
Perseverance in prayer, 110
Persons of Godhead, distinction in, 127 f.
Petition, 15, 22, 31 ff., 70 f., 123 ff., 217, 218
Philo, 53, 66, 201
Place of prayer, 42 f., 212 ff.
Plato, 26, 48, 54, 103, 172, 180, 211
Platonism, 61, 134, 142, 155 f.
Polycarp, St, 6 f., 43
Posture in prayer, 41 ff., 210 ff.
Poverty, temptations in, 193 f.
Praise, 15, 22, 30, 216 f.

236 GENERAL INDEX

Prayer,
  assistance of Christ in, 5 f., 110
  through Christ, 128 ff., 216 ff.
  Common, 213 ff.
  in the corners of the streets, 140
  to the Father, 125 ff.
  for heavenly and great things, 121 f., 131 ff., 166 f.
  to men, 125 ff.
  ostentation in, 138 f.
  parts of, 21 ff., 30 ff., 216 ff.
  standing in the synagogue, 139, 141
  without ceasing, 27 ff., 148
  and work, 15, 34 f., 114 f., 147
Pre-Christian prayer, 86 f.
Predestination, 94 ff.
Pre-existence of the soul, 56, 155 f.
Preparation for prayer, 104 f., 138 ff., 209 f.
Prestige, G. L., 52, 53, 54
Pride, 193, 195
Priesthood, Jewish, 189
Priests, 186, 188 ff.
Problems of prayer, 10 f., 31, 33 f., 70 f., 92 ff.
Προσευχή, meaning of, 91 f.
Puech, H.-Ch., 65, 66
Punishment, 58, 202 f.
Purgatory, 202 f.
Purpose of God for the soul, 199

Quadratus, 13

Ransom theory of Atonement, 185
Ratcliff, E. C., 8, 37
Rational beings, declension of, 55 f.
Reading, William, 74
Recollection, doctrine of (ἀνάμνησις), 155 f.
Recollection in prayer, 105 f., 209 f.
Reign of God over the Saints, 158 f.
Reign of sin, 158 f.
Resurrection of the body, 58
Ribet, Abbé, 63
Riches, temptations in, 193 f.
Rigorism, 190
Rise and fall of souls, 55 f., 199, 203
Rufinus, 51, 56, 64

Saints,
  assistance of, in prayer, 44, 111, 213 f.
  prayers of, 44, 111
  prayer to, 43 f.
Satan. See Devil.
Satiation with sin, 199 ff.
Science, ancient, 133
Seed of God, 147 f.
Servility, 195
Sext, 36 ff., 115 f.

Shadows, 133 f.
Shema', 39
Sickness, temptations in, 194 f.
Sin, 58 f., 119, 146 f., 159 f., 166, 183 ff., 199 ff.
Sonship, 145 ff.
Soul,
  ascent of, 57, 66 f.
  Christ's love for, 135
  of Christ, 57
  of heavenly bodies, 56
  journey of, 66 f.
  pre-existence of, 56, 155 f.
  rise and fall of, 55 f., 199, 203
  transmigration of, 56, 199, 201
Souter, A., 22
Spiritual interpretation of Scripture. See Allegorical.
Spiritual senses, 65
Spiritual wickedness in heavenly places, 162, 164 ff.
Stoa, 54
Stoics, 54, 57, 106, 172, 173
Streeter, B. H., 7
Study of Scripture, 196 f.
Subjective effect of prayer, 24, 105 ff.
Subject matter of prayer, 82 f.
Substance,
  in God, 127 f.
  philosophical meanings of (Οὐσία), 172 ff.
Successful prayer, 32 f.
Suidas, 201
Swete, H. B., 123
Synagogue, 38 ff.

Tatian, 156 ff., 222
Tatiana, 81, 218
Tefillah, 39
Telfer, W., 7, 74
Temple, Jewish, 39 ff.
Temptation, of Jesus, 208
Temptation,
  of Job, 207 ff.
  of men, 58 f., 118, 190 ff.
  usefulness of, 204 f.
Terce, 36 ff., 115 f.
Tertullian, 3, 9, 13, 15, 19, 21 ff., 38 ff., 41 f., 116, 165, 196
Thanksgiving, 15, 22, 30, 125 f., 216, 218
Theatres, 142, 185
Theoctistus, Bishop of Caesarea, 49
Theophilus of Antioch, 14
Theresa, St, of Genoa, 65
Thorndike, Herbert, 73 f.
Thought, prayer by, 28 f.
Thundering Legion, 14
Timaeus of Plato, 172
Tollinton, R. B., 64

GENERAL INDEX

Translation of Hebrew into Greek, 171, 207, 220 ff.
Transmigration of souls, 56, 199, 201
Tree of Life, 175
Trinity, the Holy, 55, 127 f.

Unanswered prayer, 10
Unforgivable sins, 189 f.
Union of Divine and human in Christ, 57, 163 f.
Unity in prayer, 143 f.
Universalism, 58, 181
Unworthy prayers, 33 f.

Vain repetition, 143 f.
Valentinians, 180
Valentinus, 146
Vokes, F. E., 7

Völker, Walter, 61 f., 65, 66
Völter, Daniel, 9
Von Hügel, 67
Vows, 88 ff.

Walker, John, 74 f.
Ways, the Two, 7
Westcott, B. F., 52, 59
Wetstein, 74, 221
Widows, 186
Will of God, 161 ff.
Williams, A. Lukyn, 13
Work and prayer, 15, 34 f., 114 f., 147
Works, good, 67 f., 69, 147, 158
Works of Origen, 50 f.
World, the visible, 56

Zeno the Stoic, 172, 173

www.ingramcontent.com/pod-product-compliance
Lightning Source LLC
Chambersburg PA
CBHW051636230426
43669CB00013B/2328